ROTTEN TO ITS CORE

by

Stephen Hayes

Grosvenor House
Publishing Limited

All rights reserved
Copyright © Stephen Hayes, 2023

The right of Stephen Hayes to be identified as the author of this work has been asserted by him in accordance with Section 78 of the Copyright, Designs and Patents Act 1988

The book cover picture is copyright to Stephen Hayes

This book is published by
Grosvenor House Publishing Ltd
28-30 High Street, Guildford, Surrey, GU1 3EL.
www.grosvenorhousepublishing.co.uk

This book is sold subject to the conditions that it shall not, by way of trade or otherwise, be lent, resold, hired out or otherwise circulated without the author's or publisher's prior consent in any form of binding or cover other than that in which it is published and without a similar condition including this condition being imposed on the subsequent purchaser.

A CIP record for this book
is available from the British Library

ISBN 978-1-80381-481-0
eBook ISBN 978-1-80381-482-7

Contents

1. ABOUT THE AUTHOR — v
2. INTRODUCTION — 1
3. A PROUD HISTORY ... Are you Joking? — 33
4. 1974–1976: JAMES WILLIAM RICHARDS — 49
5. 1976–1991: JAMES ANDERTON gods copper or total hypocrite? — 78
6. 1991–2002: DAVID WILMOTT — 110
7. 2002–2008: MICHAEL J. TODD — 120
8. 1.09. 2008–2015: PETER FAHY ... What Can You Say? — 148
9. 2015–2020: IAN HOPKINS — 171
10. JUNE 2021 – PRESENT STEPHEN WATSON — 210
11. THE SHOOTING OF ANTHONY GRAINGER — 228
12. THE UNNECESSARY DEATH OF JORDAN BEGLEY — 244
13. OPERATION AUGUSTA "a beacon of good practice"? — 250
14. OPERATION GREENJACKET — 268

THE END — 297
RESEARCH REFERENCES — 298

About the Author

I had no intention or 'saintly' community need, to join the police when I was eighteen. I always demonstrated a cavalier attitude to life generally and always wanted to be a fighter pilot in the RAF. I passed the necessary five GCE 'O'Levels as advertised in the Sunday Express and eventually travelled to RAF Biggin Hill for supposed selection.

Having completed and failed the initial four day Leadership Course, a thorough examination and flight simulator tests, I met with the Review Officer. A jovial 'fly back' to WW2 with his handlebar moustache and cravat in the shirt collar of his immaculate uniform. Throwing himself back in his chair and referring to the flight simulator and assault course "Well old boy, you are a fucking lunatic, we'd love you in a war, but we don't require anyone to fly under London Bridge for amusement just at the moment". A standing handshake and I'm gone. I mention this great memory and wonder ... why don't the police forces use various tests to assess the suitability of every applicant and then others with differing priorities to assess the senior officers as they move upwards. Cronyism would be a thing of the past as would cowardice, common sense and poor leadership.

My father was an ex-commando and having gone through five years of killing, living in s---t and being shot at himself he was a great believer in 'bottle' and particularly the absence thereof. I was an easy target, not because of cowardice, I was a lazy bastard who preferred to be part of a gang which specialised in 'spotting card hands' for pro gamblers in the King of Hearts casino reaping the benefits and bunging my hardworking mother with realistic sums for my keep. It ended in a bloody, broken boned mass as we were discovered. I got away with black eyes and a couple of cuts. With no employment on the horizon I joined the Manchester City Police in preference to unemployment, Initially to keep father quiet but actually I later enjoyed my years of fighting, preventing and detecting crime as the GMP motto now proclaims with total abandon and little accuracy.

Identified as a naturalI I was always a Constable and moved from a brief period in uniform to The Plain Clothes Department, The Drug Squad, a CID aide at Bootle Street, then to the CID in the leafy suburb of Didsbury and then the Regional Crime Squad before resigning, being totally disillusioned at the direction 'wokeism' which was affecting my black arts of criminal detection.

In early 2023 reports of dishonest and sexually perverted police officers are headlines as though such behaviour was unknown in the past. It is a culture of many years making and ignored by the senior ranks either for a quiet life or personal vendettas which had no bearing on actual police work. My potted history ably illustrates my proven credentials to criticise the Chief Constables and some senior ranks of GMP over the last fifty years. Such simple credentials allow me to report on the bent historical culture in all sub-standard ranks of GMP having 'been there'.

My dubious literary abilities stem from my GCE 'O' Level in English Language which accompanied Maths, Geography, Building Construction and Surveying. I was to be a Surveyor or Architect but didn't fancy it any longer. The lack of choice prompted me to pass an examination for 'the brain dead' to become a low ranking police officer of the late 60s and most of the 70s. After twelve months uniformed service I had already achieved such credentials and experience to ably compare my experiences with those of the charlatans posing as the 'High Ranking' so called leadership of Greater Manchester Police.

I feel confident in saying most of them have probably never experienced the wonders of my uniformed and certainly not my CID service. They will never have fought a drunken idiot in Yate's Wine Bar with a bar stool, shagged a senior female officer in a police car, planted evidence for the public benefit, accepted a 'blow job' as an on the spot fine or walked the dark back streets of Manchester armed only with a truncheon and a whistle. Would they have been commended for arrests of car thieves, burglars and on one occasion a murderer?

In this, my fourth literary masterpiece I certainly do not intend to insult the men at the pointed end of today, working the streets daily in much more danger than I experienced. I was not under the questionable leadership qualities of today working at ground level, because my respected supervisory ranks had all had the discipline of the armed services, in wars in some cases which they passed on with alacrity.

I had later in my service, often become critical of woke ranking decisions, as the days of belting prisoners for a confession was coming to an end with tape recorded interviews and whet charge office Inspectors. I decided to retire and be a Private Detective in an existing company which I eventually owned and cover in my third book 'Top Secret'. It's a long story. It may read as amusing but 'you were never allowed to retire from the police and be successful'. I was very successful, ex colleagues were forbidden to assist me but it was too late. Driving my Bentley and chirping at ex colleagues "don't believe crime doesn't pay". Often taken badly and the joke backfired and they got me twice, ambushed by a 'friend', verbally cocked up and charged with fabricated offences. Simple jealousy with an amusing abuse of authority.

I am one person in a group, I have never met, of 'Whistleblowers' on police failings who I have recognised as contributors having nicked several of their well written tweets. In our own particular style we all attempt to illustrate the long standing culture of perverted and violent sexual preferences, criminal corruption, fabrication of incident reports and crime statistics always amongst us in the form of the 'good old British bobby'.

In putting pen to paper (MacBook Pro) in my polished Manchester accent, it's very easy to self congratulate and as they say in Bolton, 'blow my own trumpet'. You may feel I am bitter and twisted in my chosen revelations from my three previous books. You would be quite right, I was a good detective, I cared and maybe skated on the 'thin ice' but I got results. However, remember that all I write is from research in many areas of the media, published in their own style but inevitably protecting named officers, from my own knowledge and that of fellow Tweeters.

My Amazon critics will be waiting to pounce again and choose to slate my grammar and occasional repetitive pointers, possibly in error, but claimed by me as the need for local colour and plausibility.

Urged on by such dedicated research by the likes of 'Woody' and in disgust for many years in retirement. I have amused and offended many having presented ten minute Facebook videos as Stephen Hayes and Stephen Hayes 'The Grumpy Gang' on my Facebook pages.

They are clearly on a Grumpy theme such as Grumpy Police, Grumpy GMP etc. with the content critical to the point of libel but never with any police reaction, which is unfortunate and in itself would have been excellent publicity ... I have shown 'power corrupts and absolute power corrupts absolutely' in my 'couldn't give a shit' style.

My previous books can be found on Amazon under ... The Biggest Gang in Britain: Shining a Light on the Culture of Police Corruption: All three books !. The Biggest Gang in Britain. 2. Shades of Black'n'Blue and 3. Top Secrets sometimes appear together. NB The first two are a continuity of my police service story and the third Private Detective revelations.

I have not mentioned any of my career in business after 1984 when I resigned from the police as this is fully covered in my third book. Suffice to say I built a large, award winning Private Detective Agency and became the market leader in covert filmed surveillance.

Introduction

"Rotten to it's Core" Unprecedented wise words from the mouth of Queens Council Leslie Thomas during the Anthony Granger Enquiry and directed firmly at Greater Manchester Police.

Let us never forget the 'wise words' of esteemed Member of Parliament for Redruth and ex Minister George Eustace when referring to the serving police officer Wayne Couzens, rapist and killer of Sarah Everard ... '"just one bad apple." It appears Eustace hasn't uttered a word since then and is confined to the back benches. A vigil for Sarah was attacked by Met officers, in supporting 'their own' they arrested six members for breaking Covid Rules in August 2022 whilst throwing them to the ground, whatever their age and painfully handcuffing them. Sensibly the charges were dropped, but the question remains "who was the ranking officer in charge, what experience did he/she really have and how could he/she honestly have authorised such violent stupidity."? More to the point on a theme throughout, were they disciplined for the command misjudgement? Don't hold your breath!

Throughout I will be adding passages in Italics, taken from my previous literary masterpieces purely as an exercise to illustrate the fact that the 'new' problems of today regarding the police generally are not new, are often a culture of many years and totally accepted as working practices. Often unbelievable, but very true.

Talking of M.Ps and their lack of real life experiences ...

Liberal Democrat Chris Huhne, the coalition Government's Secretary of State for Energy and Climate Control, had a brush with the law over his wife Vicky Pryce's driving points and it resulted in jail time all round for their conspiracy to pervert the course of justice. Yet before this Huhne had unearthed some stunning stuff and as such stated that the public cannot accept how a serving police officer can perform his duties effectively and how he could possibly give evidence in a court of law with the risk of being shown to be dishonest with a criminal record. His brief visit to one of Her Majesty's establishments – HMP Leyhill - appears to have taken his eye off that particular ball and no other MP has taken up the cudgel, probably due to all their particular skeletons in so many cupboards. Politicians and their skeletons in their various cupboards are hardly likely to rock the boat in case their little world becomes the subject of a further investigation, yet again, only to be filed away for future reference.

As I have already said and only a few paragraphs in ... this is not a new problem, it is a culture that has been allowed to develop and the many 'bad apples' of an accepted culture are now coming to the surface. Fashionable at the moment are the many prosecutions of the lower ranked police officers for blatant and often alarming sexual offences. Such offences have been disregarded and remained hidden for many years and always 'swept under the rug' of the in house complaints departments.

Senior ranking officers have moved on in this culture from the lower ranks and yet prosecutions of such 'leadership' are none existent.

From time immemorial the police have investigated the police and comparatively rarely have prosecutions resulted of officers above the rank of Inspector. I wrote in 2013 in one of my previous books. The passage could have referred to any manner of dubious police conduct.

Words of wisdom from 2013 commenting on common police practice...

Clearly, it sounds criminal but it should once again be made perfectly clear that we were not a rogue element amongst so many dutiful bobbies. Such behaviour was a culture and yes whilst serving the public and Her Majesty in taking the initial oath, we were just following a way of life encountered at every stage and practically every day in so many differing forms. As I have always said, the Hillsborough conspiracy had its foundations within such a culture and writing off so many deaths was merely an extension of such day to day thinking and beliefs we all experienced in the 60s and 70s. Enterprise was there for the taking. One just needed to watch and listen carefully. One needed only the necessary ambition, because the opportunities were everywhere. Enterprise and invention always seemed to find its way to gold. One needed to listen to the right voices above them, or to the side of them and to develop instincts. It also helps to have the right male gear. Brains and balls is an excellent combination. Maybe the police are too close to the bad guy. That in pursuit, in the art of the chase, it becomes an imperative to think like the quarry itself. Being so close, often causes a contamination, an infection of sorts. To defend against this is difficult at best, if not impossible. As I said earlier, everybody was in on it...and then some. We had cops with yachts and mistresses with fine jewellery and then other cops with the odd Rolls Royce, or top of the range Jaguar. Cops with homes that cops can't afford, bought at the price of common and fruitful infractions of the very law they are sworn to uphold. I tasted the goods. It was a taste too sweet not to. Refusal was too difficult to consider. There was no one to turn to, no one to trust, it was a culture so get on with it.

Definitely not a new problem as claimed in 2023, with headlines ...

Almost 150 employees of Greater Manchester Police were accused of behaviour relating to violence against women and girls in the last six months, the force has admitted. In the last six months to February, there were 117 complaints and misconduct allegations relating to 141 members of the force - equating to one per cent of the workforce. And in the same time period up to March last year, the force recorded 108 complaints - accounting for 9.1 per nationally, relating to 143 employees.

Such a culture has existed for many many years and the sooner this fact is recognised, the sooner the Home Office will recruit Chief Constables with real 'on the ground' experience. Maybe, even from the middle ranks of the armed services. Talking of absolute bollocks, can you recall when Conservatives were fighting the police over reforms and cuts. Now the government wants policing back onside. A little gem from the Home Office says it all with regard to their grasp on reality "Police officers perform their duties to the highest of standards and with integrity under the attestation".

The attestation sworn on employment ... "I do solemnly and sincerely declare and affirm that I will well and truly serve the King in the office of constable, with fairness, integrity, diligence and impartiality; upholding fundamental human rights and according equal respect to all people; and that I will, to the best of my power, cause the peace to be kept and preserved and prevent all offences against people and property, and that while I continue to hold the said office I will, to the best of my skill and knowledge, discharge all the duties thereof faithfully according to law".

FFS are they really serious?

Media reporting on police criminalities tend to feature the Metropolitan Police. Trust will never be restored as long as watchdogs continue to look the other way when senior officers act corruptly. Couzens and Carrick are names which resonate and require no further introduction but will eventually be slowly forgotten in the mist of time, whilst being extreme examples of junior officers committing heinous crimes.

Little is ever as regularly reported about the senior ranks, whose employment and leadership failures ignore and as a consequence encourage such outrages.

For example the Daily Mail in March 2009 featured the following article under the headline................ ON DUTY 1,000 POLICE FOUND GUILTY OF CRIMES. The article reveals that more than 1,000 serving police officers remain on duty despite being convicted of criminal offences such as assault, kerb-crawling, GBH, wounding, robbery and perverting the course of justice. There are at least 77 serving officers with convictions for violent offences which in itself proves the acceptance of violence in the performance of their duty (many chapters in my trilogy illustrate this) and 36 with convictions for theft and again seen as everyday life in the police.

However in February 2023 it was reported that one in 100 police officers faced criminal charges, including for sexual offences, last year alone. The new data shows the number has rocketed almost six-fold since 2012. The Police Federation, which provides legal support for officers who find themselves on the wrong side of the law, received 1,387 claims in 2022. A decade ago that figure was just 235. It has been established that the Police Federation, 'The toothless Trades Union (the staff association for police officers,) received 1,387 claims for legal support from members facing criminal charges in 2022. Who was it that said the indefensible defending the indefensible.?

Suella Braverman MP the esteemed Home Secretary, in 2023, in failing to recognise the full picture has ordered police chiefs to spend less time on "symbolic gestures" and more time on policing. In an open letter to police leaders in England and Wales, in which she set out her policing agenda, the new Home Secretary said diversity and inclusion initiatives "should not take precedence" over tackling crime. "Unfortunately, there is a perception that the police have had to spend too much time on symbolic gestures than actually fighting criminals," she wrote in the letter, published in 2022 "This must change. Initiatives on diversity and inclusion should not take precedence over common-sense policing." Admitting that recent years had been "challenging" for police forces, she said she was "dismayed by the perceived deterioration of public confidence in the police".

What 'a load of bull, what appears to be an attempt to right wrongs now embedded in a culture will require much more than this.

The once existing culture, which hopefully has also improved recently starts with a half hearted recruitment programme and the none existent vetting procedures on applicants. Should it not focus on the dismal leadership and the quality of what are termed the 'supervisory higher ranks', often promoted through 'cronyism'. All promoted, much too early in their careers and hence no experience of 'the pointed end' on which they can then base real supervisory decisions.

Despite the glaring leadership and the all too often criminal failings of senior officers, too many to be mentioned in a realistic volume. There are always morons in the lower ranks and civilian clerks with grand titles. In this example Colin Ramwell, the Head of GMP Recruitment who proudly boasts ... "Once a failing force, GMP has made enormous strides since it was removed from 'special measures' last year, and it is in the middle of a huge recruitment drive." Of course we should ask "how is the recruitment doing?" Well !!!

Incredibly a boy aged 17 was mistakenly sworn in as a police officer due to an 'administrative error'. Bosses only realised the mistake during the youth's training when he innocently invited colleagues to his 18th birthday party.

Greater Manchester Police confirmed to the media, details of the error, which is believed to have been uncovered during training of student officers at the force's training school. Bosses say the youth was not posted onto any police division, had no contact with the public during this period and that he has not been exposed to any harm. The boy was kept on as his 18th birthday was due a few weeks later, when he was sworn in for a second time and his warrant card was returned. He had entered his correct date of birth on his application but this had not been spotted until after he had taken the police attestation which is solemnly given at an appropriate ceremony.

The following will prove that the selection of Chief Constables must follow 'equally arduous' procedures and this now appears to be the case with the present incumbent.

CONTEXT

Improvements will remain superficial and headline grabbing, but there is an ingrained culture which will continue to fester. Whilst the entire problem relating to 'honest policing' is interesting, we need to examine the problem in real context and concentrate on a single force of the forty five individual forces throughout the UK as an ideal example of ingrained corrupt cultures which has only recently shown superficial improvements and time will tell.

The fact that there is forty six separate forces on such a small island is another story for another day but just for the moment consider the financial outlay for so many, each with a ranking structure from Chief Constable (many on salaries of £190,0000 plus additional expenses), down to several Assistant Chief Constables a couple of Deputy Chief Constables and a multitude of Superintendents before a similar number of Chief Inspectors and all 'driving desks'. Ex C.C. Peter Fahy in a rare honest moment admitted to twelve levels before the 'pointed end' retiring with over £300,000. How many junior officers for the pointed end could such a waste of senior salaries of empty men support?

Whilst a serious subject, let's remember lives have been lost as a direct result of leadership failings, deplorable standards of training and the initial quality of recruit. Despite the seriousness, I have injected a modicum of humour as I reveal the context of the dubious fifty years history of the 'illustrious' Greater Manchester Police. Such 'insightful gems' are based on my years of dubious experience and several credited sources of information, I reveal many unbelievable situations faithfully reported by the media on regular intervals with uncorroborated ludicrous claims by the police leadership to justify such appalling examples On this occasion, revealed in context, with no holds barred and names named, which is the important point so many media outlets choose to ignore unless copying supplied bull.

To affirm my protestations of a historical ingrained culture, I will additionally be referring to my previous 'whistle blowing' books with historical examples drawn from my aged memory of what has always been present. Stupid, dubious statements, honesty abuse, fabrication of crime figures and downright criminality throughout my service and beyond from the 1960s and 70s and on to 2021.

Relatively recent comments featuring in various official inquiries proliferate: "GMP's failures are very significant', *GMP's culpability is substantial. Incompetence, staggering ineptitude, shocking attempts at a cover up, levels of staggering ineptitude way beyond what was expected.*

Such failings have continued unabated until 2021, with obscene regularity and always authorised by senior police officers from the Chief Constable down in so many instances. Consequently, the following literary masterpiece will induce disbelief and often utter incredulity when seen in the context of the last six Chief Constables before the serving C.C. Stephen Watson who appears to be getting a grip. Time will tell.

The many revelations will maybe, prompt occasions of stunned silence, prompting memories of a quotation straight from the lips of the 'Geordie voice of darts' the great Sid Waddell, commentating on yet another classic 'gritty bout' of darts ... "It's so quiet in here you can hear the fat dripping off a chip".

Once occasional, but presently, what seems to be daily news articles, but all forgotten and replaced in the memory with yet another vivid incident. I have attempted to put many such media, GMP and the HM Inspector of Constabulary reports into a form of historical context. Especially in relation to the dubious leadership of Greater Manchester Police. When examined in the context I have sought, GMP of the past certainly appears to be a 'gift which keeps on giving'.

Examples of a rotten culture within the GMP are innumerable, too many to report in this simple work. Its leadership has for many years shown that power corrupts and absolute power corrupts absolutely. I am able to write with experience on the last fifty years, if not when serving, closely associated with serving members. There has always existed the ingrained culture of cover ups and all wrongdoing which eventually sinks to such depths that it becomes 'the indefensible defending the indefensible.'

Perhaps with some mistaken pride, based on numerous letters to Government level officialdom, allegedly supervisory bodies, Tweets and Facebook movies I have attempted to convince myself that I may have had some success in lighting an initial spark at Government level. However never with the explosive revelations of Maggie Oliver an ex police officer with a trust protecting vulnerable girls from the clutches of Asian Pakistani paedophiles. However her protestations continue to be ignored to various degrees.

In all I have experienced and there has been plenty, I never believed I would witness Asian Pakistani paedophiles, permitted to rape and pillage their way through various areas of Greater Manchester for the sake of 'racial harmony' with the absolute minimum of arrests.

For the continuing none-believers go to 'The latest list of Police Officers charged and Convicted of a Crime' which is published by 'Huyton Freeman and can be found with the link...." Fourteen years and constant corruption-huytonfreeman.co.uk/2023/01/police'... This detailed epic is forty pages long of separate incidents taken from media reports throughout the country. Again further efforts of an unknown believer, to illustrate the culture of dishonesty throughout the UK police force. He can also be found on Twitter ... @huytonfreeman.

Urged on by such dedicated research and in disgust for many years I have presented ten minute Facebook videos as Stephen Hayes and Stephen Hayes 'The Grumpy Gang' clearly on a Grumpy theme such as Grumpy Police, Grumpy GMP etc. with the content critical to the point of libel but never with any police reaction, which is unfortunate and in itself would have been excellent publicity ... power corrupts and absolute power corrupts absolutely.

As a relief to so many and after so many TV programmes, letters and tweets emanating from so many sources, England's so called second largest police force was placed into special measures by Her Majesty's Inspectorate of Constabulary and Fire Service (HMICFRS) It's role is to assess the efficiency and effectiveness of police and fire services in England and Wales and to suggest improvements. It is supposed to be independent of the government and police. ... Don't hold your breath.

During December 2020, Chief Constable Ian Hopkins was accused of action which represented a deliberate and unprecedented failure, but was actually a culture of many such years and in effect 'He took one for the team' The reasons were clearly a rot, a culture and acceptance of deception dating back many years within the senior leadership, trickling down from Chief Constable through the ten levels of senior leadership, eventually to the 'working' ranks' at 'the pointed end'. Inevitably 'the pointed end' constables were of course to be promoted in some cases and eventually become part of the rabble of badly trained and inexperienced officers, often promoted only on passing an examination and cronyism.

REAL DETECTIVES?

Today Murder Squads are led by senior ranks with no experience of life, let alone actual detailed detection procedures whilst leading a murder hunt effectively, which should really be based on years of experience. Today senior officers do not gain that experience as they flit from one course to another at various police training establishments and university degree courses. Of course they are taught the theory but the practical application is so very different. In my first book I detail initial basic training and how such practical demonstrations at

ROTTEN TO ITS CORE

training school differ so radically to the real world of actual police work. On leaving the training schools with so many worthless paper qualifications they soon realise that they have absolutely no experience involving the management of many men, some with the lowly rank of detective constable with much more knowledge and accordingly harbouring resentment which in itself seriously affects morale. These are good able detectives, who have made a career choice not to study for a variety of reasons usually hinging on the fact that they could be on the piss seeking their next little naked victim, or meeting informants and then going on the lash probably with the proceeds of an insurance reward. As with the very poor documentaries, the majority of murders are now just a police public relations exercise, stage-managed to hide the real enormity of their failure. Parents, relatives, and friends are paraded at televised press conferences, pleading with the culprits to give themselves up. I don't quite get that one – they generally have to be caught or at least that's what happened in my day.

Wooden television appearances by the so-called investigating officer and weeping relatives are followed by filmed coverage of masses of uniforms thrashing the living daylights out of the countryside, white latex overalls on police officers, carrying many plastic bags of potential forensic evidence away from the scene. As the story loses media interest, some insignificant young lookalike does the last walk of the victim. I can't remember when any of these scenarios resulted in an arrest, but they actually delay any real detection work whilst mountains of pointless leads provided by the local nutters flood in bringing the real investigation to a grinding halt. Then of course, if such information is regarded as important and worthy of investigation the entire procedure depends on the quality of the detective who is given the responsibility of vetting all possible leads. How many murderers have been missed with poor collation of vital evidence only to be arrested some additional murders 'down the road' when found to have been in the system already. They are often highlighted during the initial investigation, but never interviewed. There have never been so many undetected murders and so many others thrown out of court for lack of real evidence. In addition, there have never been so many convicted murderers released from prison terms of varying lengths, as evidence is proved to be unsafe. In the case of the murder of TV presenter Jill Dando an obviously innocent weirdo, Barry George, who was unable to defend himself effectively, was convicted and forgotten. He had a history of strange incidents, all sexually motivated and so tenuous was the evidence available that George was freed eight years later by the Court of Appeal.

The question must be asked whether the evidence was "made to fit?" He is now proved to be innocent, but the arresting officers have never been taken to account. If he was indeed innocent the questions must be asked regarding the fact that gunpowder residue was found on his clothing. Only recently has a witness come forward and been believed by the media, but ignored by the original investigation in relation to a good description of the actual perpetrator. A swarthy male of eastern European appearance was seen near the murder scene of the BBC Crimewatch presenter's house. Despite his release from prison as a result of evidence unreliability George continues to be denied compensation.

The conviction of Sion Jenkins for the murder of his step daughter, Billy Jo Jenkins has been declared unsafe, as it relied only on the forensic evidence of her blood on his clothes. Whilst never stated openly, the Appeal Judges must have considered the fact that the presence of the blood spots was much too convenient in the absence of other evidence. I had, in a detailed letter, informed the Jenkins' defence team that evidence such as this is commonly fabricated by investigating officers in the absence of real evidence. My assistance was acknowledged, but I was never called as a witness. Despite these publicised criminal acts of perjury and total corruption of the evidence, the so-called investigating officers are generally never brought to justice. No wonder similar acts are regularly perpetrated in the knowledge that the full force of the law will never fall on them and if it should they will inevitably be protected from any serious criminal charges as happened with such sad consequences for Stefan Kiszko.

The murder of Lesley Molseed is such a typical example of corruption of evidence and procedures on so many levels that it is certainly worthy of a detailed explanation. Lesley Susan Molseed was 11-years-old when she was murdered on the 5th October 1975. This is the same era as so many other corrupt incidents such as Jimmy Savile, the miners' strike and the paedophile Cyril Smith MP, who was well-known for his sexual activities involving children in the Rochdale area. He was protected by the same force where the murdered child lived and which *assisted with this murder investigation. Stefan Ivan Kiszko, a 23-year-old tax clerk, was wrongly convicted of her sexual assault and murder. He served 16 years in prison after being wrongly convicted of these offences in what was described as 'the worst miscarriage of justice of all time' by one outraged Member of Parliament. Kiszko was released from prison in 1992 after further examination of forensic evidence showed that he could not have committed the crime. Kiszko died one year later and Ronald Castree was eventually found guilty of the crimes on November 12th 2007. The little girl's body was found in a remote lay-by with 12 stab wounds. Her clothing had not been disturbed but the body had been laid in a 'pose' and the killer had ejaculated over her underwear. At the time of the hunt four teenage girls claimed Kiszko had indecently exposed himself to them and had repeated the act a month after the murder to one of the girls on Bonfire Night. Of course this was all the evidence required to suspect Kiszko of the murder and at the time the police concentrated on prosecuting him whilst ignoring other leads. Without doubt Kiszko had an idiosyncratic lifestyle which included a negligible social life and an odd habit of recording car registration numbers of drivers who annoyed him. There is no doubt he suffered learning difficulties. He was arrested on the 21st December 1975 and the police 'found' a bag of sweets and girlie magazines in his car. He was subjected to three days of intensive questioning after which he admitted to the offence, because in his disturbed mind he would then be released and allowed to go home whilst the investigation continued and he would be proved innocent. This belief in itself demonstrates his simple thinking abilities and clearly the police took advantage* *of this. He was the only suspect as all other 'leads' were discounted despite strong evidence to the contrary. After all he had confessed which certainly did not assist his cause. Kiszko was not automatically entitled to a solicitor as is the case today and indeed it was not until the Police And Criminal Evidence Act of 1984 that such a requirement became law. Kiszko was never asked if he wanted a solicitor and was never cautioned until well after the police had decided he was the only suspect. He was charged with the murder on Christmas Eve 1975 and his trial commenced on 7th July 1976. Kiszko was defended by David Waddington QC, who was later to become the Home Secretary, and prosecuted by Peter Taylor QC, who later became the Lord Chief Justice and the author of the infamous Hillsborough Report.*

Of course, back then the majority of the jury believed the police evidence, however flawed it proved to be. Kiszko stated his admission was purely to pacify the police who were then 'nice' to him on his admission. The conduct of his defence left much to be desired, but even his solicitor believed him to be guilty. He was found guilty after five hours and 35 minutes deliberation, but only on a 10 out of 12 majority verdict. The learned judge commended all the witnesses particularly Detective Sergeant John Ackroyd and Detective Superintendent Dick Holland. Kiszko was eventually sent to Wakefield prison where he was kept apart from other prisoners on what is known as Rule 43 for his own safety. Despite this he was attacked several times and throughout his sentence his mental health deteriorated as he was moved from prison to prison and into several mental health establishments.

For eight years Kiszko's mother campaigned for his case to be reopened. He would never admit to the offence and as a consequence would never be considered for parole. His mother contacted JUSTICE the Human Rights organisation and they eventually had the case reopened. The case was referred back to West Yorkshire Police where Detective Superintendent Trevor Wilkinson conducted the investigation and immediately found several glaring errors. Witnesses were found to confirm Kiszko's alibi of visiting a grave in Halifax and visiting a nearby shop. These witnesses had never been properly interviewed by the investigating officers and whatever evidence they gave totally contradicted the decision to prosecute Kiszko and therefore show the murder as detected. The witnesses were not called by his defence team who may not even have been aware of their existence as of course their use would have resulted in a not guilty verdict. At the time of the reopened investigation it was also established that Kiszko had a physical problem which prevented him producing sperm, so consequently could not have ejaculated over the victim. This fact was known to the investigating officers. The four young girls all admitted lying 'for a laugh.' Whilst all the detail is significant it is sufficient to say that Kiszko was by the time of his release mentally ill. He was awarded a derisory £500,000 most of which he did not receive due to his death a year after his release.

The point to all the above detail is of course what actually happened to the once commended police officers who by the time of his release had been denounced by the trial judge, the Molseed family and the local media. Detective Superintendent Holland and Ronald

Outteridge, the forensic scientist, were formally charged with 'doing acts tending to pervert the course of justice' by allegedly suppressing evidence, namely the results of the semen tests from Kiszko and from the victim's body. The defence counsel at an early pre-trial hearing before magistrates who were always police biased, proved that a fair trial was impossible for Holland. He was guilty, deliberately so and should have appeared in court to answer the charges, but it was once again brushed away.

Holland came to public prominence in yet another flawed investigation into the Yorkshire Ripper and M62 'bomber' Judith Ward, who had her conviction ruled as unsafe in 1992. Having once had these investigations regarded as his finest hours in 35 years of police service Holland was subsequently demoted, four years after Kiszko's conviction. As I have said, Holland's defence barrister had argued that his conviction would be unsafe due to the passage of time and would make a fair trial impossible. In yet another example of the naivety of magistrates they agreed and the matter was not sent for trial. Holland died in 2007 at the age of 74 and remains yet another example of the corrupt practices of the West Yorkshire Police and their ability to avoid legal retribution despite the weight of evidence.

The trial judge and West Yorkshire Police have apologised for this dreadful miscarriage of justice, but surely such a miscarriage has been further exacerbated with the lack of prosecutions against the men who deliberately fabricated evidence to ensure a conviction of an innocent man. Kiszko for so many years suffered amazing hardships in prison, which eventually caused his mental illness and death on release. So long after these events David Cameron is proclaiming the police to be 'relatively honest,' but the corruption and fabrication remains.

Of course, back in 2013 such incidents caused some mild protest against a wave of police bias which allowed the commission of a multitude of criminal offences in the knowledge that they would never be disciplined. Would the entire corrupt culture end in light of these investigations, compensation reluctantly paid and apologies from Police and Judges. ... Don't hold your breath, along came ex Labour MP Andy Burnham.

The Police and Crime Commissioner for GMP was appointed in 2017 in the form of the already Lord Mayor, the ex Labour Politician, Andy Burnham. This was to become one of the biggest public service failures to hit Greater Manchester in years and yet Burnham declared."Throughout a troubled term I held the force to account." What? ... This was a paid position and in joking reality he should have been charged with 'Obtaining Money by Deception' which would have been a first.

The warning lights had long been flashing, during the 'reigns' of a procession of Chief Constables each with their own eccentricities primarily failing victims of crime and in some cases following their own 'potty' agendas. Such leadership failings sadly affected the many rank-and-file police officers, already struggling with very dubious behavioural mandates from the ranking 'desk jockeys' whilst fighting the tide of criminality, 'one arm tied behind' in a broken culture and firmly at 'the pointed end' risking life and limb.

In reality, the creeping army of honest police officers had no where to complain and being fearful to report higher ranks followed the culture of lies whenever interviewed by those attempting internal and external enquiries. Such a culture, was so often reflected from the senior ranks that making misleading and inaccurate statements became a way of life. Whilst indulging in total denial of any official criticism and legal stonewalling easily became a life's work as was ably reflected during the times of Peter Fahy, Chief Constable between 2008 and 2015 and Ian Hopkins 2015 - 2020 limply following the ingrained culture and 'falling on his sword'.

Due to such a history of an unbelievable culture of lies, fabrication and dishonesty (HMICFS) Her Majesty's Inspectorate of Constabulary and Fire Service, in 2019 'investigated' (using the term lightly) GMP and identified yet another decline in performance and warned that too many crimes were being wrongly downgraded to less serious offences and even recording crime reports as unworthy of investigation to embellish the year end statistics. They discovered that GMP also exhibited a lack of strategy within neighbourhood policing and the forces treatment of vulnerable victims also caused concerns. Basically in layman's terms ... 'They didn't give a f--k and never even visited scenes of burglaries, choosing to discuss the serious experience over the telephone. Similar, I suppose to the conduct of G.Ps today.

Alarmingly, HMICFS only chose a specimen brief period for this 'investigation' which established that it had actually dumped 80,000 crime reports, an action in addition to actually failing to record such a crime which then had the desired effect of showing a relatively successful detection rate.

Whilst this was a chosen specimen year, it did not take into account what was most probably in my experienced opinion, a historical system of concealing crime reports and including evidence fabrication dating back many years. The Inspectorate, made no attempt to investigate the much deeper concerns of an existing culture of lies and deception emanating from the Chief Constable and down the ranks to be recognised as 'the way it is'. Of course, it may not have been a deliberate omission, but surely not. It could have just been based on poor training and experience within HMRCIFS,, but whatever the reasons they never recognised and naively misunderstood the existence of such a corrupt history.

The continual legal abuses and systematic failures could not continue, elements were being recognised as serious.

Prince Charles, in recognition of the total failure of the police at the highest levels of security, announced in the Daily Mail that Royal Security is now in the hands of the army in the form of an ex-special forces officer. The Royal Protection Department and its Old Etonian head, Commander Peter (Lord) Loughborough, who is responsible for day to day security, has had to accept this embarrassment. It has, at last been recognised by the faceless powers that be, that security is no longer a game. It is no longer a promotion exercise, but a department where experience rather than examination results is the vital ingredient. When one compares the service records of the two, there really is no contest.

The history books and accounts up to the present day are littered with similar examples of fabricated evidence. With regular monotony tragic individuals are released from lengthy prison sentences amid a blaze of publicity having had evidence re-examined, DNA checked again with modern methods and the like. The culture existing in the police during my early days ran amok in the knowledge that there was no one to effectively criticise their conduct and any corruption of flimsy evidence was fair game to ensure a conviction. Should the police of today continue in this manner with selected cases, involving so much public sympathy then people would be falling in behind their police again, they would believe they were being protected and give their support accordingly. The old adage of 'your turn' comes to mind. Unfortunately the police generally do not know where to 'draw the line' and attack all and sundry with corrupted evidence, so badly prepared that this conduct is being recognised and prevented, wherever possible but still no prosecutions of police are taking place as a result of such actions, except on very, very, rare occasions.

With such a failing culture and public protestations comes the Robin Hoods' of the legal profession. Not taking money from the rich to give to the poor, they took money from anyone, guilty or not, without a care in the world for public service.

Such evidential fabrication is what Manchester 'legal eagle' Mark O'Connor relies upon. His ability to swoop and dissect a police prosecution file is legendary among Manchester's accused population. He successfully identifies the breaks in evidence continuity, the abuses of process, the downright fabrications and police lies that are all his bread and butter. His successful acquittals of those initially facing an apparent wealth of irrefutable evidence, is as I have already mentioned legendary.

There is little doubt that his address book of learned counsel is second to none, all wishing to represent his clients in the knowledge that the initial investigation has left no stone unturned and a successful end result is considerably enhanced by Mark O'Connor's initial preparation and detailed instructions.

Mark O'Connor continues today (2023) with such dramatic results.

The public inquiry into the death of Anthony Grainger, shot dead, seated, unarmed in a car by a GMP officer in 2012. Even today the Enquiry is remembered as a one-stop-shop for the kind of cultural criticisms levelled at GMP in recent years. Anthony Grainger deserves a separate chapter later but several critical comments are so damning they are worthy of an early mention on the book cover.

The Inquiry findings, in June 2019 after initial hearings in 2017, were explicit to the extreme. Judge Teague QC, blasted the force's lack of candour, both at an organisational levels and amongst several individual senior officers. Testimony from Assistant Chief Constable, Steve Heywood, was heavily criticised by the judge. Testimony from a second officer, namely Assistant Chief Constable (ACC), Terry Sweeney, was described as 'seriously misleading'.

Firearms logs were presented and were supposed to represent the notes to have been jotted down at the time in relation to what they were doing. The inquiry examined the evidence in some detail, concluding that the officers must have adjusted them later in order to show themselves in a better light. Unbelievably Heywood was even accused of using two different pens to give the impression of a contemporaneous record. He also insisted some evidence be heard in secret, because it relied upon sensitive intelligence. The inquiry then discovered that there was, in fact, 'no such intelligence'. It's worthy of mention that such practices were not a one off, committed by ACC Steve Heywood, but an accepted practice dating from well before my service. To be perfectly honest most officers wrote their notes later and yet gave evidence on oath that the notes were made at the time committing the offence of Perjury. This practice will continue today and is demonstrated by the fact that notebook pages will be held by elastic bands in the supposed interest of security of 'confidential information' when giving evidence at Court. Barristers often request the notebook to see what notes were made 'at the time'. They only have to open the banded pages to reveal the truth but are usually prevented in doing so by the 'learned' Judge in the interests os security of information into relation to other enquiries.

The accepted culture of dishonesty was every where in my early days and with it came an acceptance of such a failing, in so many areas, even 'Cop on Cop' and not just shooting each other, as related later.....

Below the Charge Office, in the basement, was the parade room and lockers. Each locker had padlocks, which were provided by the officer who used the locker, but nothing was left in them because many officers specialised in removing the locks and the property therein. Helmets were often stolen. They were sold as souvenirs to American tourists in the St Ann's Square area. Tourists loved to photograph us. The PC was evidently the very height of Englishness. "Gee, an English

Bobby!" the jubilant tourists would say. Some enterprising officers just happened to have a spare helmet in a Marks and Spencer's carrier bag, which was sold for a few dollars, on top of the bung for the photo opportunity to any trusting American or Japanese visitor. All unaware of the fact that there was a constable minus one helmet still at Bootle Street being disciplined for the loss of issued uniform. That was Number 3 beat. I used to enjoy that beat. It had little trouble, a lot of tourists, all the 'fur coat and no knickers brigade' and the leggy hopefuls of Kendal Milne's, the Harrods of Manchester. It was commonplace to be bunged a pound to be photographed with a tourist. By today's standards a pound would be an insult, but my weekly wage at this time was a take home packet of £20 per week. A coach load of Yanks, could double that. It was also, at this time, that the longer serving, more experienced earners amongst us would sell a colleague's helmet. To prevent this everyone took their helmets home with them in a bag. Wearing a civilian overcoat over their uniform made concealment much easier.

Criminality didn't remain in the simplistic realms of helmets ...

This behaviour was, of course, blatantly dishonest and it came as a great surprise to the rookie, the cherry that I was. It was even more of a surprise to find myself involved, not as a participant, but as a silent observer. I can honestly say I never committed an act of dishonesty such as theft or burglary during my service, but I was guilty in that I did nothing about it. This again is a culture, brainwashed into every young officer and indeed the same old-fashioned culture on which the hierarchy of South Yorkshire Police relied upon in tidying up the evidence for the Hillsborough Inquest.

When I eventually got a car, I also had an excellent sound system, gifted by a 'colleague'. But where could you turn when even the Inspectors arrived at scenes of crime and not just for supervision? Everybody was in on it. It left stains on everything. But it was all so normal, so widely accepted, silence was the only response I could seem to make. Who would or could I tell? In bringing down one, you bring down all. And that wasn't my style and I suppose in truth I just did not care enough.

I remember, on one occasion, many months into my service, driving to a 999 call because a shop window had been broken near Manchester Cathedral. The shop was a tobacconist's and had a display of lighters behind the security grill. The officer of the beat stood with his truncheon in his hand and his back to the hole in the window, keeping back two other officers from adjoining beats, who wanted to empty the window.

Heywood would remember such early days and the risks involved but even he apparently cringed at the ferocity of the cross-examination and as he crumbled in the face of it 'lacked candour', while 'very little of ACC Sweeney's narrative is accurate', said Judge Teague in relation to one section of evidence. The officers were a product of years of habitual evidence fabrication and were unaccustomed to having the illegal practices questioned.

However the prickly comments of His Honour were not restricted to individuals who in reality should have been reported to the Director of Public Prosecutions (DPCC) for consideration of prosecuting them for the offence of perjury, as was often the case in relation to the public and lower ranked police officers.

Judge Teague accused GMP of being "unduly reticent, at times secretive attitude" and accused "a failure to disclose relevant material promptly to the inquiry". Such comments would prove to be the norm in later years as in 2019 when the latter criticism was levelled in court in later months when GMP were branded 'diabolical' by a grieving relative during the Manchester Arena Inquiry. Yet again it had failed to provide key evidence on time, in fact seven months after being requested. GMP got away with an apology. Peter Weatherby QC acting for families, remarked "one would have thought' the force might have learned its lesson."

The force's own self-commissioned review in the wake of Anthony Grainger's death was heavily criticised when it instructed the College of Policing to look at what had happened. GMP's terms of reference, were attacked by Justice Teague and deemed skewed from the outset towards 'generating conclusions that would tend to favour the force and enhance its public image'. 'Turkeys voting for Christmas'?

The Judge also blasted the so called Independent Police Complaints Commission the ex police staffed watchdog had also failed during its own inquiries to retrieve Steve Heywood's original log. Can you believe that the paperwork mysteriously vanished during the five-year period between the shooting and the public inquiry, before reappearing, with GMP unable to explain why. Despite the enquiry being mired in perjury and deliberate deception no prosecutions were ever formulated.

LESLIE THOMAS QC, REPRESENTING GRAINGER'S FAMILY, LABELLED GMP 'ROTTEN TO ITS CORE'

IOPC (Independent Office of Police Conduct) Director of Major Investigations Steve Noonan ex Royal Military Police reported ..."We are disappointed that, two years after our investigation concluded, Greater Manchester Police (GMP) has decided to offer no evidence in this matter. "Anthony Grainger's family, and the wider public, deserved to hear the evidence and Mr Heywood account for his actions. "We acted quickly and decisively to examine Mr Heywood's conduct once it was brought into question during the Anthony Grainger Public Inquiry in 2017.

In May 2018, after our seven month investigation, we concluded he should face a public hearing to answer allegations that the evidence he provided to the Inquiry may have breached police professional standards relating to honesty and integrity and performance of duties. GMP agreed with our findings. "Today's developments mean that there can be no ruling from the **police panel** as to whether or not Mr Heywood committed gross misconduct to a degree that would have justified dismissal, were he still serving."

Three new investigations stemming from evidence given at the Anthony Grainger Public Inquiry, which reported its findings in July 2019, began earlier this year, and we will continue to work hard to ensure those allegations are thoroughly examined, that actions are accountable and lessons learned.

What is 'The police panel'? I hear you say and to be honest, myself, an ex police officer had no idea and I had to Google for the answer ...

Made up of ten appointed councillors from each of the Greater Manchester local authority areas, and two independent members, the panel is consulted on regarding precept proposals and the police and crime plan. They are all said to be totally independent of GMP and the Lord Mayor and there must have been a proviso that they are 'totally deranged'. Googling as I did, I could find no trace of a full GMP police panel and only three members, but of course, silly me, Burnham was in charge. GMP are shown to have agreed to the inquiry which must 'ring alarm bells' until the totally unwarranted decision was made, apparently with some pre discussion or even collusion.

No Action was the inquiry result and Former ACC Steve Heywood was allowed to retire from the force in 2018 on a full pension. He had signed off on sick leave the day after giving that evidence and never returned to duty, thereafter. It was reported that, during his eighteen month 'sickness' absence, he received salary and benefits worth a sum over £250,000. He 'retired' in October, 2018 on a full police pension, having reached 30 years service.

GMP accepted the few HMI's positive assessments but with 'an ostrich, head in the sand approach', totally rejected its critical conclusions in reporting "Whilst we accept some of these findings, there are others which we have challenged. In particular we do not agree that our performance has declined since the last report," "We have made many improvements since the last report and we already have a plan in place to continue to make further improvements where we need to do so." Chief Constable Hopkins and Co. didn't agree with the HMI's assertion that they don't attempt to prevent or investigate crime well enough and performance has declined.

GMP's standard, ill considered denial would ultimately catch up with it the following year. At the end of 2020, it was placed into special measures after HMI visited again, largely as a result of the same failures which just continued and worsened, led from the top as usual.

It was not only by the failure to record crime and monitor victims, but by the way GMP treated the Manchester public in ignoring the initial report by Her Majesty's Inspector of Constabulary (HMI). The force had responded to the criticism effectively with two fingers to an unbelievable 100 HMI recommendations, some five years old, remaining outstanding. It was inevitably and yet unsurprising, with GMP deliberately failing to accept the Inspectorate's latest assessment. Such deliberate failures with the ever growing illusion of being 'untouchable' and above the law even to the point of critiquing their own investigative body, were unbelievable.

Dr Graham Smith, a senior law lecturer at Manchester University, who had been called in by Deputy Mayor Baroness Beverley Hughes to investigate GMP's Professional Standards Branch which deals with internal bad conduct issues. In the past this inglorious department had exhibited 'mind boggling' bias to the 'mind boggling' indiscretions of the senior ranks whilst happily sacrificing the junior ranks 'for the figures'.

He regarded the acquittal of senior officers charged verbally with several offences arising from the Hillsborough crowd control and resultant deaths as yet another example. He believed GMP to be a 'case study' in that kind of behaviour.

There has always been a tendency within the GMP at all ranks to lean towards the culture of obfuscation, denial, secrecy and an instinct to defend the indefensible as displayed during 2008 and 2020 under CCs Fahy and Hopkins. To pompously tell the HMI that they had "got it wrong in their critical report was stupidly wrong. The risk of reputational damage is extremely important to policing and chief officers at any expense especially in the knowledge that 'they can literally get away with murder'.

A proud history ... are you joking?

It is written that Greater Manchester Police has a long and proud history. It is not clear from whence that rather misguided piece of prose emanated. Its Chief Constables have traditionally been awarded Knighthoods for their leadership achievements and qualities. However during the last fifty years it has not been the case and the break with such a fine tradition must be questioned. It should be asked how the fine line of accepted corrupt practices had not been seen sooner but instead, confined to a rather 'Ostrich head in the sand' scenario.

What should also be questioned is how those Knighted contributed to the 'general well being' of the citizens of Greater Manchester and importantly why? In my research I find, a respected retired senior detective who actually pens in the the twenty first century that the so called 'Proud Force' is actually 'a broken force that's lost its moral compass' A relatively mild comment from a man with so much inside knowledge.

I never believed I would witness Asian paedophiles permitted to rape and pillage their way through various areas of Greater Manchester for the sake of 'racial harmony' with the absolute minimum of arrests.

As shown below, perhaps as confirmation of what will appear to be the unbelievable, are excerpts in *Italics* and such informative prose will be littering pages onwards from my entire 'chequered career' in the Manchester Police Force.

My first literary wonder offers proof that whatever corruption is publicised as a rot in the police of today, it is not original and was certainly alive and festering so many years before my police service of the 1960s and 70s. What should be clear is the fact that such behaviour was accepted by most and seen as the norm by all ranks. Such an ingrained culture at all levels has continued for many years and in some cases worsened in severity. It was not unusual for senior officers to 'entertain' young police women fresh from training school with an existing reputation and hopes for promised promotion.

The Biggest Gang in Britain:

Of course, initial impressions can be wrong. My first day saw me paired with an experienced officer so I could be shown the realities, the actual wheels and pulleys of police life, details I had been denied at training school. After having the piss taken out of my bulled boots, I was told I could forget most of what I had learned at Bruche, the training school of yesteryear, that is, except how to drink beer, pillage and shag. One of my first gems of wisdom concerned the image of a policeman in the eyes of the public. Many women, I was told, love the uniform, especially the helmet. Women love the helmet? I'm not sure why. I'm not sure they could tell you why. Maybe it looked like the head of a penis, who knows? One sanctioned by the Queen. Anyway, wearing this singular bit of apparel was certainly part of sexual arousal. The helmet alone was to be worn during the act itself. Of course I thought this fanciful speech, to be first day banter and all good ribbing. I was wrong.

I was so sadly wrong that I devoted a chapter to what was simple sexual activities and whilst all consensual in my case there were incidents involving colleagues, that would today, lead to prosecutions had they been reported and possibly in greater numbers. However the following illustrates the casual culture at the time which chose to ignore/accept the intense sexual activities of some, discussed over a pint.

What an amazing day of news, as I write. The Law Lords, in their infinite wisdom have decided that the police were wrong to reject the application of a transsexual to join the Force. If he/she should ever be a serving officer, one of the many difficulties he will face will be to search both women and men upon arrest. But there is always an excellent blow job to look forward to, perhaps by his companion on nights. From the experiences I have had and witnessed, the fact that the transsexual "came out" is the only difference, considering that policewomen have always shagged other policewomen and policemen for that matter. Gay males have shagged all they can, and anywhere they can, even fellow officers, for as long as I can remember. I have known straight serving officers, pissed up, shagging a gay just for the experience.

On the lighter, more hereto side of sex, many of us made an art form of seducing the female inhabitants of the city centre. If that wasn't an option, we might engage in the 'peep,' known in school as the voyeuristic arts.

I remember a nameless colleague being disturbed. He was fully naked, with an equally naked young lady in his car on the site, which is now Piccadilly Station. The vehicle with him inside was fully concealed and he had even cleared his presence with the security man, telling him he was taking observations with a lady in the car for cover. Peepers with their own rules and their own unbelievable radar knew that no such act of serious policing ever took place and silently congregated around the car. Colleague and lady friend, with a full head of steam, and well into the act, suddenly realised they were not alone.

Colleague was happy to continue, but his lady friend was not amused, and having unscrewed and separated themselves with some difficulty in such a small car, they started to get dressed. It was only when he undressed at home to retire to bed, with his wife watching, that he realised he was wearing the lady friend's knickers. The knickers were very similar to Marks' gent's underwear, but with the artistic addition of lace on the legs and waist of the pink apparel. Wives were much more trusting in those days, and she accepted the explanation of hubby following through after a curry at the Piccadilly Indian, which was common, necessitating the dumping, so to speak, of the original underwear and wearing a replacement pair obtained from the night security at Marks who appeared amused, for what appeared to be an unknown reason. Now that I write it down and report it, it seems beyond belief to me. Are wives, like Lady Justice, really that blind?

The most extreme example of peeping actually occurred during my service in the CID at Didsbury, in South

Manchester. I accompanied a fellow officer who is now employed at the Police Museum in Newton Street, Manchester who wanted to show me the best peep on the beat, immediately behind the station. This was a residential area of terraced houses with high walls, garages, and rear entries. The best peeps were to be found through bedroom windows. I declined the offer when I realised I was to climb over and balance upon several walls, sneak through private gateways, over fences and finally balance on a garage roof to gain the perfect vantage point. Obviously, some were much simpler, and in certain circumstances the female was fully aware of her audience, and got obvious pleasure from the show she was starring in.

I had limited success with policewomen, although I did actually marry one. But that did not hamper my success with the opposite sex. It was quite a simple matter to stop women driving home. Some were married, and usually very drunk. There was no such thing as the breathalyser at this time, and enforcement of the law relating to drunk driving was very relaxed, leaving the unofficial enforcement to fines in the form of sexual favours, usually in the back seat of the offender's own car. On one occasion, I remember two females driving past a colleague and I. We smiled and waved. It was obvious just how pissed they were. They waved back. The driver didn't notice the Stop sign. She passed over the white line and collided with a Post Office van, which was hardly damaged. The postman was happy to leave his details and vacate the scene. Although very drunk, the driver was not impressed at being distracted. We wrote up the accident as 'no fault' because the Stop sign was actually broken and it was not illuminated. Well, that was the case after we hurled a couple of bricks through the illuminated plastic casing. Instant fines followed. Once again the painful vertical version came to the fore but needs must. Copulating cops or to be precise two happy constables, carrying out their civic obligations with two model citizens, giving their best to the law. I actually saw the passenger on three other occasions, until her husband stopped her coming home so late from town.

Female shop managers were also a favourite target. I had the pleasure of knowing a few. I suppose I knew them in a King James biblical sense as well. One such lovely managed a branch of a well known national name that will remain anonymous. Many happy hours were spent during the evening patrol of Market Street after closing time, in the rear stockroom. As I have already alerted you, I was expected to wear my helmet, studded collar and tie, but nothing else. This seemed peculiar at this inductee stage in my sexual career, but it was no stranger than other lessons I was learning at the time. I came to accept the helmet bobbing sex, but perhaps lost a certain fondness for it in my later years. She was eventually promoted to area manager and the stockroom was no longer available. We then met at her home in Bolton and did so for many years. I think this wonderful arrangement floundered when my entrepreneurial ambitions were on the rise. I asked her if she would put me into a situation where I could purchase seconds of the clothing sold at the shop. It didn't happen. And neither did any more tremblers.

Has any Home Secretary or one of the many underlings actually ever examined the real credentials of such rising senior ranking stars of today and considered that these individuals were once police constables, initially educated at the same 'peepers' training school, the University of Life and GMP with it's ingrained corrupt cultures, qualifying and being let loose on the unsuspecting populace. Rape allegations amongst the populace rarely resulted in a prosecution and of course led to a joint public state of mind that it was a total waste of time and very embarrassing to report such sexual events concerning a male police officer to a male police officer who appeared to experience some sexual gratification on listening to such a complaint.

The idea of reporting a police officer for such an assault was apparently never considered and whilst I personally never had any such experience. I was aware such whispered assaults occurred, but maybe were just accepted as the accepted culture of the existing dishonesty and sexual preferences, thereafter took no further interest.

Wanton sex did not appeal to all ...

The criminal activities of many 'protectors of the piece' varied on the actual shifts being worked. Thefts from cars were very popular and, it is true to say that every officer with a car had the best sound systems available, either by doing the break-in themselves, or by purchasing from the stash of stolen goods in individuals lockers at the station, or when they met at a neutral spot after work. Breaking into premises was also popular with certain officers. It was, of course, very simple in the middle of the night. You were the only defender of the peace in quite a large area which was your assigned beat. Many officers kept a jemmy (a short crowbar) in their jackets, and maybe a hammer, or a spring loaded nail punch for breaking car windows, as part of their police trappings. This handy item was kept in special pockets sewn into the inside of the jacket. Should a burglar alarm go off, you were simply the officer on the scene. The assault on the premises was phoned in as a burglary from the attacked premises. Whilst you waited for the owner to secure the premises, the officer in question, was able to rummage about and remove whatever was valuable and portable, all of which would be blamed on the escaped culprit. Difficulties with this simple procedure arose when the van crew and the section sergeant arrived as backup, now competitors for the spoils, all of them taking as much as they could in the minimum time. Now justice is blind, and slow - whereas hands are quick and certain. I remember, on one occasion many months into my service, driving to a 999 call because a shop window had been broken near Manchester Cathedral. The shop was a tobacconist's and had a display of lighters behind the security grill. The officer of the beat stood with his truncheon in his hand and his back to the hole in the window, preventing two other officers from adjoining beats, who wanted to empty the window. It is an odd but nonetheless common occurrence and in reality one to be merely accepted as life in the Queen's Police.

How can such comparatively harmless and yet totally dishonest behaviour be so readily accepted. The key appears to be that Chief Constables and all ranks below have been trained and introduced to the available levels of dishonesty and sexual behaviour immediately on leaving training school. These are the men who very early in their career decided to occasionally take part but gave actual hard case police work a miss and instead also studied hard to pass, difficult promotion examinations often based on sheep dipping, sheep shagging and the village choices of choosing a sheep or 'your sister' for the County Constabularies with no regard to City bobbies.

Another legend was Les Sim - who was then number one man in the city, with the legendary power and reach of a Godfather. Les had several nightclubs, all of which he ran with a rod of iron. In addition to his regular premises, he also had a late drinker (in the early days the extended licensing hours related to hospitality he provided in various forms, to the local constabulary, forms he reluctantly parted with). From Chief Superintendent down through the ranks there was a scale of bungs to 'keep the city vibrant.' All we enjoyed at the pointed end was a couple of pints with the doorman, a chicken leg, or maybe a smoked salmon sandwich with the chef which would have been a left over from an earlier reception. Another by-product of the flexible licensed hours, promoted by Chief Superintendent Dingwall, friend of the Greek club owners and model for the suits originating from the Greek tailors of the city, were drunk drivers wending their way home through rush hour traffic after a night's revels until the daylight hours.

Early one morning I was conducting the traffic at London Road and Whitworth Street. I signalled for the cars heading out of the city to stop. I waved a bus to turn right from Whitworth Street also going out. The bus shuddered to a halt before it was able to complete the turn and a loud metallic bang resounded from the other side. I walked around the bus to see a Ford embedded in its side. The offending driver was still at the wheel, uninjured but bemused. Opening the door I found him to be dead drunk and totally lost, having intended to drive out of the city. Unfortunately, he was travelling in the opposite direction. Such a situation would attract a number of solutions during the night, but in morning rush hour the possibility of an 'instant fine' was out of the question. The driver was unconscious through drink, not the accident and was arrested.

Leslie Phillips the comedian and legend of the Carry On Films died recently. During the same heavy drinking days of Chief Superintendent Alec Dingwall I had the pleasure of meeting the drunk and jovial Leslie, as I recalled ...

One night, at about 2am on Princess Street in the centre of Manchester, I saw a silver Mercedes driving toward me against the flow of the one way system. I signalled the car to stop, which it did, perhaps a few yards further on than I had anticipated, causing me to jump nimbly out of its path. I went to the open window, and there he was, the actor Leslie Phillips, looking as if he had stepped straight out of a Carry On film - blazer, military tie, white shirt, and beaming smile. Pissed, but nobody's perfect.

"Good evening officer, how wonderful to see you, got myself lost; these infernal streets all run in the wrong direction, I am trying to get to the Midland Hotel. Could you be so kind as to direct me, old boy?" Directions were

not an option. He was too pissed and I told him so. "Oh come on old boy, only had a couple," he slurred with his wonderful RAF Flying Officer voice. The Midland Hotel was only a few hundred yards as the crow flies, but the route included at least three changes of direction and six sets of lights. Being the ultimate protector of the public at large, I told him to get in the passenger seat and I would drive him to the Midland. The night staff were over the moon to see him, and everyone was ecstatic with his final exclamation as he attempted to buy me and the hotel staff a drink. I just couldn't leave, so I had a coffee. "Ding, Dong. It's like a party."

Sergeants and Inspectors, having passed the promotion examination and the lapse interview system are released on the unsuspecting public. More recently, proven to attract accusations of corrupted results with acts of nepotism. During their early years of self protected service, they rose through the ranks whilst doing little actual dangerous police work at the 'pointed' end.

Having been promoted in a very few years to the appropriate supervisory rank some actual arse licking shit heads, assisted in the early development of a protective shield for the Chief Constable of the day and known as The Police Complaints Department. This well conceived practice staffed by serving police officers investigating serving police officers. For many years such staffing ensured that no action was actually taken against any suspected perpetrator unless actually caught bang to rights in the act of whatever criminal offence.

Basically this proved to be akin to "Turkeys voting for Christmas" where any disciplinary action was very rare especially with regard to senior ranks. Equally any hard working officer and there were many, usually skating the fine line of honesty but in tandem believing the 'bad guys' were there to be put away. Often questionable evidence was a factor, either planted exhibits or fabricated conversations known as 'verbals'. Hard work was tended to be admired or maybe accepted by the 'investigators' who had actually barely experienced the rigours of real police work to compare and all they required was a statement explaining the fabricated, 'true' circumstances with which they could write off the complaint.

This system worked admirably for many years with a few lowly uniformed police constables and detective constables for that matter falling by the wayside, just to keep the figures for this department looking healthy. Such a practice was never to actually highlight the corrupt culture of the force, reflecting badly on the incumbent Chief Constable, ensuring his Knighthood. Greater Manchester Police has always been termed as Britains second largest police force and as such has been allowed to fester in it's own very rotten working practices. In fact and worth mentioning again it is actually 'a broken force that's lost its moral compass'.

We need to look no further for confirmation of such a damning quote than the Professional Standards Branch, so proudly titled with yet another professional bullshitter at the helm, Chief Superintendent Jon Chadwick. The Home Office has recently investigated this department. In the year up to April 2021, 251 complaints were made about officers in the Greater Manchester Police Metropolitan Area, however none were deemed to have a case to answer and were not referred to the official disciplinary process.

The Home Office figures show that the complaints involved 151 Greater Manchester police officers and noted, an officer can be subject to more than one allegation and an allegation can involve multiple officers. Figures also show there were 131 allegations of "conduct matter" offences, where there is an indication that a crime had been committed. These complaints involved 115 police officers. There were also 19 allegations against 14 officers for "recordable conduct" matters, which includes those that caused serious harm or death, and allegations of sexual offences and corruption. Clearly none of the complaints in any section were regarded as particularly serious.

To illustrate that the totally corrupt system of police investigating police does not work,'on any level' and Nationally, only one per cent of total complaints led to an official hearing, and no action was taken in 92 per cent of cases.

Head of GMP's Professional Standards Branch Chief Superintendent Jon Chadwick, said in a public statement which could have been written by C.C Peter Fahy himself: "Public trust and confidence is of upmost importance to Greater Manchester Police, and we understand our communities' expectations that our officers demonstrate the highest standards of professional behaviour. "We treat complaints with all seriousness and progress them in line with the IOPC's guidance, legislation and regulations." The figures have yet been ratified, and therefore a comment on the specifics is not yet available.

The Independent Office for Police Conduct, which investigates the most serious police misconduct allegations, said an investigated case may not always lead to a finding of misconduct. "There are a range of options including organisational or individual learning, providing an explanation, or providing an apology," a spokesperson said. "These are all designed to have a range of options to resolve the complaint." Therefore, only the most serious cases will result in proceedings."

Well that will give the citizens of Greater Manchester the utmost confidence and what can you say in reply. F.F.S. appears to cover it.

In the words of eminent Queens Council Leslie Thomas ... "Greater Manchester Police is rotten to its' core" One of many highly critical statements through many policing years but now resounding on a regular basis and too many to be ignored. As I mention 'rotten to its' core' and 'the lost moral compass' again and again I trust my critics will accept that such comments are repetitive and deliberately used in the absence of F.F.S. which may even appear on occasions in the absence of any dramatic words in my limited vocabulary, to utter my real disgust.

It was often said, possibly by Bernard Manning, the acclaimed comedian, club owner and race relations principal, that through the years of expanding boundaries Greater Manchester Police there once was a Proud History. Tell that to the hardworking lads, through the years, fighting to keep 'the pointed end' sharp and retain their employment status.

In contrast, it definitely has not, with regard to the selection of several Chief Constable who have actually even been Knighted and others ignored. To put the entire 'pantomime' into context it is important to highlight the many failings. Indeed, failings of most of these Chief Constables whether knighted or not in one document to give a true impression of all in real and dramatic context.

I have chosen to ignore the titles of some out of total disrespect as all must take some of the responsibility for the rotten culture which was developed over many years and followed by the pack of past Chief Constables.

Sadly Greater Manchester Police, a force which moulded my future in my thirteen years, proud enjoyable service, however close to the boundaries of honesty and decency. How can a once highly regarded and proud force be now regarded as "Rotten to its Core'.

For all of us, it is a simple exercise to read and forget news articles, which at the time were of an isolated incident leaving little impression over the years and maybe never seen in the same context of a continuing, festering issue. Seen so often with the usual reaction "Oh it is just the 'bent' police, move on, paying the bills etc. This 'literary masterpiece' may give an insight into the foundation over the last fifty years or thereabouts of a force which was always, even before then. very naughty but often nice, maybe good, very very good in certain areas of peace keeping, amongst the Manchester population. They did a job, perhaps not always within the law but the lid remained firmly shut in preventing the anarchy, so blatantly on show today. As a reminder, examples from my previous books, in *Italics* of such 'little gems' and my personal opinions, which whilst apparently warped are based on a great deal of historical research with ex colleagues, in various areas of the media to whom I give credit and of course my personal experiences, reflected in my writings, which I must stress, with a Manchester accent..

Let us wander through the chequered, 'long and proud history' of the Chief Constables whom allegedly deserved such a regal recognition for playing their part in what is actually the decomposition of such a once proud force through the eyes of a lowly Police Constable with proven police based common sense and a GCE 'O' Level in English Language.

1974–1976: JAMES WILLIAM RICHARDS

James Richards served a brief period upon GMP's amalgamation with other smaller forces. I penned the following excerpt fifteen years ago confirming that the problems of today are not new and have always been an accepted culture.

This period, for me personally covered some of my more informative service years of the already accepted culture of Evidence Fabrication, Manipulation of Detection figures, Theft/Burglary. Acceptable Sexual abuse of Police Women and the public for that matter. The following excerpt, somewhat lengthy, but informative with regard to an existing culture well before Mr James Richards. In 2013 I wrote ...

The murder detection rate today throughout the country is now, of course, abysmal. The most common murders usually relate to family members or close friendships in a wider group. Only such murders with family connections are now detected and only then because the actual evidence is so blatantly obvious. During the days of the 60s and 70s as I have already written all murders were detected. Whether the accused had actually committed the offence was immaterial.

Today Murder Squads are, led by senior ranks with no experience of life, let alone actual detailed detection procedures whilst leading a murder hunt effectively, which should really be based on years of experience. Today senior officers do not gain that experience as they flit from one course to another at various police training establishments and university degree courses. Of course they are taught the theory but the practical application is so very different. In my first book I detail initial basic training and how such practical demonstrations at training school differ so radically to the real world of actual police work. On leaving the training schools with so many worthless paper qualifications they soon realise that they have absolutely no experience involving the management of many men, some with the lowly rank of detective constable with much more knowledge and accordingly harbouring resentment which in itself seriously affects morale. These are good able detectives, who have made a career choice not to study for a variety of reasons usually hinging on the fact that they could be on the piss seeking their next little naked victim, or meeting informants and then going on the lash probably with the proceeds of an insurance reward. As with the very poor documentaries, the majority of murders are now just a police public relations exercise, stage-managed to hide the real enormity of their failure. Parents, relatives, and friends are paraded at televised press conferences, pleading with the culprits to give themselves up. I don't quite get that one – they generally have to be caught or at least that's what happened in my day.

Wooden television appearances by the so-called investigating officer and weeping relatives are followed by filmed coverage of masses of uniforms thrashing the living daylights out of the countryside, white latex overalls on police officers, carrying many plastic bags of potential forensic evidence away from the scene. As the story loses media interest, some insignificant young lookalike does the last walk of the victim. I can't remember when any of these scenarios resulted in an arrest, but they actually delay any real detection work whilst mountains of pointless leads provided by the local nutters flood in bringing the real investigation to a grinding halt. Then of course, if such information is regarded as important and worthy of investigation the entire procedure depends on the quality of the detective who is given the responsibility of vetting all possible leads. How many murderers have been missed with poor collation of vital evidence only to be arrested some additional murders 'down the road' when found to have been in the system already. They are often highlighted during the initial investigation, but never interviewed. There have never been so many undetected murders and so many others thrown out of court for lack of real evidence.

In addition, there have never been so many convicted murderers released from prison terms of varying lengths, as evidence is proved to be unsafe. In the case of the murder of TV presenter Jill Dando an obviously innocent weirdo, Barry George, who was unable to defend himself effectively, was convicted and forgotten. He had a history of strange incidents, all sexually motivated and so tenuous was the evidence available that George was freed eight years later by the Court of Appeal.

The question must be asked whether the evidence was "made to fit?" He is now proved to be innocent, but the arresting officers have never been taken to account. If he was indeed innocent the questions must be asked regarding the fact that gunpowder residue was found on his clothing. Only recently has a witness come forward and been believed by the media, but ignored by the original investigation in relation to a good description of the actual perpetrator. A swarthy male of eastern European appearance was seen near the murder scene of the BBC Crimewatch presenter's house. Despite his release from prison as a result of evidence unreliability Mr George continues to be denied compensation.

The conviction of Sion Jenkins for the murder of his step daughter, Billy Jo Jenkins has been declared unsafe, as it relied only on the forensic evidence of her blood on his clothes. Whilst never stated openly, the Appeal Judges must have considered the fact that the presence of the blood spots was much too convenient in the absence of other evidence. I had, in a detailed letter, informed the Jenkins' defence team that evidence such as this is commonly fabricated by investigating officers in the absence of real evidence. My assistance was acknowledged, but I was never called as a witness. Despite these publicised criminal acts of perjury and total corruption of the evidence, the so-called investigating officers are generally never brought to justice. No wonder similar acts are regularly perpetrated in the knowledge that the full force of the law will never fall on them and if it should they will inevitably be protected from any serious criminal charges as happened with such sad consequences for Stefan Kiszko.

The murder of Lesley Molseed is such a typical example of corruption of evidence and procedures on so many *levels that it is certainly worthy of a detailed explanation. Lesley Susan Molseed was 11-years-old when she was murdered on the 5th October 1975. This is the same era as so many other corrupt incidents such as Jimmy Savile, the miners' strike and the paedophile Cyril Smith MP, who was well-known for his sexual activities involving children in the Rochdale area. He was protected by the same force where the murdered child lived and which assisted with this murder investigation. Stefan Ivan Kiszko, a 23-year-old tax clerk, was wrongly convicted of her sexual assault and murder. He served 16 years in prison after being wrongly convicted of these offences in what was described as 'the worst miscarriage of justice of all time' by one outraged Member of Parliament. Kiszko was released from prison in 1992 after further examination of forensic evidence showed that he could not have committed the crime. Kiszko died one year later and Ronald Castree was eventually found guilty of the crimes on November 12th 2007.*

The little girl's body was found in a remote lay by with 12 stab wounds. Her clothing had not been disturbed but the body had been laid in a 'pose' and the killer had ejaculated over her underwear. At the time of the hunt four teenage girls claimed Kiszko had indecently exposed himself to them and had repeated the act a month after the murder to one of the girls on Bonfire Night. Of course this was all the evidence required to suspect Kiszko of the murder and at the time the police concentrated on prosecuting him whilst ignoring other leads. Without doubt Kiszko had an idiosyncratic lifestyle which included a negligible social life and an odd habit of recording car registration numbers of drivers who annoyed him. There is no doubt he suffered learning difficulties.

He was arrested on the 21st December 1975 and the police 'found' a bag of sweets and girlie magazines in his car. He was subjected to three days of intensive questioning after which he admitted to the offence, because in his disturbed mind he would then be released and allowed to go home whilst the investigation continued and he would be proved innocent. This belief in itself demonstrates his simple thinking abilities and clearly the police took advantage of this. He was the only suspect as all other 'leads' were discounted despite strong evidence to the contrary. After all he had confessed which certainly did not assist his cause. Kiszko was not automatically entitled to a solicitor as is the case today and indeed it was not until the Police And Criminal Evidence Act of 1984 that such a requirement became law. Kiszko was never asked if he wanted a solicitor and was never cautioned until well after the police had decided he was the only suspect. He was charged with the murder on Christmas Eve 1975 and his trial commenced on 7th July 1976. Kiszko was defended by David Waddington QC, who was later to become the Home Secretary, and prosecuted by Peter Taylor QC, who later became the Lord Chief Justice and the author of the infamous Hillsborough Report.

Of course, back then the majority of the jury believed the police evidence, however lawed it proved to be. Kiszko stated his admission was purely to pacify the police who were then 'nice' to him on his admission. The conduct of his defence left much to be desired, but even his solicitor believed him to be guilty. He was found guilty after five hours and 35 minutes deliberation, but only on a 10 out of 12 majority verdict. The learned judge commended all the witnesses particularly Detective Sergeant John Ackroyd and Detective Superintendent Dick Holland. Kiszko was eventually sent to Wakefield prison where he was kept apart from other prisoners on what is known as Rule 43 for his own safety. Despite this he was attacked several times and throughout his sentence his mental health deteriorated as he was moved from prison to prison and into several mental health establishments.

For eight years Kiszko's mother campaigned for his case to be reopened. He would never admit to the offence and as a consequence would never be considered for parole. His mother contacted JUSTICE the Human Rights Organisation and they eventually had the case reopened. The case was referred back to West Yorkshire Police where Detective Superintendent Trevor Wilkinson conducted the investigation and immediately found several glaring errors. Witnesses were found to confirm Kiszko's alibi of visiting a grave in Halifax and visiting a nearby shop. These witnesses had never been properly interviewed by the investigating officers and whatever evidence they gave totally contradicted the decision to prosecute Kiszko and therefore show the murder as detected. The witnesses were not called by his defence team who may not even have been aware of their existence as of course their use would have resulted in a not guilty verdict.

At the time of the reopened investigation it was also established that Kiszko had a physical problem which prevented him producing sperm, so consequently could not have ejaculated over the victim. This fact was known to the investigating officers. The four young girls all admitted lying 'for a laugh.' Whilst all the detail is significant it is sufficient to say that Kiszko was by the time of his release mentally ill. He was awarded a derisory £500,000 most of which he did not receive due to his death a year after his release.

The point to all the above detail is of course what actually happened to the once commended police officer who by the time of his release had been denounced by the trial judge, the Molseed family and the local media. Detective Superintendent Holland and Ronald Outeridge, the forensic scientist, were formally charged with 'doing acts tending to pervert the course of justice' by allegedly suppressing evidence, namely the results of the semen tests from Kiszko and from the victim's body. The defence counsel at an early pre-trial hearing before magistrates, proved that a fair trial was impossible for Holland. He was guilty, deliberately so and should have appeared in court to answer the charges, but it was once again brushed away in the culture of the day, that police officers would not be prosecuted under any excuse.

Holland came to public prominence in yet another flawed investigation into the Yorkshire Ripper and M62 'bomber' Judith Ward, who had her conviction ruled as unsafe in 1992. Having once had these investigations regarded as his finest hours in 35 years of police service Holland was subsequently demoted, four years after Kiszko's conviction. As I have said, Holland's defence barrister had argued that his conviction would be unsafe due to the passage of time and would make a fair trial impossible. In yet another example of the naivety of magistrates they agreed and the matter was not sent for trial. Holland died in 2007 at the age of 74 and remains yet another example of the corrupt practices of the West Yorkshire Police and their ability to avoid legal retribution despite the weight of evidence.

The trial judge and West Yorkshire Police have apologised for this dreadful miscarriage of justice, but surely such a miscarriage has been further exacerbated with the lack of prosecutions against the men who deliberately fabricated evidence to ensure a conviction of an innocent man. Kiszko for so many years suffered amazing hardships in prison, which eventually caused his mental illness and death on release. So long after these events David Cameron is proclaiming the police to be 'relatively honest,' but the corruption and fabrication remains.

In yet another but simpler example of the one law for us and one for them traffic constable John Wetherall, 34, was dismissed from the South Yorkshire Force in what must certainly be a first and a sign of the times. This man had 10 years unblemished service in the force, and was career-minded, looking to be promoted at any opportunity. His life is now in ruins. Clearly the offence must have been serious, much more than a Deputy Chief Constable in Manchester prosecuted for driving at 120mph on the M6 toll road. He received a token sentence which did not involve the automatic ban that the rest of the speeding public suffers for the same offence. Wetherall actually drove his car over the force boundary into Nottinghamshire which is hardly crossing into Russia, and kissed a woman who got into his car. There was no sex or even attempts at sex. Being a traffic car, the interior and exterior is constantly filmed by two separate cameras. PC Wetherall, being aware of this, removed the videos of his married lady friend's activity in the police car and put them in his locker. The grave differences in police practices of today and my day, now become apparent. A fellow PC entered his secured locker claiming to be seeking a video for evidence, found the offending videos and handed them to the supervisory officers, who, on PC Wetherall's return from holiday, took disciplinary action against him, resulting in dismissal. Obviously, he was astounded at the dual standards in the force. Because in the same week a high ranking officer in the same force was caught having sex with a blonde female inspector with no serious disciplinary consequences. Again in the same force, continuing to perpetuate the double standards and be in no doubt that every force is the same; a sergeant was caught having sex with a married woman in a police car. without any disciplinary measures.

The Manchester and Salford joint force amalgamated with portions of the Lancashire, Cheshire and West Yorkshire Constabulary forces, producing the largest provincial force in England and Wales. At that time it had an establishment of 6,628 officers (actual strength 5,545) and 1,796 civilian staff, and dealt with 102,144 crimes reported to the police.

I can safely report that Mr. James William Richards was "totally nondescript" possibly, totally out of his depth with an uncanny knack of never 'rocking the boat' of real police work. He appeared to accept the existing 'way it was' sixty eight 'night clubs', Despite many causing the City centre to be akin to Dodge City. However Chief Superintendent Alec Dingwall presided over this accepted culture within the City centre A Division.

Many of the establishments were often only the size of a 'front room' served alcohol until 8.00am as the need arose without a thought to the 2.00am liquor licence legally granted. The Greek Cypriots benefited from a motley crew of Licensing Magistrates who granted licences wholesale and favoured a few of the larger and more salubrious establishments and the freebies they offered such as The Cromford Club., later to be featured in the movie 'Hell is a City' with the alleyways of my actual beat.

Another legend was Les Sim - who was then number one man in the city, with the legendary power and reach of a Godfather. Les had several nightclubs. In addition to his regular premises, he also had a late drinker and in the early days the extended licensing hours related to hospitality, he provided in various forms to the local licensing constabulary, forms he reluctantly parted with. From Chief Superintendent down through the ranks there was a scale of bungs to 'keep the city vibrant.' All we enjoyed at the pointed end was a couple of pints with the doorman, a chicken leg, or maybe a smoked salmon sandwich with the chef which would have been a left over from an earlier reception. Another by-product of the flexible licensed hours, promoted by Mr Dingwall, friend of the Greek club owners. He was an excellent model for the suits originating from the Greek tailors of the city, sponsored by the Club owners. There were often drunk drivers wending their way home through rush hour traffic after a night's revels until the daylight hours.

Early one morning I was conducting the traffic at London Road and Whitworth Street. I signalled for the cars heading out of the city to stop. I waved a bus to turn right from Whitworth Street also going out. The bus shuddered to a halt before it was able to complete the turn and a loud metallic bang resounded from the other side. I walked around the bus to see a Ford embedded in its side. The offending driver was still at the wheel, uninjured but bemused. Opening the door I found him to be dead drunk and totally lost, having intended to drive out of the city. Unfortunately, he was travelling in the opposite direction. Such a situation would attract a number of solutions during the night, but in morning rush hour the possibility of an 'instant fine' was out of the question. The driver was unconscious through drink, not the accident and was arrested.

Chief Superintendent Alec Dingwall ruled the A Division and 'the Greeks' with a rod of iron, well before Mr Richards and the amalgamation, visiting them all, making it perfectly clear that they were to self govern at the risk of their lucrative liquor licence and heavy fine.

In return for the 'flexible' drinking hours and the none existent enforcement, gratitude abounded, usually taking the shape of an immaculate Greek tailored suit or maybe a Cyprus holiday dependant on the severity of the transgression plus of course a 'few quid' weekly and all the booze he and we could drink at the bar and in boxes at Christmas.

The occasional, forcibly ejected, badly damaged party goer, bruised, broken bones etc. was swept under the 'sticky' club carpet as was the occasional murder of a club doorman. All transgressions, some very serious always had a proffered culprit without the need for a Police investigation, affecting the thriving businesses.

Fights would break out, often resulting in quite serious injuries, which had to be accounted for. There was no such thing as a really upset complainant, even if an ear was hanging off. They had usually picked a fight with the doorman, having been told to behave, only to come off second best with blood and snot everywhere, clothing ruined, ears and noses relocated and just generally beaten up. Today a doorman would be charged with such damage, however drunk the complainant was. During these halcyon days, of beautiful sunrises such matters were treated with the flourish of the Hillsborough Conspiracy and we didn't see the crime in it.

There was plenty more, highlighting the extent of the club culture which operated at this time. It makes one wonder how so many could survive? The flexible licensing hours were obviously a major contributory factor. And the various rents paid were an economic necessity to exist. The wheel came off one memorable time when Bernard O'Sullivan – a 6ft 8ins tall doorman – attended Sid Ottie's club which also had a 'casino licence'. It actually traded as a private members club which encouraged gambling for small sums when actually sums in excess of thousands of pounds changed hands during card games and private bets on the horses.

Anyway, on this particular evening Bernard was refused entry by one of the 'Fighting' Camalleris, of Manchester, who met him later along with another member of the fearsome scrapping family. The result was a dead Bernard. He already had a steel plate in his skull, and having his head kicked in this latest brawl, pushed medical science a little too much. He was driven to the hospital in a taxi by a driver with a prepared script for the medics. When he was found to be dead on arrival the script had to be amended to Bernard butting the dashboard in an emergency stop situation having refused to wear a seatbelt. The stories scripted for the dumb driver were a little flimsy and were not in anyway assisted with the discovery of footprints on Bernard's head. A murder charge followed for one of the Camalleris – which was eventually thrown out by a jury, possibly selected from the local populace with some knowledge of big Bernard and his shovel-sized hands. The 12 men, good and true sitting in judgement on Bernard's untimely demise dismissed the murder charge. Dingwall was not impressed at all by this episode of lawlessness in his city and did not wish such a misdemeanour to cloud the oiled workings of clubland or his peaceful existence. In his eyes he feared the Greeks and Cypriots would suspect he'd begun to lose control allowing for more criminality to follow along with the inevitable raids, then tighter licensing laws that would eventually affect the income of all concerned.

The Plain Clothes posse was immediately mobilised to visit all the dubiously licensed establishments – no matter where they stood on the rental ladder. The police had to be seen to be still in control and to give the fresh invasion some credibility a few of the really shitty joints not serving hot food in the statutory seated position and with guests not signing the membership book, were closed. Our Cypriot chums had an instant lesson in the licensing commandments in place before the unfortunate Bernard departed his mortal coil.

The odd stabbing in any club would also cause police concern in the guise of outrage and instant fines, as it drew attention to the loose interpretation of the licensing legislation we were enforcing. There were many stories of violence in the name of in-house security at untold clubs, and while the severely bruised member complained, the complaint was written around and no action taken. Even so many decades ago and in the style of the Hillsborough Conspiracy such report writing thrived and with the untouchable philosophy firmly in place it blossomed into so many much smaller conspiracies. Such Enid Blyton endeavours did not come cheap and most of the senior club owners were summoned to await an audience with the 'Boss' for a public relations dressing down and all that came with it....basically nothing. It was simple PR as long as the correct palms were greased all continued running smoothly.

The Chief Inspector would write it up as he felt it should be to pass to the Chief Super who in turn took copies of the report on his next forage about the division, in one of his 'George the Tailor' suits. All the tailors, the cafe and club owners were also called George or Chris for ease of recollection. The 'concerned' Chief Super would visit the club which the previous night was a battlefield and which showed no traces 24 hours later and met with the owner. With much wringing of hands by the boss and begging for mercy from the club owner the carefully adapted report was produced and the difficulties in preparing such a document which would not be put to the licensing magistrates was produced. Of course next Christmas was covered with a 'few' bottles, a fortnight in Cyprus and spends together with a new suit, sponsored by the club owner as the tailor was by now becoming just a little disillusioned as of course he never had fights in his workshop and no real need for the police in any case. His only fault was that he was fair game as a Greek Cypriot friend of the many club owners.

With the amalgamation came what must have been a bright idea born in the Home Office, the speedy introduction of the Accelerated Promotion Scheme, a 'brain dead' idea which quickly forced such applicants with an education, through two examinations leading to promotion to the rank of uniformed Inspector and quickly onwards to dizzy heights. The working lads, both uniformed and C.I.D were busily detecting crime, protecting the public whilst relaxing with limitless periods of pissing it up and shagging the local population allowing little time for studying.

However sober, 'little dick' University types (remember my Manc accent) and such who could spend the time to read copious manuals of legislation and retain such knowledge in what was seen as a difficult examination to the working lads, easily blossomed.

Overgrown schoolboys, leaving upper school, onwards to university for an easy degree in philosophy or flower arranging or anything vaguely connected to real life, then onto the Police Force Accelerated Promotion scheme. To be perfectly clear, these men and some women (not many) had ever seen an angry man, had a fight and certainly never broken a nose, particularly in any of the four Yates Wine Lodges on Oldham Street, Manchester which had to be seen to be believed as centres for drunken violence on a regular scale. Wise words from 2013...

It is through such ranks that the promoted senior officers climb. They have spent all their few years of service hiding from real police work, sometimes out of fear, sometimes total incompetence, but always gaining little experience, spending most of their service in desk driving administration jobs to facilitate their attendance at various universities and police training establishments. Having been promoted through the ranks they are expected to lead by example and thereby lies the problem and the reasons for such lack of control.

Of course, the success of any business relies on the 'man/woman at the helm' and down the ladder through his various supervisory officers. Success thereafter depends on the experience and capabilities of the chosen 'leaders.' A police force is no different. Where it differs from business is the fact that it does not have to show a profit to survive, it will have 12 assistants and Deputies when three would do, merely produce statistics which hopefully prove at least some element of hard work and proper guidance. Statistics are an art and the detection rate can be fabricated and only since real detectives have been replaced by university graduates has the detection rate fallen dramatically. The honest detection rate has always been abysmal and has always relied on informants and fabricated TICs (offences Taken Into Consideration) as I will relate in some detail later.

In my day the drinking, pillaging and shagging always had to be curtailed occasionally in case it prevented any real police work on too much of a permanent basis. Having had a brief history lesson, a profound and honest comparison, perhaps helping to reduce the already natural disgust and surprise, but read on. Of course in highlighting such failings, what I say is difficult to believe and to consider the fact that the Chief Constable, just didn't want to know. Even Andrew Mitchell MP of Plebgate fame was quoted as saying that his faith in the police is not, shall we say, what it was before they stitched him up like a kipper at the gates of Downing St.

Of course what had once passed as honest police work, carried on unabated as the accepted culture of all that was bent, blended often with vigorous police work. The villains were arrested and the evidence was adapted to suit. Sexual pleasures continued, mostly with general consent but always with the ripple of stories concerning certain individuals going much too far with women who during this time knew that any complaint of rape would go no further, especially concerning police officers and often public members with 'connections'. Convictions were impossible, even with matters that had actually got to court and then dissected by defence barristers to be the woman's fault. This was the days of Jury members believing anything, especially 'the police gave evidence on oath, so it must be true' and the sitting Judge for that matter.

So many unbelievable issues especially if considered in the real context of 'The Biggest Gang in Britain' with many more examples and especially with part two 'Shades of Black'n' Blue' giving an insight into the CID antics. My early apologies for the length of this excerpt, but to be perfectly honest it says so much about so many blending and accepted cultures way back in the 70s.

Didsbury has always had its own synagogue and so the Jewish community has always populated this area. They maintain the standards and build an invisible barrier from the creeping body of Asians who are moving into the area. They moved in to live and also buy the larger Victorian properties to convert to flats and rent out to students, who seemed to put up with any expensive crap. Didsbury was back then known as Yidsbury and was a target area for burglars strolling the short distance from Wythenshawe. The burglars saw these posh houses as easy targets, when taking a rest from shagging their sisters and even on occasions their mothers. Be in no doubt that during these times, the majority of the population on this sprawling estate were classic scrotes, whole families of them, who had been rehoused from council accommodation elsewhere in the city. The council decided their old accommodation was unfit for human occupation. The original houses must have been deplorable as these transient scrotes were the pits of humanity. They had no real moral compass, they had no family values and went through life existing from one crime to the next, be it burglary or shoplifting, or shagging their own mothers and children.

They even expected a good hiding whenever arrested whatever the circumstances. Their experience and knowledge of the police also allowed for an occasional good kicking just in passing, purely for disciplinary purposes. Whilst hardly PC it was an acceptable practice to 'keep the lid on' and it was great training just giving the wandering scumbag a severe hiding to keep your hand in. As with planting goods on passing suspected shoplifters, such a belting acted as a deterrent and had a dramatic effect. With the younger members such a crack at least forced them to think twice before entering the realms of criminality with any serious beliefs.

Still moving South(ish) the 3rd section changed to the 4th section which encompassed the largest council estate in Europe with all its problems, thefts, assaults, murders, burglaries and incest which was very popular with the perverted drunken louts fancying their own children. In reality these sick souls didn't know any better as their own father's often fiddled with them. Such crapheads as I have already related were rehoused from redeveloped areas throughout the city and they formed a nucleus of the population. However, many older and thoroughly decent people were moved to Wythenshawe, often under loud protest to be sprinkled amongst all this human rubbish without any consideration of the nightmares they were to experience living amongst them. The majority had never seen such human garbage.

A drive through Wythenshawe easily identified which houses were populated by each section of this disjointed community. Some of the houses had gardens, with bright flowers and mowed lawns, flowering tubs and hanging baskets finishing off the lovely appearance. The privet hedges were neatly trimmed and even the garden gate had had a coat of paint. Next door could easily have an uncut privet hedge, a flagged lawn area with the obligatory rotting mattress and rusting washing machine, probably replaced by Manchester Social Services, leaving the old items to be tipped by the householder. For many the front garden seemed an ideal tipping point and an instant playground for the children with no thought for the obvious dangers.

Of course, Wythenshawe also played host to the Golden Garter Theatre Club and whether we liked it or not we would run the gauntlet through the estate from Didsbury to the club in the hope we would not be asked to assist the resident troops on this section with removing a father from his daughter, or a suspicious cot death, an event which was too common in this area to be genuine all the time. Forensic tests which developed over the years improved considerably and later proved that cot deaths were murder in several instances either by the retarded mother, not fit to have children or the pissed-up father returning from a hard day in the Benchill pub and annoyed at the incessant crying.

The 4th section was based at Brownley Road Police Station, which was right in the centre of this seething mass of life's failures. This building was a post war red brick box, unattractive, again with its own busy public desk, cells and CID offices on the first floor. Unlike Didsbury it had its own charge office where arrests were charged and either held in the cells or bailed if actually living at a set address and appearing on the voters' register, which was always the key and strangely this was more often the case. Whilst such registering appears strange for such retards it was the case that they would not be able to claim any benefits unless properly registered as a resident on the voters' register.

The CID officers based at Didsbury, but working out of Brownley Road regarded us as non-working playboys and we all only met when they came out of the wilderness to drink in the Royal Oak, opposite Didsbury nick, having no real pub where they could relax in Wythenshawe.

At Didsbury, we had a better populace, a better class of villain and better pubs with a much better choice of women, often married, usually divorced, and many students who as today were indulging in prostitution just to make ends meet. As such a wanton sexual activity came to light, usually from a whistle-blowing neighbour we investigated, not because it was a criminal offence, which it was not, but out of a perverted interest. We were easily able to frighten the living daylights out of these lovely little things to the point of instant fines, an art honed from my days in uniform on the A Division. Back then street-walking prostitutes were often fined as they walked from one hostelry to the next. These impressionable little girls even got a kick from shagging a detective and often wanted to pose in a photo with their tame detective to show to their friends, which whilst great fun could have horrendous consequences.

Most offences on the 3rd section of the D Division consisted of burglaries and thefts from vehicles which were treated in a similar manner to the A Division. There was a standard procedure laid down throughout the force where all scenes of crime were visited, fingerprints attended, the complainants regularly updated on the telephone and with personal visits, which were a must in the climate of public relations. Each incident had its own crime number and individual crime report. This form was a work of art with many sections, titled and designed to ensure that all facets had been properly dealt with. Every visit and phone call was endorsed and recorded. Visits were made by the Fingerprint Department and where there had been a witness which was rarely the case, they would be taken to Longsight Criminal Records Office where they were shown volumes of photographs of previously convicted offenders. This was a strange practice because on many occasions, viewers recognised neighbours and colleagues, causing many embarrassing moments even resulting in dismissal in employer-staff incidents.

The CID work at Didsbury differed greatly to other divisions. All burglaries were visited and the scene properly examined. The Fingerprint Department attended and covered every flat surface with a white dust. Fingerprints were often found as many burglaries were committed by the drug-taking community, who also populated flats in some of the roads in Didsbury and then elimination fingerprints had to be taken of all members of the household to establish if there was a strange print. The print was then searched in the volumes of records with a system of recognition that I never really understood.

Until I heard of a particular murder being detected on fingerprint evidence and the culprit hanged, I didn't have much faith in the Fingerprint Department, believing it to be merely a public relations exercise. Whenever I visited complainants in their homes after the Fingerprint Department had attended the first point of conversation was how much time it had taken the householder to remove the white dust, but tempered with: "Well it's nice to see that every attempt is being made."

To say eccentricity reigned with a touch of childish fiction author 'Enid Blytons' to achieve a realistic detection rate is an understatement, not by any particular individual, but the entire CID in general. I learned a great deal from the legendary senior officers of my times such as John Thorburn, Tom Butcher, Eric Jones, Roy Hartley, Charlie Horan, Douglas Nimmo, Arnie Beales, Callum McDonald and many more in the ranks below, despite my mild encounters from the other side of the fence. The actual workers such as DI John Thorburn and DI Eric Jones were slowly replaced by the John Stalkers and much worse, the James Andertons, who luckily had been very few and far between during my service, but appear to abound in the present day policing. These are men who made an art of doing the minimum of sharp-end police work, fearing that their accelerated promotion would be badly affected by a complaint imposed by some scrote or other, fearing it would tarnish their impeccable record and rise to a really protected desk.

James Anderton when Chief Constable has to accept full responsibility for this ethic in Greater Manchester Police and the resulting general failure of the force during the later years of his service. It was during Anderton's reign that no-go areas became accepted in places such as Cheetham Hill, a secondary city area to be populated by ethnic minorities, and Moss Side, a large part of which was populated by West Indians. The detection rate dropped to abysmal reality and the streets of Greater Manchester were not safe to walk. Even fabricating

ROTTEN TO ITS CORE

TICs which maintained the detection rate became a tightrope and one not worthy of the risk. It grew like an understanding amongst the force that Anderton was not working, harassing the 'troops' with his headline-grabbing antics which became so many that it became general knowledge that the Home Office had told him to shut up. With such lame leadership why should the rest of us, the ones at the pointed end make any real effort?

As I have said, the CID offices looked like a set in Hill Street Blues and I wonder, sometimes, if plots for these programmes were taken from Manchester CID in general. The plots for Heartbeat and The Bill were certainly not. The general office had just about enough seating for us all, for morning parade. There were two side offices for interviews and a bit of quiet writing and the Detective Inspector's office, where it certainly felt like being on a daily roller coaster ride for the man in the hot seat. When I started, we had Inspector John Thorburn. I have mentioned him with great respect in previous chapters, and indeed he deserves the print. There were not enough like him. I can't say enough concerning him and those of his calibre. There were so few honourable names and so many counterfeits, that a little repetition is a forgivable offence.

John was a good man, a steady man, a real detective of the old school and a little too outspoken to proceed quickly up through the ranks of inexperienced YES men. As officers progressed through the force and their rank got higher, potential promotion candidates were interviewed by several senior officers on a Promotion Board. John only had to be asked: "What is wrong with the police today, Mr. Thorburn?" The usual and perhaps safe response might have been of the "Well run, but underfunded" school. But John Thorburn told the truth. The truth didn't help his promotion prospects. It hardly ever does. There were always other, higher criteria at stake. The truth, too many times, was a mere distraction, an impediment in the way of an imperfect justice.

John appeared quite content at Didsbury and enjoyed the six o'clock pint at the Royal Oak, which was conveniently opposite the station. He used this location to mildly discuss work, but in the main judged his men fairly and formed a type of working bond. He never came on the real piss-ups, unless it was to mark one of the office stalwarts leaving for greener pastures or civilian life depending on the circumstances.

'Tricky' JB didn't have time for a leaving do. He was arrested for a series of offences which so many serving detectives treated as the norm, but in reality, not to such extremes as Jack. He was jailed in 1983 at Manchester Crown Court for offences of corruption and brutality whilst a Detective Chief Inspector. He was sentenced to about seven years imprisonment, but served only about four. The fact an officer of such a rank could be investigated and charged with such offences highlighted to us all that the 'the times they were a changing' and 'there but for the grace of God go I.'

JB was a one-off. He took pride in being known as totally bent and a raging psychopath to boot. Where it was the norm to plant evidence, beat up prisoners and bribe informants to set up another criminal individual,

Jack always went that bit too far and his treatment of prisoners and the beatings he gave them caused concern to real seasoned detectives. Jack's conviction and imprisonment sent ripples throughout the CID and eventually other matters he had dealt with where he had secured convictions were investigated and properly examined. This action was seen as a very alarming deviation from the norm where such behaviour had been accepted for so many years by the 'troops' on the ground, but supported by the senior supervisory officer ranks in their quest for the perfect detection figures. Once a successful investigation had been completed and filed away it was of course the unwritten rule that the file would remain closed. Jack's example was an alarming deviation from this practice and could have affected us all with other matters, but perhaps with less heart-stopping examples.

One such case which became known as the UK's longest running miscarriage of justice involved a man named Robert Brown who had the misfortune of being interviewed/tortured/beaten close to death....you choose, by 'Tricky' JB. He led the interview and worked with other officers who beat a confession out of Brown, which resulted in a signed statement confessing to a murder. Brown who was 20-years-old at the time was charged with the murder of Annie Walsh, a 51-year-old factory worker. As a result of Jack Butler's convictions for offences totally unrelated to the murder investigation, the Criminal Cases Review Commission found multiple grounds for doubts in the safety of Brown's conviction. They revealed that Jack's 1983 conviction related to crimes he committed in the 1973-5 time frame, pre-dating Brown's 1977 trial.

Of course the jury was not to know of JB's activities and his reputation and was left only with the summing up of Mr Justice Milmo, who gave the jury the simple decision of believing the police or the accused whose only defence was the fact that his confession had been beaten out of him. The confession was found to be the 'chief plank of the case' by the Review Commission.

The conviction was found to be unsafe because of JB's conviction on the other unrelated matters. Brown was now found 'not guilty.' There is a great difference here. It must be remembered when pitying Brown for the 25 years he spent in jail before the Court of Appeal released him on November 13th 2002, that he was not just picked up off the street and charged with this offence. Evidence pointed to him, but it was not enough and his statement added the finishing touches. It must be asked, whether an innocent person would sign such a statement which would result in a life sentence and what did B have to gain by fabricating all the evidence without even a glimmer of truth. A murder such as this necessitated the use of many detectives and to suggest JB was alone in the commission of this offence is ludicrous and itself, a serious omission. As with the Hillsborough conspiracy there were many officers of various ranks involved in this corruption of evidence and as time will tell only a few prosecutions if any at all will follow with the majority using the tried and trusted SS explanations of WWII: 'I was acting on orders' as has occurred in so many other such investigations.

What differs with the Hillsborough conspiracy is the fact that it is indeed a proven conspiracy, which totally explodes the constant plea of a rogue element of a few people with values of yesteryear. Examine the proof to date which itself will cause some serious attempts at avoiding the truth in the final report by virtue of the ranks and numbers of conspirators. Consider the facts? There are already named four Chief Constables, four Superintendents, several members of the Police Federation, a Coroner, three Judges, two Members of Parliament and at least 200 uniformed police officers. The inquiry is dragging on, probably in the hope that the main suspects will die giving everyone someone to blame.

In the case of Brown and JB there was a statement for the media, from the usual police spokesman after the appeal court judgment which said: "We would like to reassure the people of Greater Manchester that procedures under the Police And Criminal Evidence Act now provide safeguards for both suspects and officers." These include recording of the interview process and advanced forensic techniques.

Surely such a culture could only improve in the highly regarded and protected world of 'police leadership' ... Don't hold your breath. No one had ever considered the Christian carnage which was to follow.

1976–1991: JAMES ANDERTON... GODS COPPER OR TOTAL HYPOCRITE?

James Anderton, having taken a course in criminology at the Victoria University of Manchester, was tipped early on for high office. He served in Cheshire, Leicestershire and then in the inspectorate of constabulary in London. Always behind a desk and totally out of touch with reality before becoming chief constable of GMP at the age of 44, a role he held from 1976 to 1991 and which took him on to the national stage. How did he really survive such a lengthy service? Doesn't it just show the diabolical initial selection process and even worse the actual monitoring of the entire Force throughout.

Incredibly James Anderton was Knighted in 1990, despite a very chequered verbal history and a total failure in lowering all crime figures, due mainly to his persecution of minor infractions by the working lads at 'the pointed end'. Luckily I missed most of the nonsense but in having a pint with my ex colleague detectives, I had never known so many individuals looking to resign. In effect they went on strike to protect their careers and maintain an income until other employment could be found. He became known as 'God's copper', despite managing to be a total hypocrite on many important issues involving the conduct and training within the force, which he chose to ignore as had his predecessors and then all who followed. He preferred instead to obsess with his own crusades. He said he felt answerable to a higher authority than the Home Office during his time as a senior police officer rising to the rank of Chief Constable of Greater Manchester. I actually experienced Anderton when a Chief Inspector at Bootle St. All I remember is that he viewed seized porn films from the dirty book shops he harassed, locked in his office to the sound of a cine projector.

My early recollections and memories of James Anderton in Shades of Black'n'Blue, published 2013, give a firm impression of how the unseen rotten culture within GMP percolated at an alarming rate ...

James Anderton when Chief Constable has to accept full responsibility for the the general carnage in Greater Manchester Police and the resulting failures of the force during the later years of his service. It was during Anderton's reign that no-go areas became accepted in places such as Cheetham Hill, a secondary city area to be populated by ethnic minorities, and Moss Side, a large part of which was populated by West Indians. The detection rate dropped to abysmal reality and the streets of Greater Manchester were not safe to walk. Even fabricating TICs which maintained the detection rate became a tightrope and one not worthy of the risk. It grew like an understanding amongst the force that Anderton was not working, harassing the 'troops' with his headline-grabbing antics, which became so many that it became general knowledge that the Home Office had told him to shut up. With such lame leadership why should the rest of the troops, the ones at the pointed end make any real effort?

Although he led one of Britain's largest police forces for 15 years it will be the piss take, being "God's Copper" that James Anderton, will be best remembered. He claimed that he had divine guidance in his policing duties and his inflammatory remarks about queers ensured that he became, for a while, the most controversial police officer in Britain taking any 'Home Office 'eye off' his actual policing failures.

He continued with his Christian ravings at the height of the Aids crisis in the 1980s. Anderton, when Chief Constable of Greater Manchester attracted a great number of fans and outraged many by describing queers as "swirling around in a cesspit of their own making" and suggesting that "sodomy in males ought to be against the law". We believed he was absolutely losing it, especially when he advocated castration for rapists and urged a return to corporal punishment so that offenders could be thrashed until "they repent of their sins"

Anderton made it clear that he felt answerable to a higher authority than the Home Office. "God works in mysterious ways," he said. "Given my love of God and my belief in God and Jesus Christ, I have to accept that I may well be used by God." Thus was born "God's copper", a figure of mockery even ridicule to some, a bastion of old-fashioned values to others and an absolute nutcase to most of the serving lower ranks who struggled against the rising crime rate. Anderton did not lead and offered no support to 'the lads' at the pointed end and who preferred to instal a level of discipline which meant even minor infractions were met with sacking. Moral became at an all time low and the accepted practices of the CID dragging prisoners from their homes with the inevitable violence complaint ceased. Once just ignored but under Anderton, could easily suffer terminal consequences, career wise. Actual physical detection ceased and fabricating the detection rates was preferred. being the safer option.

The CID officer yet again filled in their little box on the crime report accumulating the proof of action points, eventually resulting in the division's answer to the Blue Peter badge which was the signing off of the paperwork. Yet another statistic, an unsolved crime, waiting to be written off at a later date by a clerical exercise known as a TIC, which stands for Taken Into Consideration

When a prolific thief or burglar was arrested the 'friendly detective' caring and wishing the best for this young man, explained that all the offences he was suspected of committing previous to his arrest, would now be investigated by all the CID on the division and that he would become a priority investigation. It was explained that whatever sentence he got for the arrested offence, would pale into insignificance with the numerous added charges in the future and indeed if he got a suspended sentence he would then be immediately rearrested and the sentence of imprisonment would be imposed.

The prisoner's new best friend explained that this was to be his chance to 'clear the decks' and start afresh. With such a simple ruse and the fact that the prisoner was not aware that the local women, the Royal Oak and the Golden Garter actually took priority, he was inevitably tricked into admitting other offences with which he would not be charged. Being brainless scrotes they really believed that if they admitted all they had done they would not be pursued for other matters and 'the slate' would be cleared. Should they not do so it was stressed that they could be rearrested on leaving prison, if imprisoned or if not pulled out of the pub any Friday night.

In stupidly believing this, the happy villain, confident that his caring officer was looking after his welfare, would sign a statement to the effect that he had committed say, 30 burglaries over a 12 month period and in doing so had travelled throughout Manchester and Cheshire. Now therein lies the problem. There is no value in detecting burglaries in Cheshire, or on another division, as they would benefit from the detection in their figures and not the arresting officers of Didsbury. We couldn't have that and so we selected the 30 from our division. They were all undetected crimes with no chance of success, specially saved for just a day The boss knew the story and all 30 were stamped up as TICs with a red rubber stamp that was kept in his drawer.

Through the following months they would be fed into the system and passed through the statistics department, who were apparently oblivious to this deception and again Enid triumphed in yet another way. Each section of every division had a constant detection rate which was acceptable and the TICs in the boss' drawer were there to bump up the figures in a bad month.

There was lots to say in 2013 and to be repeated for the benefit of accurately depicting the low moral and tactics to maintain the detection rate. Systems, which could easily continue today.

ROTTEN TO ITS CORE

The A Division in the city centre always had the best detection rate because of all the shoplifters, who again were adopted by a new friend and as a result also admitted other offences but in a greater volume. Each shoplifted item was treated as a single crime, only in the event of an arrest and where a house had been searched many items were inevitably recovered. The prisoner would be charged with two specimen charges and the remainder accepted as TICs. This entire system was condoned from the top and as corroboration. One only has to consider the fact that there was even a special form printed by the force printers with its own reference number. This form was filed with the two specimen charges, but never actually sent on to the statistics department as they would then have refused to allow all the crimes to be treated separately. The statistics department must have been vaguely aware that they were being tricked and that the detection rate was being adjusted. Occasionally, they would look out for a mass of TICs from the same prisoner and insist on them being treated as the same detection as the two charges, but they could not trace them all if fed through the system over a period of weeks and months. The injection of poor leadership, men who had never seen an angry man, or even made an arrest, was causing serious moral issues amongst the rank and file. These so called leaders had no idea of reality out 'in the field' and should an officer be found to have cocked up evidence, or beaten a confession out of a thieving scrote, the arresting officer would be investigated and often with dire consequences. The days of planting, verballing evidence, tampering and the like were coming to an end.

The old stalwarts attempted to ignore the not too subtle changes to what was expected of their conduct in protecting and serving Joe Public. The sharp practices ground to a halt and with them the detection rate plummeted and as a result. The bosses decided that some further detection ingenuity was required to keep the public happy. A detective constable on each division was given the duty of visiting prisons and discussing further admissions with prisoners who were again subjected to the same script of being met at the gates on release. Such admissions were again treated in a similar manner to TICs and again the detection rate blossomed and the boss was happy. Again, a special form was printed for this further crime rate deception. Very few crimes are actually detected by good old fashioned investigations, enquiries, door knocking, witnesses and great reliance is placed on the villains being caught at the scene, or selling the property later. It is from such arrests that the fabricated confessions were developed and in turn this maintained the good old detection rate, which was and maybe still is for that matter, later published for public consumption in the annual, 'aren't we doing well' report which of course was written with similar flair to the Hillsborough, Jimmy Savile and the miners' strike reports.

In the present day police force where thousands of frontline men are being made redundant to save money the crime rate is continually shown as dropping as related earlier in the introduction. Of course, this is impossible and again the present day statistical Enid Blyton's must be at work. ... words of wisdom by yours truly in 2013, to be so true in 2020 when Chief Constable Ian Pilling fell on his sword for so many Chief Constables before him, when GMP was found to be dumping thousands of crime reports before any investigation.

Life's full of disappointments, including God's authority because the Home Office, staffed as usual with pompous tiny minds told God's disciple as did the Manchester Police Authority to "shut up" "make no further public announcements" or find evangelistic glory elsewhere, basically in good old Mancunian/Wigan ... "Piss Off if ye can't keep thee gob shut."

Anderton continued with his queer vendetta and we complied as I wrote ...

During these wonderful, informative years it was an offence for a male person to importune another for what was then regarded as an immoral purpose. The law in its wisdom felt that if a man was prepared to enter a gents toilet urinal and wave his dick about in a display of arousal then he was more than likely to engage in an immoral act. Such acts were not only the actual act of copulation and in this case, man on man which still defies my imagination, despite my years of warped heterosexual practices. It's just not the same without the kissing and how on earth can they keep it up looking at a bald head and surely stinking of shit and Vaseline. Homosexuals met in 'cottages,' which I have already explained as actually being gent's urinals. The participants having identified a potential 'lover' probably from the waving erection, would reach into the adjacent stall and masturbate each other whilst stood at the urinal in case an occasional straight guy in need of a piss walked in. 'Daisy Chains' were the end product of them all joining in, where they all had hold of the 'member' each side. Who said romance was dead? Getting carried away, due I am reliably informed to the drifting aromas of urine and cig ends often resulted in actual oral sex. However, they might simply meet and when all the Old Spice, stale urine blended with soaked tobacco bringing all the chemistries and temperature to an agreed conclusion, they would simply leave the urinal together and depart in a car, to perform elsewhere in a little more privacy.

Many were arrested and taken to Court and in my early days, the CPS solicitors were not there in force and evidence was given by the arresting officer. Great delight was taken in relating the sordid details of the offence to the Magistrates, particularly if we had a tweed-suited ex- headmaster who had never experienced any real sexual encounter involving anything other than missionaries. In true Albert Steptoe grimace we would relate all the finer details, often to the amusement of the clerk sat in front of them. Every sentence was splattered with the terms penis, erect, masturbating etc but in such lurid detail that a hush fell over the courtroom. They usually pleaded guilty and often offered a charitable donation to keep it out of the Evening News. Stan the honest reporter of the day was never approached and printed whatever he liked without any such interruptions.

Locking up 'wankers' as 'male importuners, as they were fondly referred to, was the only thing to do on some days. It wasn't that we were homophobic in any real way, it was just that they were there for the locking up. Something I learnt very early in my police service was the fact that, whatever the offence, the arrest and the conclusion, however damaging was of no real concern. It was just a figure and a means to the end of going on the piss. It became a sort of competition amongst us all. To arrest a wanker granted an award of one point, whereas a street theft brought you three. We would stroll the parked car areas in the hope of an early thief, who had probably wet the bed, having had a deprived violent childhood as they so often claimed through their legal aid solicitor at court. In the absence of a bit of luck in the real arrest department, we went for the 'cottages' where success was guaranteed. These guys couldn't help themselves. It was as much an addiction as it was desire, or some combination of the two. The thought of the damage such an arrest would do to the prisoner's family, work, and the rest and for something so minor, was never a consideration. Police work was never confused with horrendous family consequences for the 'victim.' It was just a joke and basically a game.

The wankers were often out and about the cottages from as early as 11.30am. They were usually reps with their own cars and often used them with their newly found pals. Daylight prevented the daisy chains of the dark hours because toilets in the daytime were also used by straights, innocently coming in for a pee. Limited observations had to be taken to differentiate the wankers from the straight members. Knott Mill cottage was a favourite daytime haunt and still is today. Cars remained outside for much longer than is usual to relieve oneself. Inside the importuners were standing in a stall, getting a buzz from the smell and showing all and sundry their raging hard. When anybody entered they turned into the stall until the leanings of the new boy had been assessed.

The only way to establish what was really happening, was to occupy a stall and pretend to be one of the boys and being a proven heterosexual with a well earned pedigree I did not have the necessary hard to wave about. I pretended to be shy and covered it with my hands. (Forgive my referring to that in the immodest plural). Anyway, the act served its purpose. 'Members' were waving in the breeze, and one or even two culprits were grabbed as the others ran hysterically screaming from the entrances at each end. We tended to choose the ones who appeared to have the most to lose. An expensive suit, a wedding ring, a concealed dog collar of a vicar, or even a well-known face off Coronation Street and a couple of those were captured both in my day and after. This usually assured us of a guilty plea, without any publicity, or an instant fine in some cases. As with the parking and instant fines of the uniform days, they had to know a mutual friend, the name was dropped and the settlement agreed, ensuring no comeback or being set up in a sting operation by the Y department. (Police Professional Standards in 2020)

Even early in James Anderton's career, it is claimed in his self written 'blurb' he actually worked as a beat officer in Manchester's Moss Side district as though a heroic feat of bravery. This area was not the 'war zone' it is today with its many shootings and machete attacks. In those 'heady' days of respected police, Moss Side was populated by first generation Jamaicans, coming here on the Windrush etc. and settling to be hard working Gospel Church goers. Anderton was liked and seen as harmless. He, as all officers in Moss Side, were instructed by the senior officers, Chief Inspector and above, to ignore the unlicensed drinking establishments and small brothels which were a source of 'rent' (money paid to various senior officers to allow illegal harmless 'doings')

At this time no desk bound senior officer ever believed the amount of cannabis being smuggled from Jamaica would ever amount to the incredible volumes of today.

In return, Jamaicans as a show of mocking respect knew him as "Bible Jim" because of his frequent references to God and Christ amongst other derisory terms, too many to mention. Having moved on from the 'queer bashing, dirty book brigade, I happily served in the Drug Squad during these early days and whatever arrests were made were students at Manchester University who when arrested, terrified gave information on Jamaican suppliers and given such continuity the unofficial guidance could be by passed and some very serious Jamaican arrests were made but the main trade was still the white English who were not under the general protection umbrella and who negotiated there own protection deals.

The documents of this time also showed that Sir Lawrence Byford the Chief Inspector of Constabulary, in an under statement of those days, reported that Anderton had "brought ridicule" on the police service and indeed he had. He was a laughing stock to all that 'worked' in the glorious religious arena of the City of Manchester.

It's very strange, pathetically weak and a reflection of the times as senior officers below him did not engage in a form of legal coup to remove him at Government level. It appears that Anderton always enjoyed the strong support of the Prime Minister, Margaret Thatcher who defended him behind the scenes and is believed to agree with his religious rantings with regard to Queers and Aids.

Documents showed that Thatcher had personally suggested it would be "outrageous" if Anderton had to clear his public statements with the Greater Manchester police committee, who had asked him to temper his comments on several occasions. Such requests should surely have been collated and passed to Government level with examples of his stupid religious ravings with high expectation of much stronger action than the Home Office verbal directive.

He was soon known for praying in the back of his car as his police driver chauffeured him to work, and one of his first symbolic acts was a crackdown on pornography and prostitution in Manchester. Dirty bookshops who weren't paying enough rent and newsagents, mainly Asian were raided and many books, films and magazines were seized. As I wrote ...

Anderton ran GMP for 16 years between 1975 and 1991 - crusading whenever he was able against the many dirty bookshops, wankers and, later, saunas in the city. As the detection rate was falling because of the poor morale and refusal to work due to attention from the Y Department, who by then were picking on every detail under the instructions of Anderton. At the bookshops we would seize, pin-up books, salacious novels and porn films which in those days were cine films. They all had to be vetted and sent off to the Director of Public Prosecutions with the appropriate pages marked for easy reference so that the DPP staff didn't wank themselves to death reading them all. We took to this duty with some considerable alacrity leaving us to later desperately seek any 'granny' at the Ritz for a serious scrotum emptying or a passing brass for an instant fine off the wrist. God's own servant, leading Methodist and righter of all wrongs would personally 'assist' with this film vetting. Not with the lads but tucked away in his office, door secure leaving only the sound of a whirring projector for us to form the obvious conclusion. There was never a final report.

It was this moral zeal that was to define his career and plant the seed of the '**rotten apples**', so many examples all '**rotten to its core**. Eccentric, to say the least, in many ways, he made a record of his dreams and believed that even when he was asleep, God was sending him messages. His religious path took him from a devout Church of England childhood to Methodism and then to Roman Catholicism, which surely should indicate mental issues and he even had an audience with the pope in Manchester in 1982.

Anderton did very little to introduce any new ideas on policing whilst the moral in the CID was rock bottom. Whilst he bashed the Bible when it suited him he delighted in sacking men, working hard at the pointed end and actually engaging in real police work which often required an evidential nudge or just a 'good hiding'.

Talking of nudges a little more was necessary in the CID of the 70s ...

The CID officer yet again filled in their little box on the crime report accumulating the proof of action points, eventually resulting in the division's answer to the Blue Peter badge which was the signing off of the paperwork as yet another statistic, an unsolved crime, waiting to be written off at a later date by a clerical exercise known as a TIC, which stands for Taken Into Consideration.

When a prolific thief or burglar was arrested the 'friendly detective' caring and wishing the best for this young man, explained that all the offences he was suspected of committing previous to his arrest would now be investigated by all the CID on the division and that he would become a priority investigation. It was explained that whatever sentence he got for the arrested offence, would pale into insignificance with the numerous added charges in the future and indeed if he got a suspended sentence he would then be immediately rearrested and the sentence of imprisonment would be imposed.

The prisoner's new best friend explained that this was to be his chance to 'clear the decks' and start afresh. With such a simple ruse and the fact that the prisoner was not aware that the local women, the Royal Oak and the Golden Garter actually took priority, he was inevitably tricked into admitting other offences with which he would not be charged. Being brainless scrotes they really believed that if they admitted all they had done they would not be pursued for other matters and 'the slate' would be cleared. Should they not do so it was stressed that they could be rearrested on leaving prison, if imprisoned or if not pulled out of the pub any Friday night.

In stupidly believing this, the happy villain, confident that his caring officer was looking after his welfare, would sign a statement to the effect that he had committed say, 30 burglaries over a 12 month period and in doing so had travelled throughout Manchester and Cheshire. Now therein lies the problem. There is no value in detecting burglaries in Cheshire, or on another division, as they would benefit from the detection in their figures and not the arresting officers of Didsbury. We couldn't have that and so we selected the 30 from our division. They were all undetected crimes with no chance of success. The boss knew the story and all 30 were stamped up as TICs with a red rubber stamp that was kept in his drawer.

Through the following months they would be fed into the system and passed through the statistics department, who were apparently oblivious to this deception and again Enid triumphed in yet another way. Each section of every division had a constant detection rate and the TICs in the boss' drawer were there to bump up the figures in a bad month.

The A Division in the city centre always had the best rate because of all the shoplifters, who again were adopted by a new friend and as a result also admitted other offences but in a greater volume. Each shoplifted item was treated as a single crime and where a house had been searched many items were inevitably recovered. The prisoner would be charged with two specimen charges and the remainder accepted as TICs. This entire system was condoned from the top and as corroboration one only has to consider the fact that there was even a special form printed by the force printers with its own reference number. This form was filed with the two specimen charges, but never actually sent on to the statistics department as they would then have refused to allow all the crimes to be treated separately. The statistics department must have been vaguely aware that they were being tricked and that the detection rate was being adjusted. Occasionally, they would look out for a mass of TICs from the same prisoner and insist on them being treated as the same detection as the two charges, but they could not trace them all if fed through the system over a period of weeks and months. The injection of poor leadership, men who had never seen an angry man, or even made an arrest, was causing serious moral issues amongst the rank and file. These so called leaders had no idea of reality out 'in the field' and should an officer be found to have cocked up evidence, or beaten a confession out of a thieving scrote, the arresting officer would be investigated and often with dire consequences. The days of planting, verballing evidence, tampering and the like were coming to an end.

The old stalwarts attempted to ignore the not too subtle changes to what was expected of their conduct in protecting and serving Joe Public. The sharp practices ground to a halt and with them the detection rate plummeted and as a result the bosses decided that some further detection ingenuity was required to keep the public happy. A detective constable on each division was given the duty of visiting prisons and discussing further admissions with prisoners who were again subjected to the same script of being met at the gates on release. Such admissions were again treated in a similar manner to TICs and again the detection rate blossomed and the boss was happy. Again, a special form was printed for this further crime rate deception. Very few crimes are actually detected by good old fashioned investigations, enquiries, door knocking, witnesses and great reliance is placed on the villains being caught at the scene, or selling the property later. It is from such arrests that the fabricated confessions were developed and in turn this maintained the good old detection rate, which was and maybe still is for that matter, later published for public consumption in the annual, 'aren't we doing well' report which of course was written with similar flair to the Hillsborough, Jimmy Savile and the miners' strike reports.

Anderton soon became better known for his public pronouncements rather than for his innovations and 'love' for his men. He called the 1984-85 miners' strike the work of a "politically motivated industrial mafia" and frequently dismissed his critics as "subversives", portraying the police as the last line in the defence of democracy and yet within the force he had all the makings of a 'raving' dictator.

Talking of innovations, however negative, Anderton, based on his experiences in HMICFRS expanded the half hearted Police Complaints Procedures to be a fully staffed department entitled 'the Y Dept', as I wrote from recollections of my service ...

My particular methods of crime detection and that of the other originals when I joined, was becoming more politically incorrect to the degree that Duty Inspectors of the nervous variety paled as we threw yet another bleeding prisoner at the counter. In addition and at every turn was the new breed of supervisory ranks creeping in like a dose. Several colleagues, all of the old school, including myself, were constantly being referred to the Y Department that dealt with complaints. These were being taken more seriously and were even being investigated, but still by officers with some real field experience and sympathy for our style of working.

I was doing my job out in the field and, for a reason I now forget, I had a prisoner in tow when I was summoned to the Y Department. No excuses. 'Stop what you are doing', with no consideration for real police work, 'and come immediately'. The excuse for a real policeman doing the summonsing over the radio clearly felt everyone hid behind a desk and wrote all day like he did. Thinking of 'bringing my work home' and giving this desk jockey a surprise of his own, I declined the van crew's offer of minding the prisoner. Instead, I handcuffed the prisoner to me. We marched into the Y Department offices, wrist to wrist. To see the look on the face of a man who had never seen a prisoner, and certainly not an angry one, was well worth the effort. My 'partner' complained profusely that the cuffs were too tight, and I think the Y big shot was actually in fear of being assaulted. When my new partner 'accidentally' collided with the desk and stamped about in agony the Y guy nearly pissed himself. He could not believe he was now a witness to a typical 'accident' involving a struggling prisoner.

How sad, and what a travesty, that a man with no backbone and no real police experience should have the right to criticise me, and worse, to fabricate his report, putting my career and my name in jeopardy. The power over me was unearned and undeserved. I don't really remember the rest. I can't say I was even remotely concerned at the time either. My aggravation was too present in my thoughts. Whatever he was investigating, whatever he thought he had over me wasn't proved. So it all went in such a way, forgettable and childishly stupid, the 'blind leading the blind couldn't care less' brigade. It's almost sad, not really boasting but a fact and even pathetic, to have to make such a confession, but nonetheless, for the record, to the day I resigned ... nothing was ever proven against me.

Little has changed with the Y department except the title. Even years ago, the detection and arrest rate within the uniform branch and the CID was visibly falling. An attitude of 'Why should I stick my neck out, and risk dismissal?' was becoming even more common, especially as the Y Department was increasingly becoming staffed with career jockeys who only wanted to progress through the ranks. The 'offender,' the poor beat cop at the pointed end, the man with wife and kids to support, was given little consideration at all. Most of the men on the ground had little or no higher education, a few had passed the entrance exam to the police and then with some difficulty. Therefore, they had little other employment options. The exam was an insult to anyone with a semblance of intelligence and remains so today.

Courses were offered to the politically incorrect, by the inspectors who were rapidly losing interest in writing creatively around our exploits. In truth, they were scared and wanted to see the back of us. But we were getting the results. Newton Street nick was thought to be the ideal exile because the inspector visited rarely and the station sergeant ran it like a Beirut outpost, with few rules and excellent results. It was always fully staffed and there was an unofficial waiting list, not of volunteers, but the bent psychopaths dotted about on other sections.

It was in 1986 that Anderton made his remarks about Aids and queers, claiming that he was channelling God when he spoke – and later telling a BBC interviewer that "if Jesus were here today, he may well have spoken in terms similar to the ones I used". There was a huge backlash, which he dismissed as the response of "moral lepers" and continued to urge the arrests of 'wankers' as practicing homosexuals were known at every opportunity. So we did, just for the figures under the guise of Anderton's moral crusade.

However, the furore did not halt his passage to the presidency of the Association of Chief Police Officers, although many fellow officers by then found him an embarrassment. Anderton was aware of the reaction, although he claimed that his own officers saw him as a cross between the American evangelist Billy Graham and Oliver Cromwell. Actually I can swear, they certainly had no such views at 'the pointed end' of police work. The following year he stirred fresh controversy by telling Woman's Own magazine that "corporal punishment should be administered so that [offenders] actually beg for mercy". and yet he would sack a hard working officer for minor but violent infringements when 'interviewing a suspect.'

Anderton had a row with, John Stalker the Assistant Chief Constable during the latter's inquiry into allegations of a shoot-to-kill policy operated by the British army and Royal Ulster Constabulary in Northern Ireland. Anderton's Irish 'friends' were becoming embarrassed as several were paying the IRA rent for a quiet life or actually sympathising with the 'cause' but not the violence. The inquiry eventually came to nothing after allegations of what were politely termed murky, behind-the-scenes action to derail it. The 'truth' which was popular at the time was that the Royal Ulster Constabulary was mainly a Protestant force of Masons. Stalker was a Catholic. I was a close friend of Manchester businessman Kevin Taylor who was also a Catholic a professional gambler and ex car dealer.

Our resident Christian, true to form went 'off the radar' anticipating that several of his own skeletons may arise. He had his own circle of mainly wealthy sometimes pro IRA, Irish contractors and attended several of their charity dinners often on the top table at their expense. Some of them were appointed as Magistrates as an ego trip for them. I was informed, but couldn't prove it that Anderton had accepted a large diamond ring from the Portuguese Consul at the time who amusingly worked as the wine sommelier at the exclusive Midland Hotel French Restaurant, frequented by the Irish crowd and Anderton.

Worth mentioning again ... It was during this time that the documents also showed that Sir Lawrence Byford the chief inspector of constabulary, reported that Anderton had "brought ridicule" on the police service.

Stalker was suspended while his relations with Kevin were investigated, and although he was exonerated and reinstated, it was despite masses of common knowledge 'evidence' to the contrary amongst the Manchester underworld. It was felt by many of his colleagues that he had been shabbily treated by the crusading christian who ignored Stalker throughout the enquiry. Of course he was reinstated, but the real truth was never known. Stalker socialised with Kevin on many occasions, he holidayed on his yacht, he accepted invitations to charity dinners, he accepted 'gifts'. Kevin held lavish parties at his converted stone mill. I sat in the jacuzzi with Stella, Stalkers wife which was situated prominently in a large lounge close to the grand piano, like a piece of furniture. Stella had a suspect reputation for activities with a senior CID officer which led to Stalkers speedy promotion when he discovered the facts. Somewhat alarmed in a friendly way, Kevin told me to leave the bubbles and Stella who was in danger of becoming yet another notch.

Later, I appeared on the front page of the Manchester Evening News as the criminal associate of Kevin Taylor and Stalker was soon history. I looked very smart in my white dinner jacket.

I had a great deal to say in the second book 'Shades of Black 'n' Blue ...

John Stalker intervened in Northern Ireland. In his naïve and confused aim for further promotion it appeared he believed he could actually prove there was a 'shoot to kill' policy in Northern Ireland. He chose to ignore all advice from friends, usually Catholic as he was, not to get involved. Manchester businessman Kevin Taylor at a dinner in Swinton Rugby Club told Stalker, who was sat next to me yet again, that it was suicidal in a career sort of way to accept this position and conduct a full investigation into such practices. He was to leave his own force he knew to be perpetrating the same brand of violence, but without the shootings and complaints of a shoot to kill policy, to such a degree that he could not fail to know about it. The level of such violence inflicted by the police is, of course, always relative to the violence and murders committed by the civilian population. Much more violence was dished out in the ghettos of Wythenshawe than the leafy suburbs of Didsbury where a simple threat would suffice. Such violent interrogating practices were the rule in Northern Ireland and with Government approval. Stalker who caused so much trouble with his ill-fated investigation was eventually removed, but having done so much damage, things were never the same. His own career came to an abrupt halt as warned by Kevin Taylor, who was eventually to be the unwitting key to his dismissal. The IRA took advantage of the unrest within the police that remained and committed further atrocities in the knowledge that any complaint would be treated seriously, despite the fact they were murdering hard working officers and innocent members of the public.

Whilst the Prime Minister's support may have helped Anderton remain in post (and he was knighted in 1990), his remarks almost certainly cost him the chance of taking the top job of commissioner of the Metropolitan police. Anderton continued his religious pronouncements, growing a thick beard and appeared more than ever to be modelling himself on an Old Testament prophet but with a malicious badly considered streak ...

I was playing rugby when I first met Bob Sharpe. I liked his sense of humour, his fitness, and his overall size. He dished it out on the field, as well as the streets, and was respected for it. Later in his career he decided to grow a beard. There was nothing in Police Regulations to prevent this, provided it was tidy. By this time, Chief Constable James Anderton who was happily living in his strange politically correct world - never having been criticised by the "crusading Manchester Evening News". Devout Christian Anderton was known as God's Cop and regularly pontificated about officers being smart only to later validate the hypocrisy he became famous for. In his newspaper interviews, his conduct of the Force and later in the removal of John Stalker and so much more, none very Christian and often malicious. Unbelievably, and so very him, he grew a beard of such unkempt proportions that he looked every part of the cartoon character depicting a cross between God and Jesus He became famous for his AIDS pronouncement in 1986 that homosexuals with the disease were 'swirling in a cesspit of their own making.' God's Cop's own daughter eventually came out as a lesbian.

Kevin's business and bank dealings came to an abrupt end due to the investigation into Stalker's criminal connections and of Kevins commercial dealings and his tenuous big money banking facilities. It's a long story, for another time but suffice to say the businesses suffered a 'domino effect' and most failed as did Kevin's overdraft. As Stalker was reinstated Kevin sued Anderton personally with the Greater Manchester Police for his substantial losses of several millions with the intention of forcing 'God's Cop' into the witness box on oath. Many people joined the furore, giving Kevin evidence of Andertons none Christian dealings.

The legal pre-amble went on for a couple of years with many attempts by Anderton's and GMPs legal team to have the case thrown out. The entire matter eventually ground it's way to Court and a full civil hearing. It was going well and Anderton was to appear in the witness box when out of the blue an offer slightly in excess of £2M was made as a final settlement. Kevin refused, he wanted to see Anderton squirming in the witness box.

Immediately Kevin's legal aid was withdrawn as he was offered the relatively small sum but had to settle for £2.5M in June 1995 three years after Anderton had actually retired. He was seeking much more but had to accept due to his personal financial situation caused by the GMP and their enquiries. They even charged him with defrauding the Co-op Bank but the bank had not even complained and it was dismissed.

Only a week later Anderton appeared on the top table of a charity dinner run by ex Manchester United player Willy Morgan on behalf of Destination Florida a charity for terminally ill children with a last holiday to Disney Land. I was an active fund raiser for this charity and objected to Andertons presence at their expense. He was free loading with nothing to offer as the 'yesterdays man' that he was. I approached the top table looked at Anderton and said "are you having a nice time Mr Anderton?" he confirmed he was and then realised who had spoken and paled. I continued "just think if you had got in the witness box you would be in a prison cell by now" and walked away, leaving him aghast.

He walked out, with his protesting wife, his evening ruined and job done.

There can be no doubt that Anderton's eccentric Christian claims in public and moral destroying disciplinary directives, eventually led to the negative actions of today where moral continues to be at such a low state. Hopefully with C.C Stephen Watson now in 2023 things will improve. There is little doubt that Anderton was the start of a boost to the perpetuating rot of a childish disciplinary culture having no regard to the needs of real policemen, leaving so many careers in ashes, giving way to the rising tide of unskilled, inexperienced 'yes men'.

Look back again at my words of wisdom in 2013

Didsbury has always had its own synagogue and the Jewish community has always lived within walking distance. They maintain their impeccable standards and build an invisible barrier from the creeping body of Asians who are moving into the area. They moved in to live and also buy the larger Victorian properties to convert to flats and rent out to students, who seemed to put up with any expensive crap. Didsbury was known as Yidsbury and was a target area for burglars strolling the short distance from Wythenshawe. The burglars saw these posh houses as easy targets, when taking a rest from shagging their sisters and even on occasions their mothers. Be in no doubt that during these times, the majority of the population on this sprawling estate were classic scrotes, whole families of them, who had been rehoused from council accommodation elsewhere in the city. The council decided their old accommodation was unfit for human occupation. The original houses must have been deplorable as these transient scrotes were the pits of humanity. They had no real moral compass, they had no family values and went through life existing from one crime to the next, be it burglary or shoplifting, or shagging their own mothers and children.

They even expected a good hiding whenever arrested whatever the circumstances. Their experience and knowledge of the police also allowed for an occasional good kicking just in passing, purely for disciplinary purposes. Whilst hardly PC it was an acceptable practice to 'keep the lid on' and it was great training just giving the wandering scumbag a severe hiding to keep your hand in. As with planting goods on passing suspected shoplifters, such a belting acted as a deterrent and had a dramatic effect. With the younger members such a crack at least forced them to think twice before entering the realms of criminality with any serious beliefs.

Wythenshawe was part of the largest council estate in Europe with all its problems, thefts, assaults, murders, burglaries, rape and incest which was very popular with the perverted drunken louts fancying their own children. In reality these sick souls didn't know any better as their own father's often fiddled with them. Such crapheads as I have already related were rehoused from redeveloped areas throughout the city and they formed a nucleus of the population. However, many older and thoroughly decent people were moved to Wythenshawe, often under loud protest to be sprinkled amongst all this perverted humanity without any consideration of the nightmares they were to experience living amongst them. The majority had never seen such human garbage.

A drive through Wythenshawe easily identified which houses were populated by each section of this disjointed community. Some of the houses had gardens, with bright flowers and mowed lawns, flowering tubs and hanging baskets finishing off the lovely appearance. The privet hedges were neatly trimmed and even the garden gate had had a coat of paint. Next door could easily have an uncut privet hedge, a flagged lawn area with the obligatory rotting mattress and rusting washing machine, probably replaced by Manchester Social Services, leaving the old items to be tipped by the householder. For many the front garden seemed an ideal tipping point and an instant playground for the children with no thought for the obvious dangers.

Of course, Wythenshawe also played host to the Golden Garter Theatre Club and whether we liked it or not we would run the gauntlet through the estate from Didsbury to the club in the hope we would not be asked to assist the resident troops on this section with removing a father from his daughter, or a suspicious cot death, an event which was too common in this area to be genuine all the time. Forensic tests which developed over the years improved considerably and later proved that cot deaths were murder in several instances either by the retarded mother, not fit to have children or the pissed-up father returning from a hard day in the Benchill pub and annoyed at the incessant crying.

The 4th section was based at Brownley Road Police Station, which was right in the centre of this seething mass of life's failures. This building was a post war red brick box, unattractive, again with its own busy public desk, cells and CID offices on the first floor. Unlike Didsbury it had its own charge office where arrests were charged and either held in the cells or bailed if actually living at a set address and appearing on the voters' register, which was always the key and strangely this was more often the case. Whilst such registering appears strange for such retards it was the case that they would not be able to claim any benefits unless properly registered as a resident.

The CID officers based at Didsbury, but working out of Brownley Road regarded us as non-working playboys and we all only met when they came out of the wilderness to drink in the Royal Oak, opposite Didsbury nick, having no real pub where they could relax in Wythenshawe.

At Didsbury, we had a better populace, a better class of villain and better pubs with a much better choice of women, often married, usually divorced, and many students who as today were indulging in prostitution just to make ends meet. As such a wanton sexual activity came to light, usually from a whistle-blowing neighbour we investigated, not because it was a criminal offence, which it was not, but out of a perverted interest. We were easily able to frighten the living daylights out of these lovely little things to the point of instant fines, an art honed from my days in uniform in the city centre. Back then street-walking prostitutes were often fined as they walked from one hostelry to the next. These impressionable little girls even got a kick from shagging a detective and often wanted to pose in a photo with their tame detective to show to their friends, which whilst great fun could have horrendous consequences.

To say eccentricity reigned with a touch of the 'Enid Blytons' to achieve a realistic detection rate is an understatement, not by any particular individual, but the entire CID in general. I learned a great deal from the legendary senior officers of my times such as John Thorburn, Tom Butcher, Eric Jones, Roy Hartley, Charlie Horan, Douglas Nimmo, Arnie Beales, Callum McDonald and many more in the ranks below, despite my mild encounters from the other side of the fence.

The actual workers such as DI John Thorburn and DI Eric Jones were slowly replaced by the John Stalkers and much worse. The James Andertons, who luckily had been very few and far between during my service. Unfortunately they appear to abound in the present day policing. These are men who made an art of doing the minimum of sharp- end police work, fearing that their accelerated promotion would be badly affected by a complaint imposed by some scrote or other, fearing it would tarnish their impeccable record.

James Anderton when Chief Constable was responsible for this ethic in Greater Manchester Police and the resulting general failure of the force during the later years of his service. It was during Anderton's reign that no-go areas became accepted in places such as Cheetham Hill, a secondary city area to be populated by ethnic minorities, and Moss Side, a large part of which was populated by West Indians. The detection rate dropped to abysmal reality and the streets of Greater Manchester were not safe to walk. Even fabricating TICs which maintained the detection rate became a tightrope and one not worthy of the risk. It grew like an understanding amongst the force that Anderton was not working, harassing the 'troops' with his headline-grabbing antics. Such antics, resulting in the Home Office telling him to shut up. With such lame leadership why should the rest of us, the ones at the pointed end make any real effort?

As I have said, the CID offices looked like a set in Hill Street Blues and I wonder, sometimes, if plots for these programmes were taken from Manchester CID in general. The plots for Heartbeat and The Bill were certainly not. The general office had just about enough seating for us all, for morning parade. There were two side offices for interviews and a bit of quiet writing and the Detective Inspector's office, where it certainly felt like being on a daily roller coaster ride for the man in the hot seat. When I started, we had Inspector John Thorburn. I have mentioned him with great respect in previous chapters, and indeed he deserves the print. There were not enough like him. I can't say enough concerning him and those of his calibre. There were so few honourable names and so many counterfeits, that a little repetition is a forgivable offence.

John was a good man, a steady man, a real detective of the old school and a little too outspoken to proceed quickly up through the ranks of inexperienced YES men. As officers progressed through the force and their rank got higher, potential promotion candidates were interviewed by several senior officers on a Promotion Board. John only had to be asked: "What is wrong with the police today, Mr. Thorburn?" The usual and perhaps safe response might have been of the "Well run, but underfunded"

A lengthy excerpt which says it as it was, and now James Anderton who?

1991–2002: David Wilmott

Sir David was born in Fleetwood, Lancashire and started his policing career during the 1950s as a cadet. He joined Lancashire Constabulary's regular force and was posted to Stretford. One of his first beats took him along Boyer Street, which would become the site of Greater Manchester Police's headquarters and where he would end his service as Chief Constable over thirty years later. While still serving with Lancashire Constabulary he was posted to Liverpool, being based at both Maghull and Seaforth. The area became part of Merseyside Police during the police force amalgamations of 1974. In 1983 he transferred to West Yorkshire Police as an assistant chief constable. He later became the Deputy Chief Constable of the force. In 1987 he was appointed Deputy Chief Constable of the Greater Manchester Police serving under Sir James Anderton until 1991 when he was appointed the Force's third Chief Constable already suffering from many issues and already bequeathed with the stupidity of Anderton, which to be fair he tolerated for his first two years at Greater Manchester. He continued to accept the relaxed policing methods of the CC James Richards era.

Each division had a crime prevention officer and the main office of this group of ageing stalwarts was situated in our headquarters building. An inspector and a sergeant ran this fine group of men who visited premises which had been burgled throughout the city. Their objective was to explain to the complainants how poor their security measures had been and how to improve them to prevent a future incident. Such improvements usually included an expensive burglar alarm system and luckily they had the contact number for the local representative of an installation firm. The reasons for such a reference was obvious to all except the complainant, who, in paying such a price, was including the CPO's bung. On retirement from the police, Crime Prevention Officers were usually found in employment at their favourite alarm suppliers.

Controversy followed as comments Sir David made in 1998 during a hearing in Manchester of the MacPherson inquiry, which examined the Metropolitan Police's investigation into the murder of black teenager Stephen Lawrence in 1993. Five years later the BBC's damning 'Secret Policeman' documentary exposed racism among trainees within a number of forces, including, shock horror, Greater Manchester Police. He could have caused a bigger ripple with the mention of CID conduct with a culture of everything that is wrong to get a result.

Today the police is populated at all levels with officers of similar suspect mentality and very concerning working practices and beliefs. Whatever their deviations, dishonesty or sexual perversions they could all hide in the police in the knowledge that very few were prosecuted to the point of prison. Most were allowed to resign and in many cases were allowed to remain as serving officers. Set a thief to catch a thief comes to mind or indeed, set a perv to catch a perv. Savile, Hillsborough, the Plebgate affair and so many more haunting examples have all proved that there is a police force for the police force and another for Joe Public. There are departments at all levels to house the mixture of police excuses for specialised departments. Lesbian Community Relations and Black Community Relations, usually staffed by black officers which appears to defeat the object and innumerable others, all of which are difficult to be taken seriously in the knowledge of all the ingrained prejudices within the police force. It does not really matter how many ethnics the police recruit and whatever accelerated rank they reach there will remain the ingrained racial prejudice and with it a total lack of respect.

The bosses from Superintendent down were actively aware of the level of prejudice, criminality, evidence fabrication and the rest. There were many participants in one or perhaps all of the above. In taking part, they were merely abusing the blasé platitudes from Chief Constable down, following their own guidance on training and supervision... 'Only get involved if the wheel comes off'

I think the wheel very nearly came off with the following saga, related in 2013 as I wrote ...

'Tricky' JB didn't have time for a leaving do. He was arrested for a series of offences which so many serving detectives treated as the norm, but in reality, not to such extremes as J. He was jailed in 1983 at Manchester Crown Court for offences of corruption and brutality whilst a Detective Chief Inspector. He was sentenced to about seven years imprisonment, but served only about four. The fact an officer of such a rank could be

investigated and charged with such offences highlighted to us all that the 'the times they were a changing' and 'there but for the grace of God go I.'

He was a one-off. He took pride in being known as totally bent and a raging psychopath to boot. Where it was the norm to plant evidence, beat up prisoners and bribe informants to set up another criminal individual, Jack always went that bit too far and his treatment of prisoners and the beatings he gave them caused concern to real seasoned detectives. J's conviction and imprisonment sent ripples throughout the CID and eventually other matters he had dealt with where he had secured convictions were investigated and properly examined. This action was seen as a very alarming deviation from the norm where such behaviour had been accepted for so many years by the 'troops' on the ground, but supported by the senior supervisory officer ranks in their quest for the perfect detection figures. Once a successful investigation had been completed and filed away it was of course the unwritten rule that the file would remain closed. J's example was an alarming deviation from this practice and could have affected us all with other matters, but perhaps with less heart-stopping examples.

One such case which became known as the UK's longest running miscarriage of justice involved a man named Robert Brown who had the misfortune of being interviewed/tortured/beaten close to death....you choose, by 'Tricky' JB. He led the interview and worked with other officers who beat a confession out of Brown, which resulted in a signed statement confessing to a murder. Brown who was 20-years-old at the time was charged with the murder of Annie Walsh, a 51-year-old factory worker. As a result of JB's convictions for offences totally unrelated to the murder investigation, the Criminal Cases Review Commission found multiple grounds for doubts in the safety of Brown's conviction. They revealed that J's 1983 conviction related to crimes he committed in the 1973-5 time frame, pre-dating Brown's 1977 trial.

Of course the jury was not to know of Jack's activities and his reputation and was left only with the summing up of Mr Justice Milmo, who gave the jury the simple decision of believing the police or the accused whose only defence was the fact that his confession had been beaten out of him. The confession was found to be the 'chief plank of the case' by the Review Commission.

The conviction was found to be unsafe because of JB's conviction on the other unrelated matters. Brown was now found 'not guilty.' There is a great difference here. It must be remembered when pitying Brown for the 25 years he spent in jail before the Court of Appeal released him on November 13th 2002 that he was not just picked up off the street and charged with this offence. Evidence pointed to him, but it was not enough and his statement added the finishing touches. It must be asked, whether an innocent person would sign such a statement which would result in a life sentence and what did Tricky have to gain by fabricating all the evidence without even a glimmer of truth. A murder such as this necessitated the use of many detectives and to suggest Butler was alone in the commission of this offence is ludicrous and itself, a serious omission. As with the

Hillsborough conspiracy there were many officers of various ranks involved in this corruption of evidence and as time will tell only a few prosecutions if any at all will follow with the majority using the tried and trusted SS explanations of WWII: 'I was acting on orders' as has occurred in so many other such investigations.

What differs with the Hillsborough conspiracy is the fact that it is indeed a proven conspiracy which totally explodes the constant plea of a rogue element of a few people with values of yesteryear. Examine the proof to date which itself will cause some serious attempts at avoiding the truth in the final report by virtue of the ranks and numbers of conspirators. Consider the facts? There are already named four Chief Constables, four Superintendents, several members of the Police Federation, a Coroner, three Judges, two Members of Parliament and at least 200 uniformed police officers. The inquiry is dragging on, probably in the hope that the main suspects will die giving everyone someone to blame.

In the case of Brown and 'Tricky' there was a statement for the media from the usual police spokesman after the appeal court judgment which said: "We would like to reassure the people of Greater Manchester that procedures under the Police And Criminal Evidence Act now provide safeguards for both suspects and officers." These include recording of the interview process and advanced forensic techniques.

Having successfully ignored everything in the festering pool of corruption, namely GMP and 'always' serving as a protector of the suffering public, 'Nice Guy' David

Wilmott was awarded the Queen's Police Medal in 1989 and appointed a Deputy Lieutenant for the County of Greater Manchester in 1996. He was Knighted during the Queen's Golden Jubilee Year of 2002 and stepped down the same year following the Commonwealth Games in Manchester after he delayed his retirement so he could police the sporting spectacular and enjoy the associated hospitality whilst successfully delegating any real responsibility as he did throughout his 'service'. All the black athletes and supporters must have had an effect on the powers that be and GMP became diverse as they say today with a variety of ethnic departments.

Today the police is populated at all levels with officers of similar suspect mentality and very concerning working practices and beliefs. Whatever their deviations, dishonesty or sexual perversions they could all hide in the police in the knowledge that very few were prosecuted to the point of prison. Most were allowed to resign and in many cases were allowed to remain as serving officers. Set a thief to catch a thief comes to mind or indeed, set a perv to catch a perv. Savile, Hillsborough, the Plebgate affair and so many more haunting examples have all proved that there is a police force for the police force and another for Joe Public. There are departments at all levels to house the mixture of police excuses for specialised departments. Lesbian Community Relations and Black Community Relations, usually staffed by black officers which appears to defeat the object and innumerable others, all of which are difficult to be taken seriously in the knowledge of all the ingrained prejudices within the police force. It does not really matter how many ethnics the police recruit and whatever accelerated rank they reach there will remain the ingrained racial prejudice and with it a total lack of respect.

Sir David served as High Sheriff of Greater Manchester in 2005-2006. It is thought he is the first former Chief Constable in history to have held the position of High Sheriff. He served until his retirement in 2002 just after Manchester hosted the XVII Commonwealth Games. In the same year he received a Knighthood in Queen's Birthday Honours. Sir David served as High Sheriff of Greater Manchester in 2005-2006. It is thought he is the first former Chief Constable in history to have held the position of High Sheriff.

Sir David Wilmott died June 17th 2015. Ex Chief Constable Peter Fahy in his official capacity of 'bull shitter extraordinaire' said: "Our thoughts and prayers are with the family and friends of Sir David. He was a well-respected Chief Constable who made a huge contribution to policing and to the people of Greater Manchester. This was both as Chief Constable between 1991 and 2002 and in 2005-2006 as High Sheriff. Sir David showed brave leadership after the Stephen Lawrence Inquiry by publicly stating that GMP was institutionally racist and by establishing Operation Catalyst which was set up to take the Force forward. "He led the force through many other challenges and the day to day pressures of policing such a busy area. He was involved in much charity work before and after his retirement and was an important contributor to the national policing debate during a time of much change. He was a thoroughly decent man and very good company."

All true in a Fahy glowing manner, but hardly making a huge contribution but certainly survived following the Anderton era.

Racial prejudices within the police generally were always present as C.C David Wilmott admitted and to be honest were often well justified. Asian Pakistanis soon to feature as paedophiles in large gangs throughout the GMP area, raping and sexually assaulting girls as young as nine already in care and very vulnerable. Prior to 2013 this existing problem had not become public knowledge. Pakistani households were often a store for stolen property which in itself was not a reason to prompt racial prejudice, but to see the living conditions which arose certainly added fuel to the 'prejudice fire'. As I highlighted...

On another occasion we raided a Pakistani-occupied council house coincidentally close to the same park. Whilst not being particularly prejudiced I can honestly say that I had no real time for any of them. They were not fit to be treated as equals, they were not used to it in their own country, so why should we bend over backwards with over the top PC. The house was filthy, smelt like a farmyard and even had a goat and two chickens in the front room, wallowing in their own excrement. Also living in the three bedroomed house were 10 adults, who appeared to sleep in shifts, in the same bed with the same unwashed bed clothes, and six children. There is no doubt that during this time such immigrants were treated as the second class citizens they clearly were, just by virtue of how they chose to live. Today of course, many still reside in the same conditions, but are considered equal in the eyes of the law and politicians. The judiciary and the politicians should have a crash course on the conditions the police, even today are forced to work in whilst remaining so PC. And alarmingly even today, officers can be suspended and even sacked for calling them a Paki. What is going on, when they don't behave as civilised in a Western society and then expect all the frills that go with it?

Perhaps I should relate a matter of a similar theme, purely to be of the same context and nothing to do with my general theme, but maybe amusing to some....

After leaving the police I employed Don Robertson, an ex-detective sergeant, who had suffered a 'there but for the grace of God' moment that ended up as a criminal charge for which he was found not guilty. I had discredited his main prosecution witness by simple, but difficult door to door enquiries in Liverpool. Whilst he escaped imprisonment with my endeavours and a not guilty verdict as a result, he had to resign from the police on what they said were disciplinary issues which usually meant: 'You lucky bastard, we know you are guilty.' So they got rid of him.

When he left the police he got a security job at Manchester International Airport with a firm which refurbished airplane interiors. Planes used on Pakistani routes from Manchester to Islamabad, were refurbished more often, as some first-time travellers urinated and defecated where they sat, totally oblivious to the fact that the plane had toilets. Eventually the metal components, when treated to a quick dose of what Pakistani bowel movements had to offer rusted and rotted through the entire seating frame. I suspect that Hammerite could have patented Asian bowel movements as a rust remover.

2002–2008: MICHAEL J. TODD

Michael Todd attended the University of Essex. He graduated with a first class honours degree in government in 1989 and a master's degree in politics in 1994. The university named him the alumnus of the year in 2003 for his contributions to policing and the community. Todd joined Essex Police in 1976.

After progressing through the ranks he attained the level of Inspector via a management exchange programme with the Met. As an example of the dubious promotion procedures in just twenty years In he was appointed Assistant Chief Constable of Nottinghamshire Police initially managing support services and then operational policing.

He returned to the Met. in 1998 when appointed Deputy Assistant Commissioner and in 2000 he was promoted to the rank of Assistant Commissioner. Throughout his tenure as Assistant Commissioner he was responsible for Territorial Policing covering all 32 London Boroughs. He oversaw the policing of several high profile public events, such as the Notting Hill Carnival, the Golden Jubilee Celebrations and the anti-capitalist May Day protests, for which he received a Commissioner's Commendation from then Commissioner John Stevens.

In 2002, he was selected as Chief Constable of Greater Manchester Police overseeing a City then notable for its extensive gang-related gun crime and a force with a record of poor performance, inefficiency and mired in claims of institutional racism. Could it have got any worse.... Don't hold your breath.

Todd was probably selected as Chief Constable by what must have been the same naive morons who chose Anderton with a CV which appeared to be top class when compared with the morons who had gone before. He was to oversee a City, which by this time was notorious for its extensive gang related crime, a City now nicknamed 'Gunchester'. The force already had a record of poor performance, inefficiency to put it mildly and a notoriety for institutional racism admitted by CC David Wilmott in a media interview. C Peter Fahy of Cheshire Constabulary claimed Wilmott had restored GMP's reputation within the local community in his funeral tribute. What incredible bullshit, obsessed Christian zealot James Anderton will have 'turned in his grave' especially when he supported police officers marching in gay Pride parades and welcomed the 2003 Europride celebrations to Manchester. Todd's enlistment quickly gave the 'pointed end' the rights to the existing culture of the old days and they again took to it with vigour.

When repeated several times over several days, the case for living off immoral earnings was built. Of course actual cash could not be seen, but the evidence was adjusted to see him counting the notes in full view rather than sliding the cash into his pocket. It always assisted the evidence if the ponce resided with the prostitute. During the alleged observations the home addresses would be identified and with a few well-chosen words the residence of the two would be proved. Such a lengthy period of observations certainly interrupted the social life and editing of the truth became necessary in certain areas of evidence. However the officer concerned with this particular little fabrication took it all too far. He spent a couple of nights establishing the basic movement patterns and then adjourned to a local hostelry, sometimes over a period of days running into weeks. Such evidence certainly relies a great deal on fabrication and has to rely a great deal on a touch of the 'Enid Blytons' and in some instances it is downright fiction from start to finish. With regard to this matter, the officer was certainly over-enthusiastic with the added fiction even to the point of stressing how well he knew the subject and so identification could not be an issue, the officer had decided that the Jamaican brother was taking the piss and now it was 'his turn.' This was a common attitude which reigned at this time among hard working officers in the mistaken belief that any evidence would do to 'get them off the streets.' The evidence in this case was totally fabricated for no gain whatsoever and basically in the service of Her Majesty, purely to keep her highways and byways safe to walk. In short, he had totally made up the evidence and written his statement perhaps in the vault over a couple of pints of Guinness. The evidence was perfect, but as the arrest was attempted the subject was nowhere to be found. This was not unusual and all he had to do was await his return to the area before arresting the subject, who was hysterical to say the least. In all such cases the arrested individuals never considered what they had previously done, without detection and certainly did not want to 'take one for the team.'

The inner core of 'hard working' experienced officers at 'the pointed end,' having little faith in the Courts for proper sentencing, tweeked the existing forms allowing for their particular form of alternative justice probably because the existing culture of the time worn so thin.

A typical example of alternative justice is that of an officer 'relocated' to the CID at Didsbury having been transferred from the Moss Side area as a result of a 'minor miscarriage' of justice. A move, akin to putting a five year old in a sweet shop. Moss Side was a notorious area for prostitution and with that wonderful trade came the ponces. These are men who claim to protect the girls and in doing so take money from them. In reality they are supervised, beaten up and generally abused to keep the 'protector' in the manner he was accustomed. In Moss Side the majority of ponces were Jamaican, not known for their hard work ethic and tending to favour drug dealing and prostitution as their chosen career. The circumstances of this particular example of 'The Enids' should have involved a lengthy period of observations on both the ponce and his girls, but didn't for various reasons. A detailed picture would be built of the girls parading for business, one going off in a car with a male punter to return a relatively short time later to continue plying their trade. At this point the ponce would appear and money would change hands.

In yet another rare Perry Mason moment as the case came to court, his smirking 'arsehole' of a barrister produced a medical report. It was prepared by Wythenshawe Hospital proving that his client was actually residing on a ward with his leg in traction having been badly broken in another arrest for a totally separate incident away from the Moss Side area, which occurred some days earlier than the period of evidence in relation to the proposed charge of living off immoral earnings. In addition to the charge which initiated the arrest the 'ponce' was also charged with police assault the age old standby to account for any injuries received either during the arrest and especially in the rear of the police van as he was being transported rather noisily to Platt Lane Police Station. Of course this station was on the same division as Moss Side, but inter sub-division intelligence was not what it is pretended to be today and the arrest never raised any other alarm bells. These were the halcyon days of outright colour prejudice, unabated and doled out in the form of violence on any passing unfortunate of the wrong colour. This man had put up a fight, was thrown to the ground and his leg stamped upon as it lay across a kerbside. Apparently he never complained in the knowledge that such a complaint would be ignored as the injuries were justified with a police assault charge.

The production of the medical certificate caused a mild ripple of the bowels, for the officer. The evidence of seeing the man on numerous occasions, taking money from prostitutes when he was in fact in hospital was certainly perjury once again and yet again there was no investigation as the court readily accepted the officer's limp explanation. "Well, he is black and it was night." And then: "I had to park some distance away to remain unseen." And the clincher: "I knew the woman to be under his control, and when I saw the man punching her, I knew it was him. I had seen him do this before."

Of course the bosses knew the truth, they had probably done similar. The officer was moved out of that division, where his duty was actually only a uniformed officer but in what is known as the Plain Clothes Department. Yet in recognition of his endeavours, however suspect, even illegal, he was moved up the invisible ladder to the CID. Get done and get on was always a popular phrase at this time in the police and there are many examples.

Somewhat out of his depth, and clearly believing his own bullshit, Todd investigated on behalf of the Association of Chief Police Officers the extraordinary rendition flights conducted by the CIA to transport detainees. The Rendition Project suggests aircraft associated with secret detention operations landed at British airports 1,622 times. Reported by The Guardian in 2013 but with no final conclusions and probably the reason why Todd was delegated this task with his Met experience of fabrication and lies.

Todd was a proponent of the use of the taser and advocated for the weapon to be more widely issued to front line Police Officers. In 2005, in order to demonstrate that the stun guns were safe and effective, he allowed himself to be tasered on camera. After recovering he said "I was completely incapacitated, and if I was carrying a weapon there was no way I could have done anything, as I just couldn't move. And yes, it hurt like hell and no, I wouldn't want to do it again.

There could be little doubt that such blatant bias towards GMP has been damaging to the Greater Manchester public and indeed the hardworking lower ranks of the force generally and certainly ensured that the festering culture never came to light in the expose it should have been. The closest the Manchester Evening News ever came to real reporting was the investigation and presentation of a two part story by Jennifer Williams.

In September 2021 on the appointment of 'hard nosed' C.C Stephen Watson she penned ...

When England's second largest police force was placed into special measures last December, it represented the single biggest public service failure to hit Greater Manchester in years. Yet by the time the crisis at GMP officially started emerging last year, the warning lights had long been flashing, for victims, external organisations and many rank-and-file police officers themselves. For while the headline criticism of the force was that it missed 80,000 crimes last year, according to the policing inspectorate, behind that sat something harder to measure: a broken culture. It is something impossible to count in a spreadsheet, or to list in a league table, hard to trace its history or arrest its development. But it is just as fundamental to understanding both what went wrong in the force and to turning around its fortunes.

A six-month investigation by the M.E.N. has uncovered a pattern, believe experts, that has echoes of policing scandals such as Hillsborough and, more recently, the findings of the Daniel Morgan Inquiry into the Metropolitan Police - a tendency towards obfuscation, denial, secrecy and an instinct to defend the indefensible. It takes in misleading and inaccurate statements, denial of official criticism and legal stonewalling; police officers fearful to report failure and those attempting external scrutiny being brushed off. GMP is now under new management, with its latest Chief Constable due to announce his transformation plan on Friday.

Understanding and fixing the causes and solutions of what was dubbed a 'rotten' culture four years ago will surely have to be central to that, however, if GMP is to truly turn the page. The article caused a political stir and a question by Mary Robinson MP gave it credence.

This very well researched two part article, remaining disappointingly polite and lacking in certain areas of criticism, must still have been a real 'kick in the balls' to the army of colleagues with grand crime reporting titles and pedigrees of only printing GMP approved bullshit. It is doubtful that promotion followed as she is now the Social Affairs Editor. A grand title and maybe a raise but apparently moved sideways to prevent the ruin of the MEN's police bias and their culture of many years, protecting GMP in a swap of daily arrest information etc. The Manchester Evening news has never since this article continued with the criticism and tried to hold the forces hierarchy to account. The same culture has festered onwards unabated.

The inquest into Todd's death was reported as follows with passages of unnecessary detail removed to aid the reading. ... I urge you to read this fully and remember a Coroner actually reports the death is not the suicide of a man who had behaved as a 'headless chicken" and already fooled a selection committee headed by the Lord Mayor.

"One of Britain's top cops sent a series of desperate text messages before he died from hypothermia on Snowdon after taking a cocktail of drink and drugs, an inquest heard yesterday. Greater Manchester police chief Michael Todd had pleaded for forgiveness from one unnamed person, saying: "I'm sorry for what I have done, forgive me in another life. His body was found the next day, on March 11, near an empty bottle of gin at Bwlch Glas in appalling weather following a massive search. Tests

showed he had drunk gin and taken Nytol sleeping tablets. It emerged married Mr Todd's life had unravelled after his wife confronted him about an affair he was having.

Recording a narrative verdict, North West Wales coroner Dewi Pritchard Jones said there was not enough evidence for suicide or an accident through misadventure verdict. He said: "Mr Todd died of exposure when his state of mind was affected by alcohol, a drug and confusion due to his personal situation."

The last emotional text message from Mr Todd had prompted the person who received it, known only as C, to call police. But the message was the last contact he made, following his spiral into despair after his wife Carolyn found out about his infidelity with another woman. A call from another person, known only as B, got through to his phone and was 'unintentionally' or 'accidentally' answered – the implication Mr Todd was slumped on his phone. As Mr Todd apparently lay dying, B could only hear an 'urgent heavy breathing sound', the inquest was told.

Angie Robinson, the married chief executive of Greater Manchester Chamber of Commerce, was linked to the police chief following his death. But she was just one among a string of women involved with Mr Todd – and it emerged another person, G, had spent the night at his flat days before his death.

The inquest heard how the 50-year- old searched the internet for ways to kill himself, sending increasingly desperate text messages to friends and lovers. The texts culminated in him admitting he was intending to kill himself and apologising to his wife, telling her he still loved her. Michael Todd visited suicide websites and sent numerous text messages to friends and lovers in the days before he died, the inquest heard. His last text, sent from the slopes of Snowdon, said: "I'm sorry for what I have done, forgive me in another life." The texts included messages suggesting he intended killing himself and apologising to his wife, Carolyn, about his affair with another woman. In one message Todd said he was in a 'dark place' and had 'destroyed himself' before an aborted suicide attempt two days before he was found dead.

Detective Sergeant Kevin Evans of North Wales Police read out details of the text messages, emails and internet activity. The first message of significance was on March 6 when Mr Todd was called by his wife and asked about an affair. The following day he spoke to person A and was 'cold, hard and calculating', saying the discovery of the affair was a 'nightmare scenario'. He said he needed a week to sort out his affairs and then he would kill himself. On Sunday, March 9 Todd accessed suicide websites before driving to Cumbria where another series of text messages was sent. One said: "Thanks. Not your fault...remember the good times." Det Insp Gerwyn Lloyd said he was found face down, lying uphill. He had taken his jacket off and an empty gin bottle was found in his rucksack. The weather had been cold and windy. His wife stated, "The tragedy is that Michael never felt able during his career to seek the help he badly needed and he never knew that we could and have forgiven him. Close to tears she was escorted away by police officers and driven away

Police investigated the significant movements and contacts made by Greater Manchester Police chief constable Michael Todd over the weekend of Friday, March 7 to the finding of his body near the summit of Snowdon on Tuesday, March 11, 2008. Between March 1 and 11 Michael Todd sent 319 texts to several people - mostly female - and made 47 calls to slightly fewer. Significant texts and calls are summarised. Some of the details came from police inquiries by North Wales Police officers and colleagues from Greater Manchester Police.

Thursday, March 6 *During the evening Michael Todd was phoned by his wife and challenged about an affair. He admitted to the affair with person A.*

Friday, March 7 *The following morning Michael Todd spoke with person A. He is described as cold, hard and calculating. Michael Todd saying discovery of the affair was "just the nightmare scenario he'd imagined" He added he needed a week to sort out his affairs and then he would kill himself. At 4pm they spoke again. Michael Todd sounded distressed and asked A to obtain him some sleeping tablets from a GP as his "Nytol" was not working. The same day he texted an ex-colleague (person B) that he was "losing it," "depressed" and "couldn't see the point in anything". To another ex-colleague (person C) he sent a similar message adding that he was "sorry for being a pain" and that he did not wish to talk. During the afternoon Michael Todd used his laptop to* *visit several websites on methods of committing suicide, in particular the use of paracetamol.*

He also texted person D that he was "fed up" and not in a good place at the moment. Late afternoon Michael Todd texts a colleague at Greater Manchester Police (person E) he "was a bit fed up and might take Monday off". Texts are exchanged between both, Michael Todd adding "just need to clear my head and think through the leadership stuff. Might go for a walk or hike. On Friday evening he has dinner with person F saying "it's not easy...it's getting worse"

Saturday, March 8 11.06am Michael Todd's credit card *was used in WH Smith's in Manchester's Arndale Centre to purchase leisure guides to the Lake District and to North Wales. (Both these items were later recovered from his Range Rover).11.35am Michael Todd texts a colleague his intent to take Monda (March 10) off in order to "get his head round leadership stuff" adding that he "may try a walk in the hills". Saturday evening Michael Todd texts person G "I'm in that dark place that you were in not so long ago". Michael Todd spends the night with G. Michael Todd is described as "sad" as if nothing mattered to him and he had no cares in the world.*

Sunday, March 9 9am G leave Michael Todd's flat. Says *Michael Todd appeared anxious, looked like he was crying...like a man who had lost everything. They did however arrange to meet later in the week. 10.53am following a series of texts between Michael Todd and persons B and C. Michael Todd texts person B "...thanks* *not your fault but mine. Remember the good times though. Bye."11.53am Michael Todd spoke with his wife Carolyn, he sounded extremely drunk and distressed. Early afternoon Michael Todd uses laptop to visit web sites on the Lake District and methods of committing suicide. 2.30pm Michael Todd calls Greater Manchester Police fleet office to his flat to jump start his Range Rover. They attend at 3pm, start his car, drives off at 3.15pm stating his intent to go walking. He appears fit and well.* **And you wait over 24 hrs for a burglary visit.**

3.17pm he sends person C a text saying he was sorry for all the pain caused and would not do it again. Cell siting of his mobile suggests he is heading north. 3.42pm Michael Todd's use of his mobile at this time now suggests he is in the Bolton area. 4.34pm he sends another text to person C "Have just had enough of everything..and am so depressed...has fallen out with me as well. All is shit at mo". Cell site of his mobile now suggests he is heading back to his flat. 5.54pm Michael Todd texts C telling them not to worry and that he was going for a walk in the hills to clear his head. Cell siting now indicating the text was sent from the kendal area of the Lake District. 7.29pm he sends person E a text "just need to clear my head and think through this leadership stuff. Might go for a walk or hike" Use of his mobile shows Michael Todd is close to Seascale in Cumbria. 7.58pm Michael Todd sends his wife an e-mail apologising and now admitting he had been ill for a long time and that he had destroyed himself

Monday, March 10 *00.02am Michael Todd texts person C "will be honest...was going to end it all tonight. Drove*

115 miles to what had planned but bottled out and just got back after another 115 miles. Need time to get in control" Cell siting now puts him in his Manchester flat. 00.14am Michael Todd adds to C "Just got back to Manchester from Lake District. Really fallen out with Carolyn but will now go to see her tomorrow and try to sort it out. Don't worry will get in control. About the same time person A phones Michael Todd. He said he was at his flat in Manchester working from home. He wanted some sleeping tablets as he "needed them as insurance" informing A he had researched the internet over the weekend on ways of committing suicide.

He tells her of his journey to and from the Lake District in order to end his life but had "bottle it". He wants to meet but person A refuses. Between 10am & noon he texts person F and concluded saying "I'm just saying goodbye. I'm not going to see you again". Around the same time he texts person A, who having now agreed to meet him, is told "no, its too late". 11am Michael Todd emailed his wife. He agreed he was ill, unable to sleep, eat and was weak claiming he was too drunk to drive home. He again apologised and said he would come home the next day when they would talk. 11am onwards Michael Todd uses laptop to visit number of websites of mountain ranges in Greater Manchester area including the "warnings or dangers on Saddleworth" and mountain rescue. 2.37pm Michael Todd's black Range Rover was seen by police cameras entering the Trafford Centre in Manchester. At about this time he sends a text which also shows he is in the Trafford Centre

12.57pm cctv in Black's outdoor shop in the centre clearly shows Michael Todd purchasing waterproof trousers, a hat and an OS map. All of these items were later recovered from Michael Todd's rucksack. 1.29pm he texts person C that he'd had "a big fall out with Carolyn", use of his mobile phone puts Michael Todd in the Warrington area. 1.49pm Michael Todd enters services on the M56 near Runcorn and cctv clearly shows him re-fuelling his Range Rover. 1.59pm Michael Todd sends person A further text along the lines of "going for a walk to clear head then going home." Phone now shows him to be close to Chester. He was heading towards North Wales. 2.02pm Michael Todd's Range Rover is seen by North Wales Police cameras entering North Wales westbound on the A550 at Deeside but at 2.09pm seen on the A55 at Dobshill heading east. 2.40pm a further text to person A is made from the Llangollen area indicating Michael Todd was entering North Wales via the A483 Wrexham by-pass and A5 which leads directly into the heart of Snowdonia.

4.30-5pm Michael Todd and his vehicle sighted in the Church Road area of Llanberis. The area where is vehicle was parked is popular with hikers intent of ascending Snowdon as it is very close to the start of the most popular route to the summit, the Llanberis Pass. He is seen doing up his boot laces at the rear of the vehicle and dressed as if he was about to go walking. He is aone. The weather was closing in and with sunset at 6.10pm daylight was soon to go. Another member of the public also sights Michael Todd looking agitated and avoiding eye contact. 5.30pm Michael Todd texts a colleague along the lines of "been for a hike. All wrapped up in thermal gear see you tomorrow" It is clear from phone intel tat this text was sent from the area of

Snowdon. 7.30pm Michael Todd sends another text and this too is sited to the area of Snowdon. 7.33pm Michael Todd texts person C a worrying message "...don't snd any more messages as will cause you grief. Am sorry for what I have done forgive me in another life" Cell sited to area of Snowdon.

(This was the final outgoing activity on Michael Todd's phone, he sends no further texts and makes no further calls. It is also at this point at which persons B and C instigate contact with GMP after fruitless attempts to solicit an answer fom him)

9.28pm person B tries once more to obtain an answer from Michael Todd's mobile phone. An unintelligible answer is obtained that causes much distress. Person B records on their mobile phone an "urgent" heavy breathing sound but no words were spoken. The call last over one and a half minutes.

Can you believe that the North West Wales coroner D. Pritchard-Jones said "there was not enough evidence to rule that Mr Todd deliberately intended to take his own life in the isolated spot on Snowdon where his body was found." This is a man who had purchased Blacks best and yet chose to ignore it. It was a popular theory at the time that his sexual behaviour was about to be made public and accordingly he took his own life. What a surprise and yet with all the evidence of intent the Coroner ruled against suicide. The coroner ruled that Todd had died from exposure essentially freezing to death having been only lightly clothed on the slopes of Snowdon, and while "his state of mind was affected by alcohol, a drug and confusion due to his personal situation.

Following Todd's death several allegations were made about both his personal and professional conduct.

An enquiry undertaken by the Chief Constable of West Midlands Police and 'fired' with the typical police culture of protecting their own at all costs, found that while his lifestyle damaged the reputation of the Police Service it did not compromise the discharging of his duties as Chief Constable. He was also cleared of any inappropriate professional misconduct such as that relating to expenses, promotions and misuse of Police equipment. Clearly this Chief Constable shouldn't be let loose in the 'brain dead' traffic department let alone an important and sensitive investigation such as this. The Coroner had already commented on his complex private life.

Private life! are you joking? Such a private life which included being a transvestite or at least dressing as a woman, actually filmed in the Midland Hotel, Manchester. He was dressed totally as a woman and accompanied by a woman who was thought to be a prostitute. The film taken on the security cameras during a National Police Conference in the nearby G Mex and was held by Bernard Del Soldarto the Security Manager. The film was common knowledge in Bernard's circles and in saying that, most of Manchester's dubious characters. Unbelievably the West Midlands CC and his crew never even established the presence of such a film in their 'thorough investigation'.

Well! what a surprise the Senior Ranks of the police yet again closing ranks on one of their own at the expense of the truth whatever the evidence. In fact Todd's failings were so transparent and there was more to come, he was not awarded a posthumous Knighthood.

Can you believe such a corrupt result and that a Chief Constable could endorse the unbelievable conclusion "it did not compromise the discharging of his duties as Chief Constable." Not an example of GMP but worth a mention, if only to prove the dual standards are throughout the UK Forces...

In yet another but simpler example of the one law for us and one for them traffic constable John Wetherall, 34, was dismissed from the South Yorkshire Force in what must certainly be a first and a sign of the times. This man had 10 years unblemished service in the force, and was career-minded, looking to be promoted at any opportunity. His life is now in ruins. Clearly the offence must have been serious, much more than a Deputy Chief Constable in Manchester prosecuted for driving at 120mph on the M6 toll road. He received a token sentence which did not involve the automatic ban that the rest of the speeding public suffers for the same offence. Wetherall actually drove his car over the force boundary into Nottinghamshire which is hardly crossing into Russia, and kissed a woman who got into his car. There was no sex or even attempts at sex. Being a traffic car, the interior and exterior is constantly filmed by two separate cameras. PC Wetherall, being aware of this, removed the videos of his married lady friend's activity in the police car and put them in his locker. The grave differences in police practices of today and my day, now become apparent. A fellow PC entered his secured locker claiming to be seeking a video for evidence, found the offending videos and handed them to the supervisory officers, who, on PC Wetherall's return from holiday, took disciplinary action against him, resulting in dismissal. Obviously, he was astounded at the dual standards in the force. Because in the same week a high ranking officer in the same force was caught having sex with a blonde female inspector with no serious disciplinary consequences. Again in the same force, continuing to perpetuate the double standards and be in no doubt that every force is the same; a sergeant was caught having sex with a married woman in a police car.

Yet again "Does not compromise the execution of his duties". What an amazing statement, and what does the senior level truly believe is actually police duty in GMP and forces countrywide for that matter, whilst they wallow in the corruption festering in their own forces. Such news usually breaks as an isolated incident but when examined in context as one example (GMP) as I am attempting to show, there is a real existing culture which has festered for many years and which fails the public again and again.

Shagging was and clearly is today an obsession in the ranks

Not so sexually different from the heady days of my uniformed service at Bootle Street, Manchester. Everybody from the Superintendent down had secret liaisons both on and off duty. Officers had the comfort of their own offices whilst us lower sprogs had to make do with any position available. On nights, there were more police cars on deserted car parks, rocking from side to side than there were patrolling the streets. Most officers had a favourite female on every beat. Some of the less choosy had the same one and a change was as good as a rest as far as the 'lady' was concerned. If a beat boundary had to be crossed to achieve "the end" so to speak, then it was. Whatever the circumstances the job got done, in a fashion, the figures showed some effort, arrests more by accident than deliberate police work and everyone was happy.

I must repeat ... the greatest very detailed example of such a culture, researched every year and published by a guy known as Woody @huytonfreeman with the **hash tag** Police Officers Charged or Convicted of a Crime.

The list illustrates fourteen years of a constant police culture of crime throughout the UK and runs to approximately 25 A4 pages.

There is little doubt that grooming and sexual abuse of children is continuing throughout the UK. Local authorities and the police have committed to improving and to be honest many gangs of Asian Pakistani Paedophiles have been arrested throughout the UK. Such arrests have demonstrated the absolute failures of GMP in this area and so must the Home Office in investigating this mammoth failure.

Todd in the once, wrongly and highly regarded, Greater Manchester Police, had very suspect sexual preferences which may have allowed him to give less priority to equally perverted paedophiles and choosing to ignore the sexual abuse of young white girls by Asian Pakistani males whilst other forces were actively arresting such individuals.

However in February 2004 Chief Constable Todd and the high echelons of Greater Manchester Police clearly found they could hide the facts no longer and Operation Augusta was initiated following the death of 15-year-old Victoria Agoglia while she was in the care of

Manchester City Council. Since the age of 13 she had been sexually abused and assaulted by Asian Pakistani men. She was finally injected by a fifty year old Asian Pakistani with heroin.

Augusta commenced with gusto, foremost was the honourable aim of finding and protecting children in a similar situation to Victoria. They were of course to identify and arrest the many paedophiles who openly regarded white girls as second class citizens to be raped and sexual abused at will. Augusta of course, initially had real detectives who cared, at the pointed end and who actually identified 57 girls at risk and 97 suspects. Augusta was inexplicably closed down after sixteen months. (Operation Augusta is fully covered below in a separate chapter.) The closing down left the gangs of paedophiles free to continue their abuse in plain sight. Possibly only four men were prosecuted and their activities continued.

Augusta was later said to be a litany of poor leadership, lack of resources, territorial disputes within Greater Manchester Police and a reliance on difficult-to-obtain evidence from victims which in truth was never going to be easy. This conclusion was not totally accurate. This policy was abandoned as the diligent officers prepared all the intelligence compiled for arrests and prosecution, when Chief Constable Todd believed that such actions would damage community relations.

A ruling factor remained that most of the perpetrators were Asian Muslims of Pakistani origin which meant that many hardened police officers already racially prejudiced themselves in a force already a culture admitted by CC Wilmot. As a result they were now careful of racial prejudice accusations. They were reluctant to carry out their duties. Wanton accusations of racism were dumped on GMP in the form of official complaints by a couple of solicitor firms jumping on the bandwagon. Such complaints against any officer concerned could easily result in their sacking in line with the aggressive and naive policy introduced by C.C James Anderton and which deteriorated thereafter into a force of low moral and fear of conducting their duties.

Operation Augusta is a significant and corrupt milestone in the history of GMP culture and a just example of how such corruption of the truth can remain and go unpunished. It thoroughly deserves the further chapter below with what became of the further investigation named, Operation Greenjacket and the introduction of an Asian Pakistani Assistant Chief Constable to head the heralded investigation into the deplorable abuse of white young girls. Something akin to 'Turkeys voting for Christmas' as it has proved to date.

The services of this officer ACC Mohammed Hussain have now been terminated by the 2023 Chief Constable, Stephen Watson quietly without any Manchester Evening News coverage that can be found on Google. The MEN was responsible for many glowing articles regarding this man. He now 'serves' in the North Yorkshire force, hardly known for anything except Traffic Cops on TV with excellent monitoring of motorway drug dealing villains.

Whilst honourable actions read well concerning local authorities and the police committed to improving in GMP and the UK for that matter that's where it ends and there is little doubt that grooming and sexual abuse of children continued into the 'reign' of Peter Fahy.

As highlighted in the Death of Anthony Grainger chapter below, Fahy inherited the inquest/enquiry result of a training accidental shooting of a police officer which culminated with the usual 'slippery' statement and a sacking of an officer to pacify the outcry.

However sad, the death was an accident clearly due to poor training standards carried over and from the days of C.C. Todd. The abysmal training standards were recognised by C.C. Peter Fahy who vowed to improve them, but of course were in fact only words and the the usual bull, to be confirmed by the comments of the Chairman into the Manchester Arena bombing inquest, Sir John Saunders. There should be no doubt with regard to the circumstances and the deplorable training standards which prevailed and yet never admitted by Fahy over a period of six years.

GMP announced ... A police officer was today shot and killed during a training exercise in Manchester. Ian James Terry, 32, was shot in the chest in 2010 on Thorpe Road, Newton Heath, about one mile from the city centre. He died in North Manchester General hospital. A full inquiry has been launched that will involve the coroner, Greater Manchester police's professional standards officers, the Independent Police Complaints Commission and the Health and Safety Executive.

In typical GMP fashion the acting Chief Constable of Greater Manchester police, made a brief statement about the incident, but refused to go into detail of how exactly Terry was killed. "Shortly after 11.30 this morning the firearms training exercise was taking place in Newton Heath in a disused factory site completely away from any members of the public, involving experienced firearms officers." The police would not comment on whether officers used live or blank bullets or both in the training exercises.

It was stressed there was no risk to the public through Greater Manchester police "not being able to respond to firearms incidents". "I can't go into circumstances of how the officer was killed at this time, but what I can say is there was no risk to any members of the public, no one else was hurt during the incident.

The shooting happened at a large disused warehouse, formerly a distribution centre for Sharp, the electronics company. Forensic officers were this afternoon examining the goods yard outside the warehouse, which was cordoned off with yellow tape. As news coverage grew a photograph taken unofficially by a freelance photographer emerged of the scene and the investigation officers standing about. Of course this proved that any member of the public could be in danger from a stray bullet from a gun with range must greater than that of a camera.

Speaking in the House of Commons and only casually briefed, the Home Secretary, Jacqui Smith, told MPs: "The whole House will be saddened to learn of the tragic death today of a police officer during a training exercise with Greater Manchester police. With a typical blasé statement without any grasp of the facts she states "This demonstrates the dangers that police officers face on our behalf." The shocking truth of this incident was that the police officers concerned killed one of their own on private property, creating the actual danger themselves. with the innocent public being close by.

It was later reported ... A police officer who organised a bungled firearms training exercise which resulted in a colleague being shot dead has been forced to resign from GMP. Another, who fired the fatal shot, has been reprimanded over their role in the the exercise which ended in the death of police marksman Pc Ian Terry.

Pc Terry, 32, a father of two, from Burnley, died during a firearms training exercise on 9 June 2008 involving GMP's Tactical Firearms Unit (TFU) in a disused factory premises on Thorp Road, Newton Heath, Manchester. The two officers faced a misconduct hearing organised by Greater Manchester Police under CC Peter Fahy. One officer, known by the pseudonym "Chris", who fired the fatal shot, was found guilty of gross misconduct. The second officer, known by the pseudonym "Francis", who was involved in the organisation of the training and the way it was conducted, pleaded guilty to gross misconduct at the start of the hearing. Fahy was the Chief Constable and under him the panel decided that "Francis" should be required to resign with immediate effect. The panel decided "Chris" should be given a reprimand. In its decision making the panel focused on the risks posed by the training exercise and the organisational failures by Greater Manchester Police.

IPCC Commissioner James Dipple-Johnstone said: "The IPCC investigation was concluded prior to the inquest into Pc Terry's death in 2010 and the fact it has taken more than four years to reach this conclusion must have compounded the distress of Pc Terry's family. Two officers have now been disciplined over their role in this tragedy. This training exercise was poorly planned and high risk. Everyone involved will have to live with the fact that a popular and well respected officer lost his life as a result of the mistakes made on that day."

The IPCC conducted an independent investigation into PC Terry's death and the resultant disciplinary matters in response to the IPCC's recommendations had to await the conclusion of an inquest and a subsequent Health and Safety Executive prosecution against Greater

Manchester Police and two individual officers. Greater Manchester Police in the form of Peter Fahy the C.C. pleaded guilty at court and received a fine, while "Francis" was found guilty of failing to discharge his duty under the Health and Safety at Work Act and fined. The second officer, known by the pseudonym "Eric", was found not guilty. This officer had retired prior to disciplinary matters.

Significantly the purpose of the training exercise was to practise tactics for challenging and arresting the occupants of a vehicle who were suspected of committing serious offences. Clearly subsequent training was inadequate and yet again a firearms officer shot and killed Anthony Grainger in very similar circumstances.

PC Terry and a colleague were in a Suzuki Vitara playing the role of suspected criminals. Both officers were wearing thick jackets, balaclavas, gloves and special face masks designed to protect them from possible impact from paint rounds. Incredibly neither officer was wearing body armour. 'Chris', who was performing the role designed to disable the vehicle by blowing out the tyres, ran to an area next to the front passenger door of the Vitara carrying a shotgun loaded with Round Irritant Personnel (RIP) rounds. These training munitions were filled with an inert powder, whereas in a live operation they would be filled with CS incapacitant. RIP rounds are used in 12-bore shotguns and, according to the manufacturers, can penetrate timber up 65mm thick, cell type doors and fire doors clad with thin-steel plate on both sides. 'Chris' discharged the shotgun at PC Terry from close range and he was struck directly in the left hand side of the chest, sustaining fatal injuries.

The investigation found that risk assessments for the training exercise were inadequate, the training had not been authorised and that RIP rounds only been introduced to firearms training a week before the incident. Mr Dipple-Johnstone said: "This was a shocking wake-up call for Greater Manchester Police firearms unit. Firearms officers have a very difficult and dangerous job to do and their training does need to be challenging.

Yet further deception when Fahy said: "It is six years since Ian died, six years that Ian's family has had to wait for a conclusion to what has been a complicated and frustrating series of legal and multiple investigative processes which have caused additional delay in bringing this to a conclusion. "This hearing was the final stage in a very long process and I hope that this decision provides Ian's family with some form of closure and that they can all now begin to move forward. "Since Ian's tragic death we have introduced a number of rigorous measures to ensure that the risk to our officers on such training exercises is minimised and that their safety is our number one priority." So! that's alright then, job done., what a disgrace. Rest in Peace Ian Terry and God Bless his family.

Even with the Hillsborough experience fresh on the horizon and their flawed thinking, they should have realised there was nowhere to hide, the results were publicised Nationwide and even in the Manchester Evening News. It must so often have hurt readers, seeing the local newspaper publish stories of Manchester police glorification in the past when the truth was so incredibly different. Even this newspaper could not hide from these facts and once again the police were a laughing stock in the eyes of the public.

In such a total public relations failure of laughable proportions they would surely have affected the morale of their colleagues who had to continue in a climate of ridicule particularly amongst the Asians of Manchester. The city in parts is said to be a terrorist hot bed and in turn, this has given the militant Muslims a clear account of their actual capabilities. They have probably also convinced the non-militant Muslims that their intelligence, and use of such information, is so poor that they are at risk if they pass on any information to the authorities.

In the climate of 'No Smoke Without Fire' they must surely have believed that these men were guilty, they must have had other information and therefore rather than cause so much embarrassment, and in the heartfelt traditions of my days, they would have added a little more evidence and 'verbals.' There is no doubt that many officers with whom I served would have made sure that traces of explosives in the form of forensic evidence were found in the flat, or would even have fabricated evidence in a manner which would leave no doubt, such as finding a stick of explosive preferred by Al Qaeda in a car or business premises. The fact they were innocent, mattered little. Prisons today have many prisoners serving life sentences regarded as unsuitable for parole purely because they continue to protest their innocence. Nobody considers the fact that they could be yet another example of corrupt and fabricated evidence and purely out of an amazing strength of principle were refusing to bow to this antiquated system. Typical of todays policing.

01.09.2008–2015:
Peter Fahy... what can you say?

Earlier comments in relation to absolutely unsuited wastrels rising through the police ranks in very short order supported by the useless degrees they accomplished, comes to mind. Such degrees embellished C.Vs and clearly looked good to simpletons on selection committees, but in fact were actually no use in real policing at any level. Peter Fahy is 'a gift which keeps on giving' and features as he holds a Degree in French and Spanish from the University of Hull and a Masters degree from the University of East Anglia. Isn't that just typical of poorly qualified and uneducated committee members appointing just anybody on a whim, fuelled with what appears to be an excellent education but in truth qualified in degrees, usually from internet usage, which are absolutely pointless in any police force but great for holidays.

Prior to taking up this post at GMP on 1 September 2008, he was the Chief Constable of Cheshire Constabulary a post he held since 2002. He had been Assistant Chief Constable at Surrey and had had positions with Hertfordshire and West Midlands forces. He had two years later, left Cheshire Constabulary, when in March 2017, Her Majesty's Inspectorate of Constabulary and Fire & Rescue Services (HMICFRS) conducted a crime data integrity inspection of Cheshire Constabulary.

What they discovered was a serious situation that could not possibly have deteriorated to such a level of gross incompetence and deception in just a few months. It had to be a long standing culture in light of the many recommendations they implemented to bring the force to a reasonable standard.

They reported with what was a cursory examination, possibly neglectful, over a disappointedly specimen short period as follows. It is clear that had the examination had expanded over a wider period, say three months the actual figure would have been a much larger figure than the 11,600 shown. The report follows....

Based on the findings of our examination of crime reports for the period 1 June 2016 to 30 November 2016, we estimate that the force fails to record over 11,600 reported crimes each year. This represents a recording rate of 83.6 percent (with a confidence interval of +/- 1.79 percent). The 16.4 percent of reported crimes that go unrecorded include serious crimes such as sexual offences, domestic abuse and rape. The recording rate for violent crime is a particular cause of concern at only 80.9 percent (with a confidence interval of +/- 3.00 percent). This means that on too many occasions, the constabulary is failing victims of crime. In addition to the investigation into the criminal crime recording the Inspectorate examined other failing features and thereafter in 2017 returned for a further examination. They published the report of the inspection in June 2017 and concluded that the crime-recording arrangements in Cheshire Constabulary were not acceptable. As a result, the constabulary was given an overall judgment of inadequate. The 2017 report made a series of recommendations and areas for improvement aimed at improving crime recording in Cheshire. This re-inspection assessed the progress made since that report.

How could a man leaving Cheshire Constabulary in such a diabolical state, which was discovered only months after his final day be appointed by the Greater Manchester Police authority without any cursory investigation into his previous Cheshire Constabulary service. HMICFRS in treating the force like a child, comprehensively mapped its crime-recording processes to ensure that it had a detailed understanding of all the channels through which it receives reports of crime. A system never to cross the desk or interest C.C Peter Fahy as with many matters relating to conduct and training, a honed culture to be later carried over to his 'service' in GMP. The report suggested....

- provided officers and staff with a clear understanding of their roles and responsibilities in relation to crime recording;
- provided comprehensive training which has improved the understanding of crime-recording requirements among officers and staff;
- improved supervision and quality assurance of crime-recording decisions – both centrally within the occurrence management unit (OMU) and locally in the local policing units (LPUs) – to make sure that better crime-recording decisions are being made;
- effective departmental learning feedback processes in place which support its commitment to continual improvement; and
- strong audit and governance arrangements in place to ensure that the improvements made to its crime-recording accuracy are sustainable and ongoing.

The constabulary has also completed all the recommendations made in our 2017 report, including:

- a review of the operating arrangements of its force contact centre (FCC) (including the OMU) and its diary appointment system;
- the introduction of a call-handling quality-assurance process which includes checking that all crimes identified from calls are correctly recorded;
- the recruitment of a deputy force crime registrar; and
- creating additional crime-recording audit capacity.

A further legacy of the Peter Fahy style of management emerged with the usual excuses for such failure ..." During 2017 the constabulary was experiencing staff shortages within the FCC", (The Force Control Centre) which is at the front line of policing, providing that vital first point of contact between the public of Cheshire and operational police officers.) It is so difficult to comment on such incompetence ... F.F.S. when the force had so many individuals staffing so many ludicrous, pointless positions such as liaison with street sweepers etc. and yet none could be moved to the front line.

In his 'Mickey Mouse' style, in July 2011, Fahy commanded his officers to use their common sense in dealing with the rising tide of crime. Not his own strong point and certainly not a personality trait, so obvious in so many poorly trained recruits and surely asking for trouble. Ably and conveniently forgetting his own failures and lack of common sense he criticised police policies which prevents the police from helping victims or protecting the public in certain cases, whatever that means. In 2013 I wrote, giving Cheshire Constabulary a mention ...

I was amused, as I often am, to watch Cheshire County Police motorway patrols on a recent television documentary being filmed as they performed their daily duties. Performance is surely the ideal description as they play up to the cameras in their 'wooden' childish way. Surely the viewing public recognise these as the overweight, arrogant, and small-minded shower that is certainly damaging the force nationwide and doing the police image so much harm today, if indeed such assistance was necessary.

Purely as a point of interest, a new series has been commissioned and aired in 2023. Inspector Anton Rogers remains with the same brain dead posse, lecturing and prosecuting the driving public on the M6 and M56. Such a waste of manpower, rarely having any impact on the growing crime rate. At least 5 high powered fully equipped police cars drop everything to chase a stolen car at great speeds and danger to the public as a result of the police action. The driver would undoubtedly have trundled along at 30/40 mph in the absence of such attention.

G.M.P C.C Fahy mounted a robust defence in the face of allegations from a force whistleblower, retired Detective Superintendent Peter Jackson that he created a 'culture of cronyism' that promoted under-qualified officers into senior positions. He spoke out as a witness at the continuing employment tribunal of Mr. Jackson, who has since on retiring made a life's work in disclosing several allegations of corruption, including claims he was passed over for promotion for making a series of what was deemed to be 'protected disclosures'. The transcript of Mr Jacksons verbal assault on Andy

Burnham, the Police and Crime Commissioner, beggars belief. Burnham and his cronies showed a total lack of interest with regard to the many listed GMP failings.

Incredibly, mentioned only to further illustrate the mad selection processes, in July 2011, Fahy was one of the frontrunners to replace Sir Paul Stephenson as the Met. Commissioner but Fahy ruled himself out of that position. There is little need to consider why? Even the Met and the Lord Mayor would readily see the trail of unbelievable failures of tremendous proportions and of course he had the temerity to blame" lack of staff and funding." A claim he was to use yet again later in his GMP service in failed attempts to account for yet more failings.

Whilst a further chapter gives much more detail, it is worth giving the shortened version at the stage in the context of C.C Peter Fahy's 'service' to the population of Greater Manchester. In 2012 Anthony Grainger was shot by a GMP Police officer with a high velocity rifle, as he sat unarmed in a vehicle. Fahy initially stated the officer concerned would face criminal charges. No charges were brought and Fahy was prosecuted under Health and Safety Regulations which he defended and due to many suspicious redactions, destruction of documents and failure to produce documents by senior GMP officers, even that prosecution failed with no noticeable official attempts to prevent this.

Yes! I do have to repeat myself again ... Leslie Thomas QC acting for the Grainger family stated in one of many stark comments, ...

"Greater Manchester Police is now recognised as the most scandal ridden police force in the country. and is Rotten to its Core".

The Crown Prosecution Service announced in 2014 that they would be prosecuting Fahy under health and safety legislation over the horrific death of Anthony Grainger who was shot by police. The shooting of Anthony Grainger by police whilst unarmed and the actions which followed in attempting to secure justice for Anthony in a later chapter.

A further innocent death by GMP officers will also be featured in a later chapter. In 2013 Jordan Begley was shot with a taser gun by one of three badly trained and led uniformed police constables. He had been wrongly identified as a wanted man and died later of a cardiac arrest in hospital. The family have attempted to prosecute Fahy as C.C for several years. In July 2015 Greater Manchester Police was criticised by a jury at the Inquest into the taser death of Jordon Begley.

Incredibly in a demonstration that Tony Lloyd the Police and Crime Commissioner at the time, could not care less with regard to Fahy's antics. it was announced in July 2013 that his contract had been extended for a further three years after 30 years service, Fahy was eligible for retirement, and his contract would have ended on 31 August 2013.

Continuing to fester at this time was the shooting of an officer by another in a badly prepared training incident, again due to poor training for the training exercise itself. Throughout Peter Fahy's service the shooting of a police officer by a police officer in the training exercise was to be delayed for years until GMP could wriggle no longer when on 17 September 2014 a Greater Manchester Police officer had been sacked over the fatal shooting of an unarmed colleague during a training exercise. PC Ian Terry 32, was killed in June

2008 at a time when C.C Todd was too busy shagging and researching suicide, to deal with the running of GMP and instil the need for proper training in many departments.

The shooting was during a police firearms training incident at a disused warehouse in Manchester. The officer, known only as "Francis", to hide his identity, admitted gross misconduct in relation to the way the training was organised and conducted.

Another officer "who fired the fatal shot has been reprimanded", police said. A hearing organised by the force found that the officer, known by the name "Chris", was guilty of gross misconduct. Peter Fahy adopted the matter some four months after the initial incident, as he 'took command of GMP' and therefore led the delays and prevarication thereafter.

An inquest held in March 2010 during the suspect leadership of Peter Fahy, found PC Terry was unlawfully killed, but the Crown Prosecution Service (CPS) said there was "insufficient evidence" to bring criminal charges in relation to his death. PC Terry, from Burnley in Lancashire, was not wearing body armour when he was hit from a distance of about 12" by a blank round of specialist ammunition not designed to kill. He was playing the role of a criminal fleeing in a car.

Ian Terry's family naively, never believing that Peter Fahy and Co. would have attempted all the delays to avoid prosecution ..." The important result of this hearing is that we finally feel the officers responsible have been shown indisputably that they are undeniably to blame for Ian's death and we want them to know that we believe if they'd had the courage to face the consequences of their actions in 2008 and take responsibility for their actions, they could have saved our family six years of unnecessary pain and difficulty."

The Independent Police Complaints Commission (IPCC) called it a "shocking wake-up call" for the force's firearms unit, with "completely unnecessary risks" resulting in PC Terry's death. C.C. Peter Fahy had the gaul to speak out ... "Ian Terry was a complete professional, highly regarded by all his colleagues, who served the public of Greater Manchester with huge commitment and expertise. "Since Ian's tragic death we have introduced a number of rigorous measures to ensure that the risk to our officers on such training exercises is minimised and that their safety is our number one priority."

A Fahy proclaimed priority similar to that promised regarding Operation Augusta and the suffering young white girls at the hands of Asian Pakistani gangs to be featured later. Greater Manchester Police admitted breaching health and safety law over the shooting and "Francis" was fined £2,000 and ordered to pay costs of £500 at Manchester Crown Court. The force was fined £166,666 and ordered to pay costs of £90,000.

A third officer did not face the gross misconduct hearing as he had retired. Fahy's usual apologies to the grieving family and promises to improve training followed.

Never one to be out of the headlines, featuring anything that represented the diabolical training existing at the time of his 'leadership'. During November 2013 protests at Barton Moss in the GMP area, triggered a large-scale policing operation by GMP reportedly costing in excess of £1.6m which led to over 200 arrests and numerous official complaints about the conduct of police officers including indecent assaults on female protesters.

After demonstrations outside police stations and even a protest camp outside GMP HQ, most of those arrested during the Barton Moss campaign had charges against them dropped or the cases have since collapsed at trial. The wastage of police assets and time was incredible. The badly led policing raised significant questions about the policing at Barton Moss and specifically the way that arrest and bail powers were used by GMP. Ultimately the report raised serious questions about the nature of democratic accountability and policing in England and Wales and on this occasion featuring C.C Peter Fahy with his continuing neglect to appropriate training procedures.

In a pantomime gesture so reminiscent of Fahy's style of policing he also came under fire once again for the same GMP's policing of these anti-fracking protests when Peter May the Sheriff of Northwich rode into Salford on a horse. He had prepared the official notice for C.C Peter Fahy, to stand down under common law, citing the Magna Carta clause 61 of 'lawful rebellion'." Today I'm serving Peter Fahy with a Stand Down Notice over the current criminal investigations against him" explained Sheriff Peter May "There's three instances – the Harold Shipman case disposal of body parts by GMP, the health and safety breach in the killing of Anthony Grainger, and the unlawful killing of Jordan Begley – we want the name of the constable who unlawfully killed him."

The Sheriff is quoted as saying "Basically we're trying to get rid of corruption in high places ... police corruption, government corruption and anything else that goes with that" he explained "There's no legal standing, *'Legal'* is government created acts or statutes, *'lawful'* is common law, a natural law that basically states '*Don't do harm or injury to man, person or property*'. "I'm going to Tony Lloyd to serve these papers because we believe that Tony Lloyd is above Peter Fahy" he explained "I have here a formal Warrant to Deputise, issued by Coventry Common Law Court to deputise Tony Lloyd, which means he becomes my Common Law Deputy. The headlines in the local media, read The Good, The Bad and The Fahy. Doesn't that just say it all.

The papers were delivered to Greater Manchester Police and Crime Commissioner, Tony Lloyd, at this Salford office . Fahy, announced his retirement stating in his usual blasé dishonesty "It has always been my intention to leave during the Autumn of this year". Of course he took no responsibility for any of his obvious failures and using a similar excuse to that of his Cheshire Constabulary failings "I have led the force through four years of budget cuts and staffing reductions but despite this we have achieved significant improvements in service, increased public confidence and reduced crime and anti-social behaviour". Unbelievable and what is the alarming feature of such a statement is that he expected the public to believe this.

However, he added "It is now time for someone else to bring fresh ideas for what will be more challenging years ahead." Probably the only honest statement he had made for some considerable time but of course even he, with his confused outlook on professional policing could have foreseen what would follow.

Peter Jackson, 59, retired from the force in February 2017 after 31 years. He had told an employment tribunal he felt 'vindicated' after a top officer was served with a gross misconduct notice for disposing of Harold Shipman's victims without their families knowledge.

The former Detective Superintendent has now taken GMP to an employment tribunal and written a 226-page witness statement, including a series of allegations against former colleagues. One such allegation in his 226-page statement to an ongoing employment tribunal is that he, other officers and even a forensic psychologist had warned C.C Fahy about the 'dangerous and misguided tactic' of repeated police visits to professional criminal and violent Dale Cregan's family while he remained on the run following the murders of Mark and David Short. In his witness statement to the employment tribunal continuing in Manchester, Mr Jackson alleged Assistant Chief Constable Steve Heywood had posted a message to fellow officers at the time which read: "Public safety demands that we visit Dale Cregan's family and friends regularly until he reappears.

Following the well founded warnings, Cregan murdered two policewomen on September 18, 2012, after weeks on the run before handing himself in. He is now serving life behind bars.

A further incident referred to at the proceeding in Manchester was when GMP secretly destroyed remains of Harold Shipman's victims after 12 years without informing relatives. Talking of a 'gift which keeps on giving' Peter Fahy chose to add yet more glib comments and promised to investigate yet another diabolical instance of senior leadership by an officer below him dodging yet more disciplinary bullets.

On the 17th March 2014 it was widely reported that Greater Manchester Police were being investigated for misleading the families of Harold Shipman's victims. The allegations relate to the disposal of human tissues of the victims, according The Independent Police Complaints

Commission (IPCC). The IPCC announced on Twitter that it has launched three investigations into GMP following the allegations. The commission also confirmed that the allegations were made by an officer currently serving in the force. One investigation focuses on allegations that families of Harold Shipman's victims were misled by GMP over disposal of human tissue. Such announcements were again treated with the usual disdain and clearly no-one was holding their breath.

Mr Peter Jackson was the whistleblower who prompted an investigation into the incident by the IPCC (Independent Police Complaints Commission), which, surprise surprise, eventually found 'no evidence of wrong-doing' and that the force had acted within the law.

A disgusted Mr Jackson called the report, published in 2017, a whitewash. At his employment tribunal Mr Jackson accused Detective Chief Superintendent Darren Shenton in the witness statement of being responsible over the Shipman affair, along with Assistant Chief Constables Terry Sweeney and Steve Heywood. Both to feature later in the Anthony Grainger enquiry. On this occasion, skating very close to being prosecuted for perjury. Mr Jackson claimed: "DCS Shenton, with the knowledge of ACC Sweeney and ACC Heywood, authorised the destruction of human tissue from the victims of Harold Shipman without notifying their families."

The statement continued: "There would have been those within the victims where the religious beliefs of their families may have been that they would want body parts to be reunited with their loved ones. It was a decision for the families and they had to be told. "The decision to incinerate the body parts was not borne out of a concern to save the families heartache; it was borne out of a desire to avoid negative publicity for the Respondent (GMP) and those senior officers who had responsibility for serious crime investigation and retention and disposal of body parts from the Shipman case." ACC Sweeney was served with a gross misconduct notice and investigated by the IPCC (Independent Police Complaints Commission) in relation to the disposal of the victim's body parts, following Mr Jackson's whistleblowing. In the witness statement, Mr Jackson said he felt 'vindicated' by this. "Its a window into GMP, a broken force that's lost its moral compass," he told the hearing.

In yet another allegation, Mr Jackson said that Chief Inspector John Lyons was allowed to continue in his Acting Superintendent role 'despite being found to be drunk and abusive' while out in the Bolton town centre division.

Mr Jackson wrote in his statement: "I had become aware of an incident involving the alleged misconduct of Chief Inspector Lyons who was an acting Superintendent at Bolton had been drunk off duty in Bolton town centre, when approached by lower ranking officers and had only avoided arrest because of his position. "These were officers under his command. I became aware through the usual police gossip mill in general conversation. "Incidents of a Superintendent or an acting Superintendent, being drunk and disorderly and nearly being arrested by their own staff are far from common and for that reason news of this type of incident travelled quickly through the force."

Mr Jackson rightly claimed that no action was taken against CI Lyons. He continued: "In terms of official records, it would appear Lyons had an unblemished record, and nothing was recorded." Mr Jackson claimed that he would have been 'dealt with differently' and suggested that this was because of 'cronyism'. "What I'm trying to do in this evidence is show an officer who should have been disciplined and wasn't and it highlights cronyism," he told the tribunal. "If I'd have been found drunk and abusive in the town centre of the division by police, I'd have been dealt with differently."

Of course, remember the age old adage of GMP, 'Get done and Get on', Chief inspector Lyons was eventually appointed as Detective Superintendent to the North West regional Crime Squad, an appointment that Mr Jackson suggested came about because of his relationship with ACC Sweeney. In his statement, he wrote: "I knew that Lyons was close to Sweeney through my own knowledge and conversations from working within GMP and having seen them talking from time to time when at various events or meetings across the force.

"I later learnt that Lyons was appointed as Detective Superintendent in the North West Regional Crime Squad by a promotion interview panel comprising ACC Sweeney, who was chair of the interview panel and DCS Shenton. "My concern in short regarding the way the behaviour of Lyons was dealt with was 'what message did it send out' how could other officers be held to account when an acting Superintendent was treated in this manner and was even permitted to continue to act as a Superintendent thereafter."

The IPCC reported ... The officer who has made the allegations has accused a number of senior officers of cronyism, failure to follow correct procedures, failure to investigate complaints properly and corruption. We've assessed a range of other allegations, which include cronyism and corruption and these were returned to the force. Of course to be subjected to yet further cronyism by 'you know who'. Police investigating police yet again with the added bonus of 'never to be prosecuted' senior officers." The other GMP allegations to be investigated are the alleged unauthorised bugging of a police office & poorly managed investigations". "We've started three investigations into GMP after allegations made by a senior officer serving in the force," The three investigations will examine: Whether GMP officers misled families and the public when human tissue from victims of serial killer Harold Shipman was disposed of.

The actions of a Detective Chief Inspector and whether these put public safety at risk as well as the officer's alleged unauthorised bugging of a GMP office. The force has told the IPCC that this bugging did take place. Further, claims that an investigation into alleged sexual abuse was poorly handled and the alleged failings covered-up by GMP. True to form, following an IPCC assessment, all other allegations outside of the three investigations which were returned to GMP for the force to deal with. Officers whose actions will be investigated range from the rank of constable up to GMP's Assistant Chief Constable, Terry Sweeney who certainly showed serious inabilities in several areas under his leadership.

The replacement force computer system and his involvement in the Anthony Grainger shooting, cover up to name just two. Can you believe ACC Sweeney worked on Operation Resolve, the police investigation into the Hillsborough disaster and we all know how that ended.

IPCC Commissioner Jan Williams said: "These are serious allegations and the gravity and nature of the allegations, and the fact that they are made against senior officers within the force, means they must be investigated independently. "We will also look at the wider organisational response by Greater Manchester Police in each of these investigations. "We know that the families involved will have been through very distressing times, and we will be sensitive to this as we conduct our investigations." IPCC Commissioner Williams added that the commission have a statutory duty to conduct independent investigations in circumstances such as these, and will make sure they communicate with the families and do whatever they can to avoid further distress.

Lo and behold, speaking on behalf of GMP, with yet another empty disingenuous statement, Chief Constable Peter Fahy said: "We will be cooperating with the Independent Police Complaints Commission as we want to ensure the allegations raised are brought to a satisfactory conclusion. We hope this can be done swiftly."Assistant Chief Constable Terry Sweeney has voluntarily decided to stand down from his work with the Hillsborough Enquiry as part of Operation Resolve while the investigation takes place." He added: "I support the need for difficult issues we face to be subjected to scrutiny and for there to be a transparent process for this."

As it inevitably proved, so transparent that no action was taken against any officer and it was never heard of again.

C.C. Peter Fahy retired ignoring the existing evidence from the closed Operation Augusta, the 90 suspects and the 57 identified paedophiles throughout his six years of C.C. service. Peter Fahy, in an ITV interview in 2014, said he was 'quite happy' to look at Victoria Agoglia's death again after her grandmother Joan Agloglia, in the wake of the Rochdale sex grooming scandal, had said: "These men are still walking about".

"She needs to be put to rest and I hope if anyone is watching and they do know something, even if it's the smallest thing, to come forward so that social services will know there's a lot of people that still know they never helped these young girls." Despite the existing filmed evidence he later denied any knowledge of this interview with his glib promise and resigned in 2016 to feature, somewhat strangely having failed many children, in a variety of Children's Charities.

Tony Lloyd in his own deceptive 'wonderland' of flowery tributes, as the Police and Crime Commissioner appears to have taken some responsibility for the Fahy carnage in saying … "During his seven years with GMP, Sir Peter has worked with me to implement fundamental changes to how Greater Manchester is policed, ensuring that we protect those that are most vulnerable whilst ensuring that all of our communities are safe from harm". Effectively, 'the blind leading the blind' and the 'most vulnerable' proving to be the higher ranks of GMP.

Unbelievably he continued "Sir Peter has been a great credit to both GMP and Greater Manchester and he leaves us in much better shape than when he arrived. He is held in the highest regard, not just by his colleagues in GMP, but across Greater Manchester and the country…"

Tell the Grainger and Begley families that, tell the sexually abused young girls that, tell the imprisoned frackers that, tell the Shipman relatives that and of course the tens of thousands members of the public suffering burglaries, street thefts and street gangs vandalism due to none attendance of police officers. What can you possibly say to nonsense like that?, well maybe F.F.S. covers it admirably.

Had the wanting local media chosen with the minimum of expertise to examine the verbal and actual bilge just below the surface of Fahy's glib pronouncements, they would recognise a man with no real regret for the Anthony Grainger incident despite the legal squirming to avoid conviction. They would discover a man with no regard for the grieving family of Jordan Begley. What about the many young white girls just forgotten with the prosecutions he promised on TV of so many Asian Pakistani paedophiles.

The pantomime theme continues when in October 2015, Fahy was appointed an Honorary Professor of Criminal Justice by the University of Manchester which clearly chose to ignore such a dubious history. He gave his first public lecture on 11 November 2015. The subject of the lecture was Thinking about police and public in a more divided world: reflections on 34 years of policing. Could he possibly be reflecting on the existing culture of lies, statistical fabrication and gross dishonesty.

In a moment of honest reflection he states it is easy for a leader, to live in a management bubble and as his previous Chief Constables seeing what they want to see and hearing what those close to them think they would like to hear. "GMP is indeed defensive," he draws the line at inveterate liars and claims "as are most forces" Learning from the disasters of Anderton's reign he attempts to hide behind the force legal department, insurance companies, press office and sometimes politicians telling you to be careful what you say or, indeed, say nothing.

He agreed, that the old police authority system was able to carry out closer scrutiny but also to have the time to really understand the force and the challenges it faced'. The old police authority spent a lot of its time 'scrutinising major spending and IT projects', he notes.

Since 2017, however, there has also been an added factor for Greater Manchester, which is unusual in having a Police and Crime Commissioner who is also Mayor, therefore not focused full-time on policing and usually on his own survival. Burnham claims to have delegated the task to Baroness Beverley Hughes and since then she has barely uttered a word which is understandable, probably because she has no idea of policing and is totally out of her depth.

Fahy actually retired on 23rd October 2015 leaving yet another scandal within the force. A senior police officer was sacked for gross misconduct but alleged he was the victim of "corrupt practice" within the force's anti-corruption unit, renamed from the 'Y Department' of Anderton's days. Ch Inspector John Buttress was cleared of mortgage fraud by a jury but was dismissed by an independent panel. He was accused of breaching professional standards over his mortgage at a disciplinary hearing. GMP said Mr Buttress had "fallen below the accepted standards" of honesty. A crown court jury in Liverpool cleared him of mortgage fraud in January. GMP said Mr Buttress applied for a "specific" mortgage relating to a farm house he rented as a holiday home.

The mortgage fraud emerged when Mr Buttress failed to tell his mortgage provider Intelligent Finance about the holiday business he ran at his property in North

Wales. The case centred on whether he committed a fraud by not taking out a buy-to-let mortgage. A crown court jury sitting in January cleared him in 20 minutes. Mr Buttress claimed "at most" it was a civil contractual breach, which he admitted and said he "didn't realise I was doing anything wrong". He said at the time that the force even looked at whether his organ playing at his church was paid and said things were "taken to an incredible degree and it almost became silly".

In 2005, Mr Buttress was a rising star within the force. He was awarded a gallantry medal for disarming a gunman in Stockport. He became a poster boy for police recruitment, with his face on the walls of police stations across the country, advertising the fast track officer development scheme. Since returning to work, he has accused six GMP officers of offences ranging from misconduct in a public office to perjury. These accusations were investigated by Kent Police, a force lacking in credentials for detecting crimes especially against brother senior officers.

In May, he was told he would face a gross misconduct hearing in September where it was actually double jeopardy. GMP decided to discard the two weeks of evidence and the judgement of 12 jurors and re-try him in front of two police officers with much lower standards of proof. He was dismissed and Mr Buttress said: "I am shocked. I have been a policeman for more than 20 years. I am standing outside the organisation I joined, I am just flabbergasted to be put in this position."

Graham Stringer, the Blackley and Broughton MP, said: "What has happened to John Buttress is a disgrace. He was cleared of an absurd case in court, but instead of welcoming back an innocent officer, GMP decided to hound him."

Assistant Chief Constable Garry Shewan, no stranger to gross financial losses had presided over GMP's disastrous Police Computer IS Transformation Programme with costs rising to £80 million, said: "Ch Insp Buttress may have been acquitted in a Crown Court where the burden of proof is beyond all reasonable doubt." The burden of proof for breaching the standards of professional behaviour is based on the lower threshold of a balance of probabilities.

"He has been dismissed from Greater Manchester Police with immediate effect." ACC Sherwan denied all responsibility for what was his totally failed computer project and resigned on his full pension. Fahy left the force on October 23rd 2015 with a Knighthood and a massive pension in recognition of 'his excellent leadership' which was to be dramatically revealed as a total charade. The Cheshire Constabulary practice of dumping crime reports which does not happen overnight and requires planning, suddenly appeared in a HMRCFS investigation during Hopkins 'reign' along with the abysmal training record of all GMP officers, junior and senior, to deal with a terrorist bombing attack as detailed in following chapters.

What should be concerning to the Charity Commissioners is Fahy's new charity interests which involves children. In blurb clearly self written he says "Sir Peter has a continuing interest in counter extremism, community cohesion and race and diversity." It's a great pity he did not ensure such wonderful beliefs had not fallen by the wayside of Greater Manchester, leaving residents desperate for police protection. Delving deeper into the Charity 'world' and ignoring the fact that he had lied with broken promises and abandoned Victoria

Agloglia and so many abused children, taken from care homes by Asian Pakistani gangs and drugged, raped and groomed in alarming numbers.

"On leaving the police Sir Peter took up a position as Chief Executive of the Street Children charity Retrak which he then brought together with the modern slavery charity Hope for Justice. Unbelievably he now has lofty positions for both organisations as Director of Strucutral Change. Retrak believes that children develop best in safe, caring family settings. Retrak gets street children back to families but also work in orphanages and remand homes. They also do a lot of preventative work to strengthen families and parenting particularly against the dangers of trafficking and domestic slavery. Peter Fahy is said to have a particular interest in policies to protect vulnerable children, mobilise communities and new models of multi-agency working. He is chair of Plus Dane Housing Association and Chair the National Housing Federation Refugee Network. Could this be only as innocent as a guilt complex as a result of his historical child abuse failings or something with a deeper need?

Peter Fahy has what appears to have an obsession for 'vulnerable children's charities' and is also the founder and chair of the Community Cohesion charity We Stand Together and trustee of Care of Police Survivors (**COPS**) which is a charity that supports the families of police officers and staff who have lost their lives on duty. Is that the same man who led the fight to confuse the shooting of PC Terry and cause unnecessary grief to his family over five years. Other charities include Get in Touch. and Redeeming Our Communities... Amazing.

2015–2020: IAN HOPKINS

Hopkins joined Greater Manchester Police in April 2008 on promotion to Assistant Chief Constable. He started his career in Staffordshire Police in 1989 and has served in Northamptonshire Police and Cheshire Police. In 2011 he undertook a three-month secondment as syndicate director for the Strategic Command Course which is said to prepare police officers and staff for promotion to the most senior ranks in the service. To say that was an absolute waste of funds is an understatement of obvious proportions. Based on his amazing past which included service already in GMP as Assistant Chief Constable and therefore well experienced in the existing culture. He had been appointed by C.C Peter Fahy who had worked with him in Cheshire Constabulary. Fahy was accused of cronyism for obvious reasons. What is important is the fact that they both had a clear history of presiding over an existing culture eventually attracting the attention of HMRCFS for the fabrication of crime detection figures after their transfer to GMP.

It is worth mentioning at the outset, Ian Hopkins has not been knighted, as the honour is bestowed while serving. He was sacked under the pretext of sickness involving an ear infection. Of course even taking into account all that has gone before it is, therefore, still unlikely that he ever will be. This is a big step when one examines the previous incompetent failures and all the Knighted 'suspects".

Talking of incompetent failures, Peter Fahy having left Cheshire Constabulary only a short time before a corrupt system of crime recording was discovered and dating back many years in the form of accepted practice. Todd was taking 'one for the team' of his predecessors in having no choice but to take the blame for introducing a similar system at GMP which would of course have been a clerical impossibility in such a brief period.

A report in May 2019 issued by Her Majesty's Inspectorate of Constabulary and Fire and Rescue Services (HMICFRS) said it was left "deeply troubled" over how cases handled by Greater Manchester Police were closed without proper investigation.

Greater Manchester Police failed to record more than 80,000 crimes in a year, closing cases prematurely without consulting vulnerable victims, a report has found. England's second largest police force failed to record one in five offences committed between 1 July 2019 and 30 June 2020 - the equivalent of around 220 crimes a day. Inspectors found that around one in five of all crimes, and one in four violent crimes, reported by the public to the force were not recorded. It must be stressed that this was a trial period only and in calculating a figure for many years would be an impossibility.

England's second largest police force was placed in special measures after a watchdog raised concerns over its failure to record more than 80,000 crimes in the space of a year.

One in four violent crimes went unreported, including domestic abuse, stalking and harassment, with detectives deciding to close cases without considering victims' wishes in "too many" circumstances. Inspectors from HMICFRS said the findings were "deeply troubling". They estimated that the number of reported crimes recorded by the force fell 11.3% from 2018 - to just 77.7%.

HM Inspector of Constabulary Zoe Billingham, served as Her Majesty's Inspector of Constabulary for 12 years, she is said to have shone a light on all aspects of policing and created the new fire inspectorate. It is claimed she led the Inspectorate's national work on value for money, mental health and protecting the most vulnerable. Bingham's work on domestic abuse and violence against women and girls led to a sea-change in approach. Who could possibly have written such poorly researched, unadulterated crap in the knowledge she presided over both Fahy and Todd, a multitude of diabolical failures, collapsed to Health and Safety prosecutions and of course Operation Augusta abandoned at a whim for racial harmony. From Zoe Billingham's perspective, for a woman claiming to investigate cases of domestic abuse and violence against women and girls which led to a sea-change in approach. What's that then?

She did however say in what is an amazing understatement, "Victims of crime are too often being let down by Greater Manchester Police "The service provided to victims, particularly those who are most vulnerable, is a serious cause of concern." She described the findings as "extremely disappointing" given that the force was asked to improve its victim support in 2016. "I am deeply troubled about how frequently the force is closing cases without a full investigation, giving the reason that the victim did not support police action". She added "In too many of these cases the force didn't properly record evidence that the victim supported this decision - particularly in cases of domestic abuse, where seven in 10 are closed on this basis.

In a further comment, which should embarrass her, again adding fuel to the belief that senior police officers and associates always close ranks, whatever the circumstances," While it is simply not good enough that these concerns have not been addressed for over four years, I acknowledge that the force is taking action to address these deficiencies." "The force is investing in new infrastructure to centralise its recording of crimes and is bringing in a new assessment to make sure more vulnerable victims are identified. Unbelievably and totally naive Ms Billingham said "senior leaders at GMP are demonstrating their intent to improve, with a marked improvement recently in its recording of serious sexual offences and rapes." Tell the child victims of Operation Augusta that !

But adding, "this now needs to be done across the board". Ms Billingham warned that the "situation cannot continue" and ordered a follow-up inspection in six months. Clearly 'out of his depth' Deputy Chief Constable of GMP, Ian Pilling, clearly a career minded 'Yes Man' who followed the C.C.Hopkins culture to the letter without offering anything of note offered further GMP bull. He said "the force is treating this matter very seriously". "We have a long-term strategic plan in place to address these issues and we are determined to make whatever other short-term improvements we need to make, and to make them as quickly as possible," he said. "Although we acknowledge there has been a deterioration in some elements of recording since the last inspection, we have made huge improvements in some elements including rape, sexual offences and many areas of volume crime which are now recorded by our centralised unit." He added: "The safety and wellbeing of the public, as well as maintaining their confidence, underpins all that the force does."

The HMICFRS also reported GMP's service to victims of crime was a "serious cause of concern". Inspectors found that around one in five of all crimes, and one in four violent crimes, reported by the public to the force were not recorded. In a statement issued on Thursday night, the Inspectorate said the force had been moved into the "Engage" stage of its monitoring process. This requires GMP to develop an improvement plan to "address the specific causes of concern". The naively prepared report found that GMP failed to record an estimated 80,100 crimes reported to it between July 1 2019 and June 30 2020, amounting to around 220 crimes a day. A higher proportion of violent crime was not recorded, including domestic abuse and behavioural crimes, such as harassment, stalking and coercive controlling behaviour. What about the sad multitude of young white girls, wantonly abused by Asian Pakistanis.

There is little doubt that the HMICFRS covered many areas of conduct within the GMP in their report of 2018/2019 and many showed poor performance scores. A brief excerpt towards the end is very interesting in light of the earlier accusations of cronyism ... "It should ensure its wider workforce is trained in awareness of abuse of position for sexual purpose and its impact on the public".

'Walt Disney' must have added "The force is good at treating its workforce fairly, but we found some areas for improvement. The workforce is confident in the grievance process. But the force doesn't deal with grievances in a timely manner. It has improved in this since 2017, and improvement must continue.

In yet further un-researched bilge, "We saw that the force was working to improve its personal development review (PDR) process. This was an area for improvement in 2017, and the process still has gaps. We look forward to seeing the process fully implemented, used effectively and monitored force-wide. In 2017, we also recommended improvements to the talent management system. The force has reviewed it, but it relies on the PDR process mentioned above." So, the force may not be providing fair opportunities for its entire workforce. (Cronyism?) This is an area for improvement.

The Google definition of PDR ably describes all that is hopelessly wrong at GMP …The Performance Development Review (PDR) is not just a set of processes. Used well, it offers a constructive and flexible approach to reviewing your team members in a way that inspires and motivates them to be the best that they can be. It also forms part of a wider, holistic approach to performance management. F.F.S. GMP.

This bland and deceptive statement must surely refer to the Manchester Arena terrorist attack which killed and injured many individuals whilst attending a concert. On the 7th September a public enquiry on the conduct of the emergency services and other related matters commenced. It was a popular belief at the time of the attack there was no response by the three emergency services who remained safe distances from the scene initially it was publicly thought to be due to cowardly decisions issued by their senior officers at the time.

This was not true and the responsibility for such inactivity was laid at the door of GMP and a uniformed Inspector Sexton, badly trained and incapable of supporting the position of Silver Command before handing over to what on paper appeared to be a qualified Silver Commander in her position of ACC. But where was she when it mattered. She was in bed as you would expect. However that situation alone showed that a qualified Gold Commander was not on duty and such mammoth decisions were left to a badly qualified Inspector who failed miserably. Sadly several of the dead victims were said to "have had a chance of living" had medical assistance occurred much earlier.

Ian Hopkins had been Chief Constable of GMP since October 2015, leading a force of 6,866 officers. Following the publication of the damning HMICFRS report, Hopkins revealed he had decided to take a break from his role to recover from Labyrinthitis – an inner ear infection which affects balance.

In a statement, C.C Hopkins said he had been suffering from the condition since the end of October. "I continued to work throughout with the support of the rest of my Chief Officers team until Sunday 13 December, despite feeling very ill," he added. He failed to mention he continued to draw his full salary. "I finally made the decision over last weekend that in the interests of my health I needed to take a break and recover properly so I can return and lead GMP with the same passion and strength of character that I have always demonstrated.

"Despite feeling ill I remain in contact daily with members of my Chief Officers team." There appears to be little doubt that he was 'put in a cupboard at home' until the noise died down. It didn't, he initially sought to indicate he had voluntarily stepped aside with the ear infection but it soon emerged that he had been required to leave office by Andy Burnham the Mayor for Greater Manchester and who himself had a great deal to answer but remained as the Police and Crime Commissioner.

Further details emerged that are regarded as theft in normal Manchester citizen circles, that even though Hopkins had been claiming to be sick, he had continued to claim his full salary. Could such an act be the same as cash machines giving incorrect sums to be misappropriated by the customer and to be later charged under The Theft Act which surely hasn't a clause excluding 'bent bastards'.

HMCFRS continued, making the appropriate 'get out' excuses ... "Many of the biggest decisions taken within the force over the past decade, first under C.C. Peter Fahy and then under his successor C.C.Ian Hopkins, were taken against the backdrop of austerity. It lost 2,000 officers in the initial years of cuts, a blow even GMP's sternest critics would acknowledge was significant." Yet again favourable bullshit to allow room to manoeuvre in the inevitable final 'no action' judgement.

However, close observers noticed a corporate narrative, then used from his final days at Cheshire Constabulary and GMP by Peter Fahy, again blaming austerity to defend all abject failures, weaknesses, computer system failures to poor investigations. Of course many Labour politicians repeated the line, even if some had private concerns.

Perhaps the most significant commentary on that narrative comes not from former officers but from the new Chief Constable Stephen Watson who had himself been leading South Yorkshire Police during the same period. But on day one at GMP, he made clear that austerity was no excuse for its many problems. Perhaps words to haunt him later but we can all genuinely hope.

In a joint statement, Mayor of Greater Manchester Andy Burnham and Bev Hughes, Greater Manchester's Deputy Mayor for Policing, Crime and Criminal Justice, said the HMICFRS report "raised extremely serious issues with implications for the quality of services to victims that have been on-going for a number of years". Shouldn't they have added "to our knowledge but ignored?"

They outlined actions being put in place to improve standards of service, including investing in more police officers and recruiting more staff for GMP's Central Recording and Resolution Unit. What the hell is that department and in any case ... 'Don't hold your breath' more to come.

"A dedicated hotline, supported by Victim Support, will be available from Monday for victims who wish to make a complaint or report concerns about their treatment". Burnham deserves a later mention in a separate chapter.

The Manchester Arena bombing was a disastrous episode in so many ways in the already chequered history of Greater Manchester Police. In the third volume of the Arena Enquiry Report. In his usual, no holds barred style Sir John Saunders reported in his highly critical report on the performance of the emergency services on the night, concluding that **two of the victims could have survived had they not faced an "interminable" wait for treatment.**

Only firearms training gained recognition of efficiency, in part due to the reckless death of PC Terry of the firearms department. It was a separate unit with its own command of experienced skilled senior officers.

The overall blame was without doubt due to none existent training in the rest of the force, for such an episode and above all realistic leadership. Despite there being many levels of command the blame eventually fell on two uniformed Inspectors with Inspector Sexton taking the lead.

The Manchester Arena suffered a terrorist bombing attack on May 22nd 2017. by a single individual who had walked past many security and police officers whilst he carried a large heavy rucksack which contained a bomb. The terror attack shocked the City of Manchester and the Nation to its core. Salman Abedi killed himself and 22 others consisting of schoolchildren, students, mothers and fathers, sons and daughters, working men and women. The youngest victim was only eight years old. A suicide bomb was the weapon, concealed in his plainly heavy backpack, as mainly young concert-goers were leaving an Ariana Grande concert. How many Asians attend such a concert with a heavy rucksack as a norm and yet this terrorist casually walked past police constables and private security men without question, as illustrated later on CCTV film.

By this time the men at the pointed end were sensitive to malicious 'racial prejudice' complaints conducting 'stop and search' and disciplinary measures often followed. Black Asians were like a 'hot potato' and even permitted to groom young 14 years old white girls for sex, attracted from Care Homes with the offers of gifts. (Operation Augusta and Operation Greenjacket failures will follow below)

The Manchester Arena Inquiry was an independent public inquiry, led by Sir John Saunders which was established on 22 October 2019 by the Home Secretary. The Inquiry hearings commenced on 7th September 2020. The purpose of the Manchester Arena Inquiry was to investigate the deaths and serious injuries of the victims of the 2017 Manchester Arena attack. A public inquiry is set up to look at a matter of concern. There was certainly concern and I believe none of us caring Mancunians were disappointed with the results and comments.

GMP was informed that there had been an explosion at the Arena. At 22:31:52, (10.30pm in pensioner speak.)

As you would expect the official enquiry results were incredibly detailed and 'no holds barred' but equally unnecessarily polite in places. The entire set of three reports are worth reading to appreciate the significance for future training of everyone from constable upwards in relation to minuscule detail including the provision of first aid. Unusual for anything including GMP it included all higher ranks with reference to the lack of real clear minded leadership in the force. The enquiry's final comment says it all ... **"GMP's failures are very significant',** but even then chooses to polite 'speak' which inevitably is an understatement.

Throughout this literary masterpiece I have attempted to illustrate that the failings of GMP start at the top with incompetent and failing leadership born of totally incompetent selection procedures. A rare compliment emerges in the midst of so much failing leadership ... "The GMP firearms officers discharged their primary responsibility with skill and efficiency. Individual officers of GMP who entered the City Room acted with courage and resourcefulness. "At the time they were forced to make their own immediate decisions and ran into the arena despite obvious fears of a secondary bomb.

The enquiry reported ... "However, others within the GMP command structure did not make the contribution that the public was entitled to expect they would make in the event of a terrorist attack in the heart of Manchester. Although there were individual failures, **the principal responsibility for that rests with GMP at a corporate level.** Through the confusing detail of Operation Plato, the cold to hot zoning of the area and an amazing number of commanders ... bronze, silver and gold there remained the actual facts of gross incompetence and pre planning for such an 'event'

Comments such as 'unarmed Operational/Bronze Commander' 'Operation Plato, cold zone and had been for a long time' '"It's warm going cold" Casualty Clearing Station was "getting near to cold", whatever that means. Can you believe this comment in light of all the circumstances ..." **If Chief InspectorI Sexton had been adequately trained, he would have understood that.** "Inspector Sexton's references to Operation Plato zoning were also vague.

"**GMP's failures are very significant**", but are not the only explanation for why joint working between the emergency services broke down on the night of the Attack. The enquiry identified failures by GMP in planning, including in planning for the consequences of a declaration of Operation Plato. (Terrorist Attack) On the night of the Attack, those failures had consequences.

The consequences appear to have been Inspector's Sexton and Inspector Smith both of whom are probably now directing traffic in a Bolton outpost. The report continues ... Shortly after 22:47, when he had declared Operation Plato, Inspector Sexton should have informed NWAS (Ambulance) and GMFRS (Fire) that he had done so.

This **failure by Inspector Sexton** gives rise to the question of why he failed to do something so fundamental to the response to a perceived Marauding Terrorist Firearms Attack. Such a response was required by the national and regional Operation Plato plans and recognised in his own aide-memoire document. When pressed in evidence, **Inspector Sexton** had **no convincing explanation** for why he had given these accounts if in truth he had made a deliberate decision at the time to conceal the declaration, as opposed to simply overlooking the duty upon him to communicate.

It appears that **Inspector Sexton** was overburdened on the night. He simply had too much to do. He overlooked the requirement to contact NWAS and GMFRS, just as **he overlooked the need to declare a Major Incident.** No one reminded him that he should do so. No one else within GMP Control had the responsibility allocated to them for making the necessary communication or for reminding the FDO to do so. **Inspector Sexton** was the single point of failure and, under severe individual pressure, he failed that night. **Inspector Sexton** failed to ensure there was an FCP.331. Nor did he do anything to manage the confusion that developed in relation to a nominated RVP. **These failures represent an important part of the explanation for why joint working never happened, but instead the three emergency services ended up operating largely in silos.**

Inspector Sexton gave evidence that was factually inaccurate about his thinking at the time is a further example of the situation. Inspector Sexton should have concluded by no later than 22:50 that the City Room was an Operation Plato cold zone. I consider that such a clear decision at that stage would have made a difference on the night. Believing that Sexton was fully trained "The fact that **Inspector Sexton failed** to give any thought to zoning meant that, not only did he make no decision in that regard, he was not in a position to reconsider that decision. Such reviews of zoning decisions are critical, given their impact on deployment. JOPs 3 made that clear, although **in my view it was a matter of common sense.** There were a number of points in time at which **Inspector Sexton** should have reviewed his position on zoning."

"**Overall, the failures of Inspector Sexton were serious and far-reaching in effect. I am satisfied that the burden placed on Inspector Sexton on the night of the Attack was too great. It overwhelmed Inspector Sexton. While this does not excuse Inspector Sexton's failures, it does mitigate his culpability.**"

Comments made during the enquiry by the author are significant and due to the planning time frame which never existed, not only blame C.C.Hopkins but also C.C.Fahy and possibly even C.C.Anderton. ... "GMP had known, for several years, of the risk that the FDO would be overwhelmed in an Operation Plato situation. GMP should have put in place proper mechanisms of support for the FDO, such as ensuring that action cards were implemented, were well understood and utilised to achieve systems of delegation. **GMP failed to do so. I regard that failure as very serious. Looking as a whole at what went wrong in GMP Control on 22nd May 2017, GMP's culpability is substantial.**"

An Operational Firearms Commander can only implement the tactical plan if given one. On the night of the Attack, **Inspector Sexton** provided no tactical plan to PC Richardson. He should have done. This represents a further respect in which the FDO failed that night. Throughout the critical period of the response, the FDO was too reactive. He did not take the necessary step back in order to assess, in a structured and proactive way, what was needed to ensure that the firearms response, the broader police response and the emergency response worked. I am satisfied, for the reasons I have given, that the burden imposed upon **Inspector Sexton** largely explains this failure."

The following clearly illustrates the unbelievable example of promotion to the position of Inspector being due only to examination success and not competence and ability to lead ... He (**Insp. Sexton**) simply had too much to do. He overlooked the requirement to contact NWAS (Ambulance service) and GMFRS, (Fire Brigade) just as he overlooked the need to declare a Major Incident. Equally badly trained, a chain of anonymous officers did not remind him that he should do so. No one else within GMP Control had the responsibility allocated to them for making the necessary communication or for reminding the FDO to do so. **Inspector Sexton** was the single point of failure and, under severe individual pressure, he failed that night.

"The role of the Force Duty Supervisor is vital in an Operation Plato situation. **Inspector Sexton** had an expert and experienced Force Duty Supervisor in Ian Randall. **Inspector Sexton** made a decision that Ian Randall should leave GMP Control at about 23:20 to travel to GMP HQ to set up the Silver Control Room. That was a mistake." The officer who replaced Ian Randall, Sergeant Andrew

Core, lacked Ian Randall's experience. **Inspector Sexton** should have recognised that Ian Randall was better deployed in GMP Control. His departure significantly depleted the experience available to the FDO and added to the already substantial demands on **Inspector Sexton**. There should have been someone else who was capable of setting up the Silver Control Room and available to do it. "I have made clear the importance of action cards within GMP Control and the serious failure of GMP to introduce such prompts. David Myerscough stated that he had never seen CI Michael Booth's action cards, and that no action cards were in use in GMP Control on the night of the attack. **Inspector Sexton** said the same."

The report summary says it all.... "A striking feature of the events that night was that **Inspector Sexton** did not speak to Inspector Smith at any point. That the FDO never spoke to the Operational/Bronze Commander is a clear indication that not only did multi-agency communication fail on the night of the attack, but communication within GMP was also inadequate." At no stage that night did **Inspector Sexton** declare a Major Incident. The enquiry regarded it as a serious omission. It is vital that all emergency services are informed promptly that an Operation Plato declaration has been made. Otherwise, no joint approach is possible, "I just literally thought crikey no one's declared a Major Incident yet, so I'm going to declare a Major Incident." It was clear from the evidence that both of these senior officers considered that a Major Incident should have been declared very much earlier. It was not until 00:57, nearly two and a half hours after the explosion, that GMP declared a Major Incident. The horrendous pantomime continues ... While the failure to declare a Major Incident was principally **Inspector Sexton's,** others also bear some responsibility. In particular, neither Temporary Superintendent Nawaz in his role as Tactical/Silver Commander nor ACC Ford in her role as Strategic/Gold Commander declared a Major Incident. Each of them should have done so. That confusion should not have happened and should never be allowed to happen again."

Such failings, so dramatically highlighted are the sad consequence of the fact that promotions will always be based on poor selection procedures and cronyism leaving a force so badly led and exposed as in this example. The men at the pointed end lose faith totally in their leadership and declare a truce on crime fighting in there own selfish interests having established that they have no support at all from their senior officers..

ACC Ford, was at home in bed and from home drove to the force HQ and not the Arena until later when appointed Strategic/Gold Commander on the night. In keeping with GMPs existing culture of duck responsibility and delegate to an underling, she gave the following straightforward evidence passing the blame to a handy underling in the shape of Temporary Superintendent Nawaz. The Report reads ...

Temporary Superintendent Nawaz was not competent to perform the role that he was initially put into. In particular, his approach to Operation Plato and zoning was deficient

The GMP Night Silver (Nawaz) on the night made no contribution of substance to the emergency response.

You could hear "the fat dripping off a chip" as the Enquiry Chairman gave his excellent summary in making the following points ...

1. GMP strategic/gold command on the night made no effective contribution to the emergency response.
2. Prior to the arrival at the scene of the Ground Assigned Tactical Firearms Commander at 23:23, no GMP officer gave any consideration to Operation Plato zoning.
3. The importance of Operation Plato zoning was not adequately understood across the GMP command structure.
4. The Ground Assigned Tactical Firearms Commander made a significant contribution to the emergency response.
5. The unarmed officers of GMP had received first aid training that was inadequate to enable them to provide effective treatment to the injured
6. Force Duty Officer should communicate the declaration of Operation Plato to the emergency service partners of GMP. The FDO failed to do so.
7. That failure fundamentally undermined the joint response to the Attack.
8. *The FDO (Force Duty Officer) Inspector Dale Sexton failed in other important respects. The overall impact of his failures was serious and far-reaching.*

GMP had known for years that there was a material risk that the FDO would become overburdened in the event of an Operation Plato declaration but had failed to put in place proper mechanisms of support for the FDO.

GMP did not declare a Major Incident until 00:57 on 23rd May 2017, long after such a declaration was capable of making a difference to the emergency response during the critical period. A Major Incident should have been declared by GMP more than 140 minutes earlier.

The failure to declare a Major Incident occurred across the GMP command structure.

As I have written, the above summary is only a brief edited excerpt of Part 2 of the full report and clearly illustrates all that is wrong in GMP not only for planning for such an attack despite Home Office directives of such an incident, but the conduct of the force generally. There is no leadership or training procedures in many if not all areas from the top and as the above summary concludes. In true police ranking blame structure, ACC Ford blamed underlings at Superintendent level, who undoubtedly attempted to blame the fall guys Inspectors Sexton and Smith. Both certainly deserved such comments but in truth were the fabric of a none existent training regime despite intelligence warning of such an incident.

It is worth considering that the serious training failings in GMP existed over what must have been several years, that Andy Burnham as Commissioner, and several Chief Constables and so many ranks below were culpable. So many blatant failings existed that reference to the entire saga was totally ignored to hide the existing embarrassment, as one of many reason Hopkins sickness resignation.

On the 3rd November Gamal Farnbulla interviewed Burnham on Granada News regarding the Arena Bombing and the report. Burnham appeared under pressure, paled and lied that he had immediately sacked C.C. Hopkins. The softly spoken, never been known to upset anyone in interview, let Burnham get away with the blatant lie. In fact he remained until the 18th December 2020 when he resigned on health reasons on the 18th December 2020 with his full pension and spurious ear infection which certainly had nothing to do with Burnham.

SPECIAL BRANCH

At the risk of assassination by umbrella I feel the GMP Special Branch deserves a further mention in the context of the Manchester Arena attack as it was identified as having failed along with MI5 in several areas. The B.B.C. reported that a Muslim preacher Al-Anezi who was close to the Manchester bomber had been suspected by MI5 of being a radicaliser more than a decade earlier. The inquiry had already published two revealing reports before the third volume. The previous highly critical report on the performance of the emergency services on the night, concluded that two of the victims could have survived had they not faced the "interminable" wait for treatment.

The officer who led the Manchester investigation, Detective Chief Superintendent Simon Barraclough, told the arena inquiry that the relationship between Al-Anezi and Salman Abedi was "clearly a connection of significance", but police were unable to establish exactly what it was. This is a reference to GMP and its very own Special Branch claiming to be staffed by police officers in close liaison with MI5 as we would all like to believe. Even in the present 2023 the investigative abilities of the GMP Special Branch clearly remain very poor and it is to be hoped that they do not continue with a nine to five ethic as in my day.

Maybe not, possibly seen as 'after the horse has bolted' It is reported that Police are trying to close in on a suspected terror network linked to the Manchester bomber Salman Abedi during May 2017 headlines 'screamed', 14 Suspects Arrested whilst three miles away, Greater Manchester Police arrested a 25 year old man on the suspicion of terror offences. This brings the total number of arrests up to 14, with 12 still being held in custody. Two people—a woman and a teenage boy—have been released without charge. Arrests are easy for public consumption in the 'good old' Manchester Evening News, but how many charges followed.

Such close liaison must have been in it's infancy during my service, when in a dubious staffing structure decision, the Drug Squad was formed, more of an afterthought "Where do we put these scruffy bastards?" Inexplicably, The Drug Squad was attached to the Special Branch. My progression through the force led to thi motley crew, located in the brown tiled building opposite Manchester Piccadilly Station. It housed a fire station and police station and ourselves in three first floor rooms. We only had a Detective Sergeant at the base for ten of us and were in fact under the 'supervisory umbrella' of the Chief Superintendent of the Special Branch. Being an anonymous headless department no one understood the sensible thinking involved but during these halcyon days, no one really cared.

There are a multitude of stories and revelations in my second book Shades of Black'n'Blue but this one will suffice to give yet another example of police training and the exercising thereof. But for the 'Grace of God' no public lives were lost....

In Liverpool today, conditions are even worse. Drug trafficking and general gangster activities are blatant. There are many shootings and threats to police, who appear to be led with more confidence than those in Manchester, but clearly still not well enough. In both forces there are many informants to the drug world. Such informants come in all shapes and sizes and surprisingly from all areas of the judicial system, including court staff, who on the face of things appear to be the retired pensioners they are, but beneath this façade is a villain's informant fighting to get out with information on a well-protected search warrant. There is so much corruption, often borne of fear, but usually out of greed, throughout the many forces in the land. Taking a bribe is the easy option, when you have no one in authority to turn to and no guarantee of personal safety if you do. It is a culture which emanates from my early days in the 60s and 70s when the commission of crime was commonplace within the police and apparently condoned by the supervisory ranks.

It was very early in my career that I was taught always to take over the dominant high ground and use whatever tactics came to mind in doing so. These were not to include the taking of a bribe.(Thank you PC Harry Kite) During my police service I was prepared to use any weapon at hand and often did. In true Life On Mars style I have assaulted prisoners with a variety of weapons ranging from a bottle, a bar stool, a shop window, flights of stairs, a pair of scissors and even a car. The fact is that the more any detective did, the chance of confrontation will be greater as you make enemies and encounter situations that can get violent in the detection of crime. I never took a bribe and whatever threats were made, had the benefit of my punch bag training in my wrestling days.

ROTTEN TO ITS CORE

Of course, the Special Branch we had in those early days was in its infancy and now I was part of it, however loosely attached. Special Branch to me was not so much The Spy Who Loved Me more the spy who loved himself. I might even have had a licence to kill, but in my case the job was not to fire the gun and shoot anybody - something for which I was later trained and often dreamt of. They didn't have such dangerous things to contend with as the Islamic terrorists of today. There were not so many political issues as there seems to be now. Looking back, it is strange to remember that the IRA was little more than a rumour and generally laughed at by these so-called intelligence officers.

One evening we were briefed by S.B. Inspector George Dampier, who had been dragged away from his dance class. Gorgeous George, as he was known, kept a pair of patent leather dancing shoes in the Special Branch office. His evening duties generally consisted of sweeping a 'little beauty' off her feet with a dazzling foxtrot at the Ritz dance hall. On this occasion, however, we were to raid a house in the Plymouth Grove area, thought to house a man with IRA connections. Plymouth Grove, close to Longsight Police Station, was a popular area for the Irish labour contingent who resided in Manchester and, indeed, one of the best nights out in the area was the Irish club known as the Carousel.

Gorgeous George was the only man allegedly trained to use a firearm on duty at the time and was there to lead us into the house in his shiny new bulletproof jacket and clutching his Webly 38 revolver. These would have matched his patent leather shoes admirably, had he worn them. George appeared to be not very keen on the fact he was at the pointed end. Apart from being in grave danger and facing the possibility of being killed he was likely to get blood on his rather fetching floral patterned tie. Leaving the police with a posthumous Queen's Police Medal was not in his plans.

It was quite amusing to watch him as we approached the house. We dived straight in and kicked the door off its' hinges. We were good at that, it was a skill developed in the Drug Squad to prevent the occupants flushing the cannabis and speed down the toilet. Instead of rushing straight in, George stood back, as though marking time in a quick flash of the Gay Gordons. It was obvious this was not what he wished to miss a dance class for. This was a critical time and to maintain the element of surprise, we made an instant decision and ran in before the suspect could stand and act with a gun as we believed he would. He was watching TV and never moved. It was hardly surprising, George asked the trembling unfortunate a few questions and from the answers quickly deduced that we were sitting on and strangling the wrong man. Even in those days, so long ago, the Manchester Special Branch still specialised in arresting the wrong person.

Our suspect got a letter of apology, a new door, and probably a pacemaker. George knew we were taking the piss regarding his heroic style and rather than have such a situation occur again he sent some of us on the firearm shooting course. The object was to turn us into sharp shooting police marksmen, so we could be the first to be shot. Supervision from the rear was a trait becoming all too prevalent in the police leadership of the day. We went

ROTTEN TO ITS CORE

to an Army firing range, somewhere near to Glossop in Derbyshire, for one day where we were allowed to fire a military type recoilless rifle, which couldn't possibly miss because of the number of bullets per second it fired. This weapon was not issued to the police of the day. It was never used by the police as it is today.

Does that mean as I report later, the shooting of unarmed Anthony Grainger was by yet another 'trained, skilled and badly led 'crack' department.

We were rather disappointingly trained with Webly .38 revolvers, a gun that had the smallest butt possible. An effective grip was difficult for men with large hands as they could not hold the gun firmly. With my tender, lover's fingers of pianist proportions I was better suited to holding the butt. Of course I had held many butts, but most supported above high heels and often enveloped in lace. We all shot about ten rounds at a target some 20 feet away. I hit the target six times. Others didn't hit it at all. As I have said, I was declared a marksman and was to be called on in circumstances where a marksman was necessary or, in truth, they were desperate, very desperate indeed. Unfortunately, they were never that desperate and, to my everlasting disappointment, I never shot anyone. Years earlier on the mobile column we had been instructed to shoot the ring leader in any scenes of public disaffection after a nuclear war. But back in those days we never had any guns, so it was a particularly bizarre instruction – though it did appeal to me and would certainly have been a welcome addition to our armoury of bar stools and tables on a Saturday night in Manchester. The reference to such an astute body of highly trained marksmen, always evoked thoughts of intense training and a wealth of experience, observing terrorists and any individual likely to cause a threat to the Crown.

Of course, the truth begs so many awkward questions and always with lives at risk. Lives of the public sometimes, often treated as collateral damage and then of course the boys in blue who fared little better in the eyes of the struggling and badly trained, unqualified 'leadership'. Moral was very poor in all areas of real police work and rarely assisted by the 'skilled glory departments'. but this time risking a high profile life. As I wrote ...

Back in the day decades before, I was regarded as a police marksman. A title earned as I have already related by hitting the target, not far away with about six rounds out of the 10 supplied. With such skills I was attached for the night to the 'James Bonds' of the City, the Special Branch and placed on VIP bodyguard duty. Prince Phillip needed guarding in the 1970s. And strangely, yet totally in keeping with police logic, I formed part of the assignment of super-tuned 'bodyguards', but, of course, without the gun despite now being fully certificated and raring to shoot anybody.

Because of their collective darkness phobia and the 'we don't do nights' attitude, which appeared to exist in the Special Branch at all ranking levels, I was placed on night duty to assist in the protection of Prince Phillip. I was assigned with other officers from the Drug Squad and a couple of real bodyguards from New Scotland Yard. One of the regular Manchester SB officers, who had lost the office raffle, also joined us to act as liaison with the regular Scotland Yard Royal Protection contingent. In the halcyon days of no real security issues there were only about six of us for this duty.

However we were all finely honed into this small unit of highly- trained manpower, braced for any eventuality and waiting to spring into action at a second's notice, but of course armed only with our equally highly trained hands as we were not allowed the guns with which we had been drilled. On this occasion when we were assigned to guard His Royal Highness, Prince Philip, was on a visit to Salford University as Honorary Vice Chancellor.

Although, it must be said, that among us HRH was better known as Phil the Greek as Ken Chaplin, of the A Division, was a stoker on his last ship.

This was an annual visit and great play was made of the fact he would be treated as 'just one of the boys,' because he was to sleep in an ordinary student room on a normal landing with all the people as normal and ordinary as you find in any university. But one must remember that the word 'normal' is hardly ever used for the long-haired, drinking, cannabis-smoking marauders who populated this building, usually sleeping something off or shagging until the one class of the day later in the afternoon. The dormitory building was three storeys high with small single en-suite rooms. They were all clean but sparsely furnished with only a single bed, a wardrobe and a bedside table. Nobody publicised the fact that the entire floor was cleared of students and HRH had his own entrance to the building in case he bumped into one of the 'unclean' long-haired greasy reprobates. The rooms in question and indeed the landing corridor had been newly decorated and kept empty to rid them of the smell of paint and the lingering aromas of the unwashed masses of regular occupants for a couple of weeks. All the rooms had been newly furnished and yet the whole set up must have appeared to be a Vietnamese mud hut to Phil who was used to a little better even on board his destroyer.

Phil had the room farthest from the entrance staircase so in the event of an assassination attempt we would fall on our swords in protecting His Royal Highness. The room next door was occupied by his Royal Protection armed Scotland Yard bodyguard. Next to this was his valet John, clearly adept at trapping a bus ticket between the cheeks of his bottom an art ably displayed as he minced from room to room looking busy, prim and proper, but in reality doing nothing at all except to show off his tight little arse just in case one of us was to jump out of the closet. John had brought his own furniture in the shape of his trusty ironing board. There was then a gap of four locked rooms to act as a barrier from any noise for the sleeping Prince in case he woke up as a frog as in all good nursery stories. At the entrance end to the corridor was then a room, cleared of furniture, newly decorated and prepared as a buffet with every type of alcoholic drink and sandwich, small snacks, even biscuits and Horlicks – the latter apparently His Royal Highnesses' favourite night time tipple. The bodyguard contingent also occupied the room next door which again had been cleared and replaced with a few uncomfortable chairs for our use, probably deliberately uncomfortable as of course we were supposed to be warily patrolling the

ROTTEN TO ITS CORE

darkened corridors and outside perimeter in our capacity as unarmed minders.

Our duty was to initially arrive early and search all the rooms from where the students had been made homeless some weeks before, taking all their pin-up photos from the walls, books and drug paraphernalia. Of course we had to search all rooms including His Royal Highness' next best thing to a tent. It was clearly set out for the maximum of appearance, but it was still strange to see the official Palace released photo of Her Majesty the Queen, diamond tiara and all displayed on a bedside table. I think from recent events they have amply displayed the fact that they are however a very close couple and they both gain strength from each other and so a little photo may have got Phil through the night. On the other bedside table was a wooden box about nine inches by nine inches containing every proprietary medicine you could want for the prevention and cure of a cold, sore throat, reluctant bowels and all other minor ailments which could easily inflict upon him in deepest Salford.

John, the valet, continued to mince about, fluttering his eyelids with a wiggle of his tight black pants. All of us in the temporary James Bond contingent had skated a bit close to the transvestite wind, usually by a drunken mistake in some darkened club, but none of us felt any urge towards John other than perhaps to give him a swift kick. Whilst immaculately attired in full valet livery I thought he would probably have been happier in a maid's outfit, which would have been much more in keeping with all his other effeminate traits.

The Prince's accommodation was on the top floor of this three storey building. The floors below were occupied by students, females, specially selected, with strict instructions for silence and no unruly behaviour. The fact that bombs, tend to explode in an upwards direction, especially in flimsy modern buildings had not occurred to anyone. No one searched the other floors, there were no SAS snipers, no dogs, or mine detectors as today and in reality the entire security issue was a virtually unarmed, unprotected joke.

However, Manchester's finest were on hand and braced for any eventuality. During the early evening HRH was at a civic reception in the Town Hall and at the arranged time in what was a very detailed calculated timetable the Prince was to arrive at the reception doors to the student accommodation. At this time he had a bit of an entourage from the university who had also been at the Town Hall reception. We were braced at the entrance, hands crossed at waist height, as in the movies, looking unsmiling at the assembled crowd and would have worn sunglasses in typical FBI fashion had it not been so dark. We joined forces with the existing team and escorted HRH into the building and up the stairs toward his accommodation. To the right took him to his corridor and room at the end. The carefully planned timetable allowed for 15 minutes in the students bar, a fact we had not been privy to and which caused some confusion as we attempted to change his direction whilst being corrected by the men from the Yard. Turning to the left chose the route past the students bar, where despite the rigid timetable Phil, feigned surprise at 'bumping' into the bar where his 'surprise' was equalled by the surprised masses of students, chosen to occupy the bar. For such a well and acutely trained protection detail such a detour, planned or not was the makings of a nightmare, especially in the company of a crowd of glorified schoolchildren all vying for attention through childish remarks and actions, which could even have been an attempted Rag Day kidnap stunt.

Into the bar walked the genial HRH still feigning surprise as he marches right into the middle of them, shook a few hands and rested on the bar. He declined a pint, or anything else for that matter, was called "mate" by the resident 'cheekie chappie' before he was dragged off to Salford University's equivalent of the Tower of London. Genuinely pleased and somewhat pissed cheering students, jostled for position to HRH's ever so polite amusement. His 15 minutes duty completed, HRH bade goodnight saying: "Fucking off to bed now! Good night." This, of course, to those who have had the undoubted pleasure of his company will recognise it is his normal vocabulary, a stronghold from his Royal Navy days. Of course, the students loved it. The effing HRH brought the house down.

As he tottered along the corridor clearly suffering the effects of the civic reception, HRH never even looked in at the buffet and retired to his room dutifully followed by mincing John now happy that his boss had returned. He had been known to reappear some minutes later, 'just to keep the chaps on their toes' so we were all on guard. His valet, who had minced after him into his room, reappeared after assisting him into his 'jim jams' as he so fondly called them.

Then we had the night to get through, and all the food and drink left for our use. The Royal Standard was flying on the roof as it did whenever members of the Royal family were in residence and was supposed to remain so for as long as they stayed. Being an obvious target for souvenir-hunting students, it was removed to be replaced in the morning for the 10 minute exit.

Obviously, with HRH in residence and all the possible dangers associated with such an important guest, all security factors were mentioned at length at a briefing, but casually ignored by alleged experienced and expert security operatives in relation to a full and detailed bomb search. With equal concern and being trained to such a finely-tuned state we all wandered into the buffet room. We were bodyguards and of course the food had to be tasted and checked for poisons in case an assassin had tried a different method and in case HRH got up for a midnight snack. John, the valet, joined us, minced into the room, loved the masculine, hairy- arsed company as we told him a few jokes, some mildly homophobic, but harmless and by 6.30am he was as pissed as we were.

Clearly and totally out of character he had not hot showered, shaved and changed his lovely pressed outfit. His pert little effeminate face drained of colour as he heard the boss' bedroom door open. To make matters worse, HRH appeared at his door. Down the corridor, he bellowed: "John, where's my fucking shirt?" The door slammed shut. John, close to fainting, scurried along the corridor: "Coming, Sir." And in a flash he appeared with the shirt from his room, luckily ironed the evening before having then spent a night on the tiles with Manchester's finest.

Of course an amusing tale which could have had unbelievable consequences, due entirely to deplorable training and execution thereof, standards in force at the time. I recall one further occasion, being a darkness Deputy during a raid. I was still serving in the Drug Squad and so pretty much at the same time as the bodyguard incident. Under the guidance

Whilst in the Drug Squad, we were strangely regarded as part of Special Branch for the reasons I have given in book one The Biggest Gang In Britain. Hard drugs were unheard of in the 60s and 70s in Manchester, but in keeping up with the Jones', in this case the Metropolitan Force and in ticking a couple of apparent efficiency boxes at the Home Office, a Drug Squad was put together. Nobody knew what they were doing, the squad had no officers and so it was put under the control of Special Branch, Manchester's answer to James Bond. This department had a ranking structure, including a Chief Inspector, a couple of Inspectors, Sergeants and all of them were merely a paper exercise to tick further boxes at the Home Office. The IRA was in its infancy and not seen as the threat it grew to be, or at least not seen as any real threat at all in Manchester by this hardy group intent on tracing only illegal immigrants.

In being part of this department we were regarded as the in-house shit heads and then used for what was described as operational matters. In truth, our assistance involved

undertaking some of their typically minor enquiries in the evening, when the Special Branch did not work. I always found it strange that a body of men purporting to be James Bond did not work after 5pm and certainly did not go out in the dark. They were effectively Manchester's equivalent of the Gurkhas, in so much as they took no prisoners. Today the Special Branch has more to do, even in Manchester where they are claiming to be involved in monitoring terrorism with the abundance of illegal immigrants on the patch. In London, Scotland Yard has had some considerable successes with the help of MI5 and its' network of informants and undercover operatives, in making the arrests they have to date. Manchester appears to be falling behind in that area, but one hopes they're keeping calm and carrying on as the old wartime saying goes.

It's not clear what "rigorous measures" were in force when Stephen Oake was murdered during an arrest which should have had the benefit of such promised "rigorous measures" and "training exercises". Stephen Oake, was a police officer serving as an anti terrorism detective with GMP who was murdered while attempting to arrest a suspected terrorist in Manchester on 14 January 2003.

Oake's father was a former Chief Constable of the Isle of Man Constabulary. Nepotism was not a consideration during Stephen Oake's service of twenty years with GMP as a constable. At the latter end from 1999 he was still a constable and serving in the special branch as an anti terrorism officer. In 2002 he was commended for his professional skills and expertise.

Such commended professional skills and expertise were not apparent on 14th January 2003. Oake and colleagues went to a flat in North Manchester, as part of an immigration operation. Not wishing to speak ill of the dead and only as an example of diabolical police training and expertise do I relate this very sad and avoidable death. To be fair a Sergeant was also present who should have had command of the entire scenario.

It was said, the resident was not expected to be there and clearly no early observations had been taken to identify occupants and movements. It begs the question 'in that case why did they go? However they found three men, including an illegal immigrant Kamel Bourgass, who had arrived in England in the back of a lorry three years before. They had not identified Bourgas or discovered that he had attended terrorist meetings in the months leading up to the attack. Because of the lack of preparation he was not immediately recognised despite being wanted in London in connection with what became known as the Wood Green Nicin Plot, a bio-terrorisim plot to attack the London Underground. Strangely he was not perceived to pose a threat and thus was not handcuffed by the officers.

However, believing that the officers had identified him in connection with the ricin plot, Bourgass made an attempt to escape and, in the process of doing so, punched one officer and picked up a kitchen knife. Oake, who was unarmed and significantly not wearing protective clothing, went to restrain the suspect but was stabbed eight times in the chest and upper body, including one blow which penetrated his heart. Despite his extensive injuries, Oake continued trying to help his colleagues bring Bourgass under control. Three other officers suffered stab wounds before the suspect was eventually detained. Oake later died of his injuries.

The circumstances of Oake's murder led to debate over whether police should be free to handcuff any suspects, regardless of whether they pose an immediate or obvious threat of violence or escape. An inquiry into the incident criticised Oake's colleagues who led the raid for failing adequately to plan the operation.

Oake's full police funeral in what can only be seen as a display of guilt on the part of GMP was held at Manchester Cathedral. It was widely publicised and attended by over 1,000 people including prime minister Tony Blair. The cortege was escorted through the centre of Manchester by mounted police wearing full ceremonial dress, and Oake's coffin was carried by six former colleagues through a guard of honour into the cathedral. Proceedings inside were relayed to a crowd of hundreds outside by loudspeaker.

Sickeningly in 2005 the Criminal Injuries Compensation Board paid £13,000 to Oake's widow and to each of his three children, amounts which the Greater Manchester Police Federation said failed to match the sacrifice the detective had made. What typical understatement from a body, terrified to criticise anything in authority within the police.

In 2006, the police unveiled a granite stone memorial to Oake in North Manchester near the location of his murder. As would be the norm in North Manchester the memorial was destroyed by vandals in March 2007 but replaced six months later. No-one was prosecuted for the memorial damage despite a £15,000 reward was offered.

In the years following his murder, there was debate over whether Oake should be formally recognised for his bravery in Bourgass' arrest, including a call from his chief constable, Michael Todd for him to receive the highest civil decoration in the United Kingdom the George Cross. A civil service committee decided in 2006 that Oake's actions had not met the "extremely high" standards of bravery beyond the call of duty for the GC.

They had probably established that the entire operation had been badly planned and executed without arms and body protection. Behind so many failures of the training necessary would have been the appropriate senior officer, even the actual sergeant at the time, some rungs of seniority below C.C Todd He was, however, posthumously awarded the Queen's Gallantry Medal only the third-level civil decoration after the GC in 2009, only the ninth such posthumous award for a police officer since the creation of the medal in 1974. Clearly, more good luck than good management in necessary basic training. The Sergeant, who in truth, should have known better, was stabbed twice in the incident but survived, received a Queens Commendation for Bravery.

More recently, GMP Special Branch bristling with training and expertise, probably brought on by increased terrorist activities and the many successes in the efficient Met, arrested four so-called terrorist suspects for having weapons of mass destruction, allegedly to blow up Manchester United Football Club at Old Trafford. In a raid in London, they had found match tickets for an important clash with Liverpool and felt such a find was vital proof of the conspiracy. Such a find was not in retrospect, surprising because they were all long standing Manchester United supporters. The white powder 'explosive' they discovered in the raid when examined in the laboratory, transpired to be something like Daz washing powder. There was no way that even the Special Branch could hide such a result as they had foolishly shouted their 'success' from every Manchester rooftop.

Enter Mr Stephen Watson, let's hope he is not confronted with the 'top secret, not cleared for that information' barriers this department may also require his 'hard nosed' reputation.

Having mentioned the drug squad as a team of reprobates with no regard to the law or civil liberties, it may help to consider further words of wisdom from 2013 ...

It may also have had something to do with the fact that the officer in charge of the search warrant brought in the 'stash' to find in the absence of any real ingredients, especially if the users were regarded as local villains and not worthy of the 'office pardon.'

In many cases the flat occupants proved to be regular people, students seeking a career in law, or medicine, and unworthy of our fabricated finds and the dreadful effects a possession of drugs conviction could have on their future careers. In such cases, we would substitute the genuine cannabis for formula before any serious and unjust action was taken. Formula was a mixture of cannabis seeds, any old dried leaves and a few stalks. Gullible students, moving to the big city university would fall for this regularly in Moss Side. In all my wayward experience, totally innocent individuals were never arrested and charged.

However, certain individuals were often charged with offences they had not committed when evidence proving an offence they had committed was not forthcoming. This was the good old style of Life On Mars with its own particular form of justice and which certainly 'kept the lid on' by preventing wholesale criminality with a fear of instant justice. It was all known as 'your turn' and accepted to a degree, but of course, never totally as a prison sentence could have been the end result. Professional criminals had the strange belief that they were innocent until proven guilty, but where proof was in short supply on too many occasions then it was 'their turn.'

With the end of a trail of fantasists at best and absolutely corrupt liars as the norm, Chief Constable Stephen Watson is appointed and immediately criticising all that has festered before.

June 2021 – Present:
Stephen Watson

The new chief constable of Greater Manchester Police boasted as 'hard nosed' did not have the most glorious start to his service when he declared "the country's forces to be free of corruption, at least when it comes to the 'traditional' definition of the word.

Good old Google says ... Traditionally .. Corruption can be defined as **dishonest and illegal behaviour by people in positions of power.** It threatens national security, reduces access to services, erodes public trust in institutions and impedes investment.

Let's hope 'hard nosed' C.C Stephen Watson is aware of that precise definition which appears to say all that has been so drastically wrong with GMP. Let us all hope he isn't just attempting to placate the Greater Manchester public with the age old C.C Peter Fahy bilge which now having been shown in true context is quite alarming and certainly not a route to be chosen.

Mr Watson honestly stated when he arrived at the force, that "he found officers so demoralised they were failing to investigate crimes.GMP, the country's second/third-largest force, first entered special measures after a HMICFRS report revealed the force had failed to record 80,000 crimes during a comparatively brief period, highlighted by the investigation".

Surely the days of Andy Burnham the illustrious Police and Crime Commissioner for GMP, usually sat in his attic on zoom calls with Sky News spouting his usual rubbish on traffic congestion and rail services should be over. C.C Steve Watson does not need Burnham and whilst he speaks and writes with a plumb in his mouth he is momentarily believed, and already known only as 'Stevo' in Twitter articles.

Let's hope we can really believe his initial statement ... "Our success will be measured principally by whether the public feels like there has been improvement and that they are more confident in our ability to achieve our purpose. In this section we articulate those things we expect our communities to see, feel and experience in consequence of our successfully delivering upon our Plan on a Page.

These promises do not define the totality of our endeavours and are not an exhaustive list; rather they are the things we know our communities care most about and can use to easily evaluate our progress. We will develop simple indicators that everyone can use to track and measure how well we deliver these promises. Let us all hope he does not include a further report by Andy Cooke of the HMICFRS to be explored later.

Our Public Promises

- OUR PROMISES FOR A BETTER POLICE SERVICE: YOUR NEW GMP. ...
- RESPOND TO INCIDENTS AND EMERGENCIES. ...
- PREVENT AND REDUCE CRIME, HARM AND ANTI-SOCIAL BEHAVIOUR. ...

- INVESTIGATE AND SOLVE CRIME. ...
- DELIVER OUTSTANDING PUBLIC SERVICE. ...
- BUILD PUBLIC TRUST AND CONFIDENCE.

Stephen Watson, is in rather naive circles of Chief Constable selection but is regarded as an 'old school' thinker who has thrown himself head on against the 'woke' brigade when he joined GMP. He quickly blamed a 'failure of senior leadership' for its problems and promised a 'dialled up muscularity' in his approach to crime.

The force was moved into special measures in December 2020, However His Majesty's Inspectorate of Constabulary and Fire & Rescue Services (HMICFRS), ex Merseyside C.C Andy Cooke has reported that Mr Watson had made sufficient improvements and no longer needed 'enhanced' monitoring. This has to be seen as 'well give the lad a chance' but being a half hearted effort initially. Unfortunately he never mentioned the failed training throughout the force in typical HMICFRS Investigator, Andy Cooke style.

For example, out of context for a moment ... Reacting to the Elle Edwards murder in Wallasey, Merseyside Police commenced an exercise aimed at what they said were suspects but in fact appeared to be a general sweep of every known villain. They already knew where to seize stolen cars, guns, drugs and wanted persons. The questions have to be asked why such raids had not happened sooner as a daily priority. They were clearly in possession of such intelligence, some possibly dating to Andy Cooke's residency allowing them to act immediately.

Only a couple of weeks later two people were arrested in connection with her murder in Wallasey Village A 30-year-old man from Tranmere has been arrested on suspicion of murder and attempted murder. A 19-year-old woman from Rock Ferry in Birkenhead has been arrested on suspicion of conspiracy to murder.

In relation to GMP, what was the experience of C.C Andy Cooke with his precious statements of 'No longer need for enhanced monitoring" at this time and surely should have regard to 'There but for the Grace of God' in his case.

To continue, ... C.C Watson and his opening introduction. Never a mention of the many Operations against the marauding gangs of Asian Pakistanis and the continuing failures to keep up with the fantastic results by Maggie Oliver and her Trust. The trust reports that the problems of Child Sexual Abuse remain at the initial levels. The grooming gangs scandal is still claiming scores of victims, as a GB News investigation with Maggie Oliver found in early 2023. Their figures of thousands of historical and modern survivors that have come forward to the charity fighting to support victims since 2020. The broadcaster referred to an exclusive copy of The Maggie Oliver Foundation's annual report, which reveals that it is currently working on over 50 live group-localised child sexual exploitation cases. The charity has also supported over 1,000 survivors of child sexual abuse and exploitation through its legal advocacy and emotional support services since 2020.Was C.C. Watson too embarrassed to mention the failed arrest rates of Operation Greenjacket under A.C.C. Mohammed Hussain himself an Asian Pakistani? which now appear to be improving.

Never a mention of the criticisms laid to bare in the Manchester Arena Terrorist attack by Sir John Saunders in his very detailed Report and in particular Part Two of that report. Despite such glaring omissions it is acclaimed that the police chief took a 'back to basics' approach with the failing force. From information supplied by GMP and therefore 'a pinch of salt' comes to mind the following report has emerged...

'Since Mr Watson's takeover, 999 call answer times have been cut from an average of one minute 22 seconds to seven seconds, response times have been reduced and arrests have increased by 60 per cent. Watson has also put an emphasis on the force's public image, ordering officers to iron uniforms, cover tattoos, polish boots, tie up long hair and come into work clean-shaven.'

Simple claims of course should be regarded as true but during the week of 20th February 2022 Sir Kier Starmer MP the Labour Leader was filmed with Yvette Cooper MP the shadow Home Secretary walking the streets of Wigan in a staged production. They were in conversation with two specially presented polished police constables, wearing police helmets, without the usual yellow jackets, displaying all the belts and buckles necessary for the mass of protection gear. OK so far, but one of the constables appeared to be a schoolboy, all 5'6" of him and sporting a banned beard. Standing upright and with the rarely worn helmet he remained an inch shorter than Starmer. Hardly the image of authority. He was accompanied by a full sized version but with a big shaggy beard and heavy rimmed spectacles. Again hardly an image of authority. Are they the best Wigan can produce.

Mr Watson continues "The number of open investigations have been halved, while crime-solving has risen by nearly 20 per cent, with lower-level crimes taken more seriously. Can this in all reality actually be true and if it is does it not show what absolute failures his predecessors were.

Mr Watson has previously spoken out against officers displaying rainbow badges on their uniforms as 'virtue-signalling' and said he would not take the knee like other police bosses. Taking the job, he told Mr Burnham and other political leaders in the region he would turn the force around with a plan to make more arrests, go after serious criminals with 'real ferocity' and investigate every burglary and if he failed resign.'

To put any HMICFRS investigation into context at this stage.... 'Andy Cooke with very limited competition was said to have impressed in interviews for the post of HMICFRS by pledging to get forces better focused on detecting more crime and locking up more criminals. Of course, this must have been a new idea as he never attempted such drastic action whilst languishing as Chief Constable on Merseyside.

Having run the force as his own personal hobby with its alarming crime rate, more guns than Dodge City and more drugs than Morocco. Merseyside was run by crime gangs, all known to the CID but allowed to continue until they ran out of control as in the cold bloodied but accidental shooting of model Elle Edwards in Wallasey proved. The gunman shot her in the head attempting to kill two men who were only wounded.

Such amazing failures and inactive intelligence reports were never considered and he got the job. Cooke had impressed the Home Secretary, Priti Patel, who was clearly a none believer in even scratching the surface of a chequered history, although did comment that 'delivering on it will be trickier than promising it." Cooke's appointment marks a return to having a former chief constable leading the Inspectorate having previously had an ex rail regulator. FFS the choice wasn't difficult but look deeper.

In his report on GMP he identified the many failings with regard to the 80,000 missing crime reports and a list of many recommendations with regard to the general book keeping as listed earlier but never a mention of the Asian Pakistani gangs abusing fourteen years old white girls in Care. No mention of the amassed failings in training for elementary tasks such as basic first aid and upwards in priority to the declaration of a terrorist bombing incident, liaison with the other emergency services and a host of other measures to ensure belatedly saving lives.

Having done so, A.C. had the gaul to announce "'I am pleased with the progress that Greater Manchester Police has made so far'. So what progress is that then, if the figures are merely a fantasised wish list.. A well written declaration of intentions will not suffice. As far as the citizens of Manchester are concerned we need only to consider a quote by Adolf Hitler in 1945 ... You can fool some of the people some of the time, but not all of the people all of the time' and of course time will tell. The improvements took an initial turn for the worse. Local Media reported ...

Almost 150 employees of Greater Manchester Police were accused of behaviour relating to violence against women and girls in the last six months, the force has admitted. In the last six months to February, there were 117 complaints and misconduct allegations relating to 141 members of the force - equating to one per cent of the workforce. And in the same time period up to March last year, the force recorded 108 complaints - accounting for 9.1 per nationally, relating to 143 employees It comes as complaints about police officers' treatment of women and girls are highly unlikely to result in action, according to new police data for England and Wales. The National Police Chiefs' Council says nine in 10 complaints were dropped in the six months to March 2022.

In what appears to be the same Police Complaints Department there are reports of little action. "According to the new figures, where cases were completed, no further action was taken against police officers and staff accused of violence against women and girls in more than nine in 10 complaints from the public, and seven in 10 internal reports from police against colleagues. During the six months to March last year, the National Police Chiefs' Council (NPCC) found 1,539 officers had been implicated in alleged police-perpetrated violence against women and girls."

Andy Cooke, missed that report. Himself, hardly with a glowing reputation for hard work, said: 'I am pleased with the progress of Greater Manchester 'Whilst there is still more to do, I have decided to remove the force from our enhanced level of monitoring, known as Engage, and return it to routine monitoring. 'I am pleased with the progress that Greater Manchester Police has made so far'. Nothing in these welcome developments implies any complacency on our part. We fully recognise that much remains to improve still further. 'I look forward to sustaining GMP's march forward and for us to continue to make our region a safer place to live, work and visit.The force will be inspected again during 2023.

This work of literary art has already included several of Mr Cooke's glowing comments which were dramatically proved to be 'very misleading' and totally biased to the police over only a comparatively few years. This was so in the investigation report into the shooting of Anthony Grainger and the perjured evidence given by very senior police officers. His comments reflect the culture from whence he came, at a time he was actually believed, but time and public credulity move on.

Mr Watson said: 'Our route into 'special measures' has been thoroughly analysed and much discussed. There are several reasons as to how we came to bear our recent travails, a failure of leadership principle amongst them. Surely Peter Fahy in addition to Hopkins deserved a mention by name. "As I have stated repeatedly however, the fundamental failing was simply that we stopped doing the basics well, we stopped being the police and we stopped doing many of the things that our public have every right to". Never a mention of future training to accommodate a further terrorist incident which was totally lacking and criticised throughout the Arena Bombing report.

"As it approaches one year since I launched our plan to improve Greater Manchester Police and unveiled a series of promises to the public, I am pleased to provide an update which I trust will demonstrate to the people of Greater Manchester that the plan is working, and green shoots of improvement are coming into fruition".

Since September 2021, we have seen advancement in all areas highlighted as causes for concern by the HMICFRS, and the areas we know our communities rightly expect us to improve upon. In this time I have appointed effective leadership, set out a clear plan, and taken our policing approach back to basics, effectively fighting, preventing and reducing crime, keeping people safe, and caring for victims.

To ensure the plan would be delivered at pace, I established a strong leadership team. This involved bolstering the Force Executive team with experienced leaders and putting in place dedicated and accountable District Commanders at Chief Superintendent level in every district across Greater Manchester to improve local leadership and partnership working. This inspired the most ambitious senior recruitment process in GMP's history, and I'm pleased to confirm they are all in post and supporting front line officers and staff in delivering on our mission. With the right leadership in place and everyone working together in the same clear, positive and progressive direction, we are beginning to make rapid and sustained progress.

Great words, but is he rapidly promoting badly trained officers purely to fill seats and be the early leadership problems yet to develop with the majority never having seen an angry man, preferring to hide away and study. Time will tell.

"One of the very first things I committed to the public was to ensure when they called GMP in their time of need we would answer quickly and seek to get them the appropriate response as swiftly as reasonably possible. I am pleased to say that we are seeing increasingly improved call answer times, with the average call answer time for 999 calls in June at 29 seconds, which is down from 1 minute and 6 seconds in June 2021.

However just this weekend, we saw the best call answer time for 999 that we've seen in GMP memory, with call answer times below 10 seconds consistently from Friday evening until Monday morning. We're also seeing a positive trend in the 101 call answering time, reduced to 4 minutes and 19 seconds in June 2022, which is faster than its peak of 6 minutes 44 seconds in July 2021.

This marked improvement is down to new leadership within our call handling branch, the 1,100 hardworking call handlers answering calls and enquiries from the public 24 hours a day, the utilisation of technology and improved processes, and a £1million investment resulting in 40 new call handlers joining our Force Contact Centre. Recruitment in this area is very much ongoing and recruitment events are taking place throughout the summer and vacancies can be found on our website.

This goes hand in glove with our response to incidents, and I can confirm that response times for grade one calls have reduced since the peak times we were seeing in September last year. Our average response time to Grade 1 incidents in June was 10 minutes and 12 seconds, almost 5 minutes under the 15 minute target. 40% of grade 2 attendance times are now achieved within the target time of one hour. Times have fallen from 20 hours and 55 minutes in May 2021, to 1 hour and 27 minutes in May 2022. Whilst this is a significant improvement, we are continuing to work on this to achieve lower response times. Our work here is by no means complete, but we are delivering on our commitment to the public that at the very first point of contact with GMP, they receive a prompt response and turn out when needed. Mr Watson should watch The Force Manchester a TV programme featuring several good officers. It also features the urgent need to send a dog handler from Bury in the North to Stretford in the South a distance excess of thirty miles with heavy traffic. The villain had left the premises on his eventual arrival.

This in turn has led to a renewed focus on crime recording practices and process improvement. For May 2022 the force recorded 33,170 crimes, the most crime recorded for the last 9 months. We are recording around 30,000 crimes on average. This data shows that we have improved the accuracy of our record keeping to the extent HMICFRS has adjudged us to be 94% compliant with national crime recording standards, and therefore this element of the cause for concern has now been rescinded.

This supports my promise to the public - to make Greater Manchester a safer place to live, work and visit. It is imperative that our priorities are centred around getting the basics right, preventing and reducing crime, harm and anti-social behaviour. I am confident by now you will have seen Operation Avro taking place in your local community - our highly visible day of action in which our resources in that district are aligned for 24 hours of targeted action tackling the issues, and more importantly, the criminals blighting your neighbourhood. We will have shortly executed this operation in every district across Greater Manchester with optimal results.

As of June 2022, 290 individuals have been arrested as part of Operation Avro, (A new force-wide initiative - codenamed Operation AVRO - which will run each month in a different district. We will bring you real-time updates including images and video as activity continues throughout the day.) with 111 search warrants undertaken, 713 motorists reported for motoring offences, and 98 vehicles seized or prohibited from the road – demonstrating our active approach to tackling those who treat our roads like racetracks.

Our dedicated action to tackle crime is of course not limited to one day of action. As part of my commitment to investigate and solve crime, I also pledged to doubling the number of arrests made and as of May 2022 figures show our arrest number is 61% higher than of May 2021 – the highest they have been for two years. To better accommodate this and the criminal justice process, we have reopened the 18-cell Bolton custody suite which is now used full-time to increase capacity, and in support of our renewed focus on arresting offenders and investigating crime, an additional 28 custody sergeants have been recruited. Plans to refurbish other custody suites and uplift criminal justice units are well underway.

It is important that this enforcement action results in positive outcomes, and in addition to recording more crime we must seek to resolve more crime positively. Our performance is certainly going in the right direction and figures show during a rolling 12 months to the end of May overall positive outcomes were up by 19% (29,120) with 21% more crimes resulting in a charge or a summons. In May 2022 alone, we solved 1,000 more crimes than in May 2021, an increase of 46%. We're also delivering on our commitment to attend every burglary with attendance at 94% and whilst not every burglary victim will take up the offer of officer support, we will continue with this approach to ensure a prompt and a thorough investigation into these crimes.

Whilst this activity shows we are going back to basics and getting the policing approach right, we are not resting on our laurels and we continue to hit the criminals where it hurts – in their wallets. We're seeing an increased trend in the value of asset recovery each month, and our new Account Freezing Order Team which specialises in restricting criminal's access to money in accounts has returned £2million of victims' money in just six months of operation. This follows a record-breaking year for our Economic Crime Unit that saw almost £14million recovered between April 2021 to March 2022 – an increase of 26% on the year before. We continue to prove that Greater Manchester is no place to commit crime – if you are acting criminally you can expect us to seize your house, your car and your cash when we catch you.

These are just some of the key indicators that GMP is fast emerging as the most improved force in the country. This is a positive marker for everyone at GMP who, despite the inevitable challenges which come with transforming an organisation of this magnitude, have embraced this undertaking and whilst simultaneously adopting a new operational model to enable change to happen, they continue to strive towards our shared goal of awakening the giant we know our organisation can be.

Our major improvement projects for 2022-23 aligned to our improvement plan are clearly set out and fully funded. Each programme is led by a dedicated Chief Officer and overseen by improvement boards to scrutinise our progress in detail. These boards will oversee the delivery of transformational changes to operational policing, with key strategic reviews underway in both response and neighbourhood policing; as well as numerous projects to improve investigative resilience, force intelligence, digital and cyber investigations, and provide a more resilience specialist capability to meet the future demands and tactical deployments envisaged. There is much to accomplish and delivering these projects and improving services require us all to maintain a positive mindset and deliver to the very best of our abilities.

An additional focus for us as we head into the next stage of our plan to fully realise our potential is to strengthen our workforce. We are on the cusp of an enormously positive period in our history in that we will continue to forge ahead at pace, and we are recruiting into almost every area of policing the career has to offer. As one of the largest forces in the country, GMP can offer a range of specialisms and diverse experiences that you would not get elsewhere. Other forces may have some of these opportunities but here at GMP, we have them all. All information on our vacancies and information for transferees can be found on our website.

We are making excellent progress in our transition to the resurgent GMP, and it is thanks to our committed officers and staff who are determined to stay the course until we deliver what our public rightly expects of us, and that I am confident we will reach our latent potential. GMP is a force to be reckoned with, and we have positively embarked on the process of becoming the force Greater Manchester deserves. I would like to thank colleagues, our partner agencies and most importantly the good people of Greater Manchester for their continued support whilst we surge on with our mission to be the best police force in the country.

However bitter and warped I appear, I for one, am genuinely excited and look forward to future results under the leadership of Chief Constable Stephen Watson and his 'hard nosed' approach. It certainly appears that 'shy' operational junior officers will have little room to squirm, provided the examination of actual conduct by a skilled committee is implemented. Good luck Mr Watson.

In January 2023 The Police Fire and Crime Panel sat. With a variety of Councillors sat Chief Constable Steve Watson accompanied by D.C.C Terry Woods. The panel heard that almost 100 police officers in Greater Manchester are under investigation for sexual misconduct. GMP is investigating 82 officers for sexual offences or misconduct with investigations for a further 16 concluded and the officers currently awaiting a misconduct panel hearing.

The figures, in what appears to be to the 'learned eye' a bullshit exercise by the Mayors Office in the form of Kate Green to steal the glory of Chief Constable Steve Watson. The figure represents around 1 pc of the force. The new deputy mayor accompanied by a very quiet Mayor, Andy Burnham, said GMP is 'very committed' to openness and wants to assure the public that police officers who are found to have abused their position will be 'rooted out' from the force. She said: "This is a huge issue for all police forces - including Greater Manchester Police - in relation to public trust. An issue which has never bothered Burnham in the past.

"That's why immediately after we knew about the Carrick conviction, I asked for a report on the sexual misconduct cases that are current in GMP so that the Mayor and I could assure ourselves of the scale of what we face and the action that is being taken. You have to laugh, does she think anyone in the know believes that. The figures would have already been held by CC Watson and the appropriate action already being taken.

Councillors on the panel were told that all police forces are now required to check every police officer against the national database, revisit any allegations that may need further investigation and also revisit all vetting decisions. Chief constable Stephen Watson said that the recent uplift in police officers has already resulted in some 'resourcing issues' within the vetting unit at GMP. Having never had the benefit of such a unit, over many years and several Chief Constables he said the new requirements are likely to bring further pressure on the unit. However, he added: "The assurance that I can give you is that however difficult it is, we will fully comply with everything that is asked of the force. "We will do so expeditiously and if we have to find additional resources we will find those additional resources because it is so important for the public."

As promised by C.C Watson, dismissals for sexual offences or misconduct have more than doubled in the last twelve months. In 2020, one officer was dismissed, but in 2021 there were 5 and in 2022, 12 officers were dismissed for sexual offences or misconduct. However Twitter had a comment ... Cabal Of Corruption wrote as @whistleblower ...GMP recently had officers transferring to other forces, now 20% want to leave altogether. 2 years of Stevo who hasn't steadied the ship or made GMP a demonstrably better place. He's been rumbled and is quietly planning his great escape. It's worth mentioning that whistleblower is a man who should been Chief Constable but was yet another victim of nepotism, but certainly knows whet he is talking about, so time will tell.

Commenting outside of the meeting, GMP's deputy chief constable Terry Woods said: "We treat all allegations of sexual misconduct by officers extremely seriously.

Where people believe officers have acted wrongly, I encourage them to make a complaint and assure them that all complaints are ethically recorded, fully assessed, and investigated objectively." What a dramatic change of such a failing culture, totally ignoring sexual accusations in the recent past. It is regretful to note that once again the hundreds of young white girls abused by Asian Pakistani Paedophiles were not mentioned in the same breath as "We treat all allegations of sexual misconduct by officers extremely seriously." They should be investigating the deliberate acts under C.C Peter Fahy, C.C Stephen Hopkins and A.C.C Mohammed Hussain who all ignored the deplorable offences of rape, grooming and drug abuse in relation to very young girls in the care system and allowed the perpetrators to continue under the guise of racial harmony.

The shooting of Anthony Grainger

Father-of-two Anthony Grainger, himself with a petty criminal record, was behind the wheel of a stolen Audi in Culcheth, Cheshire, when a Greater Manchester Police officer, referred to in court as Q9, fired his Heckler & Koch MP5 submachine gun. A police officer might not have shot dead an unarmed man if senior commanders had competently organised the firearms response, a public inquiry has found.

The ill fated investigation and prosecution of a responsible party continued with real optimism.

The family of Anthony Grainger has called for a Public Inquiry after the 'health and safety' case against Greater Manchester Police Chief Sir Peter Fahy collapsed today. Salford's Anthony Grainger was shot dead by an officer from Greater Manchester Police in 2012. The officer didn't face the criminal charges, as promised by Chief Constable Fahy. Fahy who was to be charged under the Health and Safety at Work Act. This failed as they calling for a Public Inquiry into the shooting. The families solicitor "The family of Anthony simply want answers and are hugely disappointed at the decision not to proceed with the prosecution of Peter Fahy" it reads "They have waited three years for this trial. During that period the Inquest has not been able to progress and they now find that they are no nearer to the truth.

"The matter must now proceed to a public inquiry. If a jury in a criminal court can not deal with the case the family would question how a jury in an Inquest could consider the evidence and we will be petitioning the Home Secretary in this regard next week."

During 15 weeks of evidence in 2017, the Anthony Grainger family were represented by by Leslie Thomas QC, who is a leading Barrister at Garden Court Chambers, London and now of course K.C. In his summing up he declared Greater Manchester Police is "Rotten to its Core'. He certainly had the authority to speak in such 'glowing terms' with regard to G.M.P. He is highly regarded and has expertise in claims against the police and other public authorities, and claims against corporate bodies, with expertise across the full spectrums of civil wrongs, civil litigation, human rights, data and privacy claims.

Q9 told Liverpool Crown Court from behind a screen that he believed Mr Grainger, 36, had reached down as if to grab a firearm. The inquiry heard that no firearms were found on Mr Grainger or in the stationary vehicle in the early evening of March 3, 2012. Grainger, and one of his two passengers, David Totton, had for some weeks been the subject of a GMP operation, Operation Shire, which was investigating their suspected involvement in commercial robberies. Said to be absolute fiction by the family.

In his report, Judge Thomas Teague QC concluded: "Q9 shot Mr Grainger in the honestly held belief that he was reaching for a firearm with the intention of discharging it at Q9's colleagues. That belief was, however, incorrect." When Mr Grainger disobeyed Q9's instruction to show his hands, he was probably reaching for the driver's door handle in order to get out of the Audi. "Had GMP's firearms commanders adopted disruption as a tactical option, as they should have done, they would have avoided the risks occasioned by decisive intervention." Had they planned, briefed and conducted the deployment competently, Q9 would have been less likely to misinterpret Mr Grainger's actions and might not have shot him."

A Greater Manchester Police spokesman said: "We fully understand the heart-breaking effect that Anthony Grainger's death has had on his family and loved ones." "We also fully understand that the public inquiry will have been very difficult for them. On behalf of Greater Manchester Police, we offer our condolences to Anthony Grainger's family and to his loved ones." We have received the public inquiry report into the death of Anthony Grainger and we are considering the findings of the chairman, HHJ Teague QC."

"In his report, the chairman has made a number of findings which are critical of GMP.

"The criticisms are wide-ranging and include criticisms of aspects of the planning and preparation of the firearms operation during which Anthony Grainger lost his life on 3rd March 2012.

"The force, our commanders, and our officers do not set out on any policing operation with the intention of firearms being discharged. This case was no different and the safety of the public, the subjects of police operations and our officers is, and remains, our absolute priority.

"That being said, we undertake to consider each and every one of the chairman's findings and criticisms with the utmost care, attention and reflection. It is what the public would expect GMP to do in circumstances where criticisms have been made of the planning and preparation of a police operation in which a young man lost his life. It is what GMP will do.

First the family was forced to wait two years for the outcome of a detailed Independent Police Complaints Commission investigation into the shooting. During 2017 a criminal prosecution was brought against GMP Chief Constable, Sir Peter Fahy, only for the family to discover that the trial couldn't take place due to the existence of '*secret material*' and evidence.

The GMP has never been held to account, and Farleys Solicitors, acting for Grainger family, states that "Throughout the five year investigation, GMP has attempted to hold back huge amounts of evidence from Anthony's family, some 5,850 entries, with any evidence that has been provided being subject to over-redaction. "Just days before the Inquiry is due to commence, thousands of pages of relevant material are yet to be disclosed" the solicitors add "The family will be excluded from the first two weeks of the Inquiry as GMP representatives address this secret material."

The hearing at Liverpool Crown Court is only the second time in England and Wales that a Public Inquiry has been set up to examine a fatal police shooting. "The family want two things from this inquiry" says Jonathan Bridge, Partner at Farleys Solicitors who is leading the team representing Anthony Grainger's family "Firstly they want to understand how an unarmed man can be shot dead at close range by a police officer with a high-powered firearm. "Secondly they want lessons to be learned" he adds "No mother should face that knock on the door and be told by an officer that the police have shot and killed her son. Anthony's parents, siblings and children were all devastated by his death and deserve to know what mistakes were made leading up to that fatal shot being fired, and how we can make sure that such mistakes are never repeated.

"To achieve these objectives GMP need to attend the Inquiry with a willingness to be open" he explains "If the Inquiry becomes a 14 week exercise in GMP attempting to limit the extent of criticism for their failings, lessons will not be learned. The family are not encouraged by the conduct of GMP since they shot and killed Anthony but must put their faith in the Inquiry. They are extremely grateful to His Honour Judge Teague and his Inquiry team for the hard work they have already put in to preparing for the inquiry."

During the first four days, there will be an opening speech from Counsel to the Inquest, followed by opening speeches from the other parties and statements about Anthony from family members and his partner. There will then follow two weeks of closed hearings at which the Inquiry will consider evidence from GMP and the National Crime Agency, before the examination of all the witnesses begins.Chief Superintendent Heywood could remember such early days and the risks involved but he apparently cringed at the ferocity of the cross-examination and as he crumbled in the face of it 'lacked candour', while 'very little of ACC Sweeney's narrative is accurate', said Judge Teague in relation to one section of evidence.

In November 2018, the Crown Prosecution Service (CPS) said it would not bring charges against Mr Heywood because of insufficient evidence and the case went to a disciplinary hearing. Proceedings started on a Monday but on the following day, GMP said it wanted to stop them. Misconduct proceedings commenced in June 2020 against Steven Heywood an Assistant Chief Constable accused of misleading an inquiry into the fatal shooting of Anthony Grainger have been dropped. A previous investigation into ACC Steven Heywood, found he may have committed a criminal offence with evidence given to a public inquiry into the death. He was accused of retrospectively changing a written log and adding inaccurate information that would "retrospectively justify" his decision to authorise the firearms operation leading to Mr Grainger's death.

Gerry Boyle QC, representing the force, said it would be "unfair" to continue as the hearing would not have access to redacted material, including evidence given during a closed session of the public inquiry in 2017. Formally dismissing the allegations against Mr Heywood, the chair of the panel accused GMP of a "fundamental disregard" for all parties. Nahied Asjad for "Mr Grainger's family, said Mr Heywood and the public have been let down by the appropriate authority in this case and we note there was no contrition or apology to anyone in what was said on their behalf." Mr Boyle had initially asked for an adjournment to see whether redactions could be lifted but a lawyer representing Mr Heywood said it would not be possible for the evidence to be heard and accused the force of an incredible shambles".

Mr Grainger's partner, Gail Hadfield Grainger, requested to make a submission to the hearing but was not allowed. Speaking after the hearing, she said: "The police have fought at every stage to avoid being held accountable. "It is contrary to the public interest not to proceed with the gross misconduct hearing and offensive to Anthony's loved ones who are still waiting for justice from GMP eight years later. "GMP wishes to avoid disciplining Heywood in order to hide its own wrongdoing during the aborted criminal prosecution it faced. The system has been set up to fail."

Deborah Coles, director of charity Inquest, said: "This shameful outcome points to the impunity of the police, and a process which frustrates the prevention of abuse of power and ill treatment."

However a public inquiry concluded the decision to shoot the 36-year-old was not unlawful because of the officer's "honestly held belief" that he and colleagues were in mortal danger. But Judge Thomas Teague QC criticised "serious deficiencies in the planning and conduct of the firearms operation that led to Mr Grainger's death" and said GMP was to blame. "Firearms commanders authorised and planned the Masts operation incompetently and without keeping proper records of their decisions," his report said. "They inaccurately briefed the firearms officers who were to conduct the operation, distorting and in some respects exaggerating the risk presented by Mr Grainger."

On Monday, the misconduct hearing was told Mr Heywood admitted a firearms log from the days leading up to the shooting was completed afterwards, and he did not initially tell the inquiry he had not filled it in on the date shown. Mr Boyle said the document, which was used in evidence, contained inaccurate information about Mr Grainger's previous convictions. He said it was asserted that entries in the log were made to "misrepresent" the information available at the time and to "retrospectively justify" Mr Heywood's decision to authorise a firearms operation on 1 March, 2012.

The IOPC said three investigations stemming from evidence given at the public inquiry, relating to the conduct of six officers, were ongoing. The IOPC has said that there will be three separate investigations in relation to Mr Grainger's death. Investigation one will focus on former Assistant Chief Constable Terry Sweeney, former Superintendent Mark Granby and a former Chief Inspector in regard to their command and control of the policing operation. All three of the officers are retired. The second part of the investigation will look at GMP's acquisition of a CS dispersal canister which was not approved by the Home office. The final part of the investigation will look at the conduct of a serving GMP officer regarding their management of two firearms officers' training records, according to the IOPC. The IOPC has said that all officers have been informed that they are under investigation. SO! that's OK then, all retired and committing police disciplinary offences in a force which doesn't prosecute deaths by police action.

The watchdog's Director of Major Investigations, Steve Noonan, said: "We are disappointed that, two years after our investigation concluded, GMP has decided to offer no evidence in this matter. Surely he had sufficient powers to appeal such a travesty. Anthony Grainger's family, and the wider public, deserved to hear the evidence and Mr Heywood account for his actions." GMP's assistant chief constable said the case had involved "complex issues" on information and intelligence that could not be provided to Steve Heywood, the misconduct panel or made public for legal reasons. Steven Heywood was accused of changing a log to 'retrospectively justify' decision to authorise firearms operation Deputy Chief Constable Ian Pilling said: "Following submissions made on Monday, the force has accepted that some of these matters could not be overcome and it would be unfair to pursue the case against the retired officer. Why?? this was a criminal offence, not just an admin failure. FFS.

Continuing with a flourish of the usual bullshit Pilling continued "These are complex issues and the available options were often constrained by the law. Decisions have been made based on professional advice and in the best interests of reaching the most appropriate outcome. ... FOR GMP! However, in this case this hasn't been possible, which I very much regret." Mr Pilling admitted that the proceedings "should have been handled much more effectively" and apologised to Mr Grainger's family.

However the prickly comments of His Honour were not restricted to individuals who in reality should have been reported to the Director of Public Prosecutions (DPCC) for consideration as was often the case in relation to junior officers with similar law abuses.

Judge Teague accused GMP of being "unduly reticent, at times secretive attitude" and 'a failure to disclose relevant material promptly to the inquiry'. Such comments would prove to be the norm in later years as in 2019 when the latter criticism was levelled in court in later months when GMP were branded 'diabolical' by a grieving relative during the Manchester Arena Inquiry. Yet again it had failed to provide key evidence on time, seven months after being requested. GMP got away with an apology. Peter Weatherby QC acting for families, remarked "one would have thought' the force might have learned its lesson. The force's own self-commissioned review in the wake of Anthony Grainger's death was heavily criticised as it had incredibly instructed the College of Policing to look at what had happened. GMP's terms of reference, were attacked by Justice Teague and deemed skewed from the outset towards 'generating conclusions that would tend to favour the force and enhance its public image'. Turkeys and Christmas comes to mind yet again.

The Judge also blasted the so called Independent Police Complaints Commission the ex police staffed watchdog had also failed during its own inquiries to retrieve Steve Heywood's original log. Can you believe that the paperwork mysteriously vanished during the five-year period between the shooting and the public inquiry, before reappearing, with GMP unable to explain why. Despite the enquiry being mired in perjury and deliberate deception no prosecutions were ever formulated.

Certainly worth repeating in context ...Rotten to it's Core ... The wise, informed words of leading council Leslie Thomas QC about what is now recognised as the most scandal ridden police force in the country spoken at the conclusion of the Public Enquiry. Mr Thomas claimed that "GMP attempted to cover up failings over the death of Anthony Grainger. Key documents have been destroyed, accounts and logs embellished, police statements carefully stage-managed, evidence has been concocted, redactions made for no reason and thousands of pages of relevant material withheld. Taken together with the sweeping failures in planning and execution of this operation, this smokescreen by GMP reveals an organisation that is **ROTTEN TO ITS CORE.**"

IOPC (Independent Office of Police Conduct) Director of Major Investigations Steve Noonan ex Royal Military Police reported ...

"We are disappointed that, two years after our investigation concluded, Greater Manchester Police

(GMP) has decided to offer no evidence in this matter." "Anthony Grainger's family, and the wider public, deserved to hear the evidence and Mr Heywood account for his actions. "We acted quickly and decisively to examine Mr Heywood's conduct once it was brought into question during the Anthony Grainger Public Inquiry in 2017. In May 2018, after our seven month investigation, we concluded he should face a public hearing to answer allegations that the evidence he provided to the Inquiry may have breached police professional standards relating to honesty and integrity and performance of duties. GMP agreed with our findings." Today's developments mean that there can be no ruling from the **police panel*** as to whether or not Mr Heywood committed gross misconduct to a degree that would have justified dismissal, were he still serving."Three new investigations stemming from evidence given at the Anthony Grainger Public Inquiry, which reported its findings in July 2019, began earlier this year, and we will continue to work hard to ensure those allegations are thoroughly examined, that actions are accountable and lessons learned. Well! That's alright then."

ACC Steve Heywood was allowed to retire from the force in 2018 on a full pension. Just what do senior police officers especially in GMP actually have to do to warrant a criminal prosecution. He had committed the offence of perjury! Heywood had told in an amazing admission to the inquiry, that log entries were "retrospective" in a closed session on the day after his public having previously claimed them to be authentic notes made at the time.

*Who are The Police Panel.**

Made up of ten appointed councillors from each of the Greater Manchester local authority areas, and two independent members, the panel is consulted on regarding precept proposals and the police and crime plan. They are all said to be totally independent of GMP and the Lord Mayor and there must have been a proviso that they are totally deranged. Even GMP are shown to have agreed and yet such a strange and totally unwarranted decision could be made. A Google search appears to reveal that GMP had only three members at most at this time.

In an astonishing admission, GMP wrote to Justice Teague listing almost two pages of justifications for its failure to disclose information as requested, including noting that the inquiry's timetable had been 'very demanding' in response to the Inquiry, apologising. This apology followed another, weeks earlier with a similar GMP response to further similar criticism. GMP accepted the few HMI's positive assessments but with 'an ostrich, head in the sand approach', totally rejected its critical conclusions in reporting "Whilst we accept some of these findings, there are others which we have challenged. In particular we do not agree that our performance has declined since the last report," "We have made many improvements since the last report and we already have a plan in place to continue to make further improvements where we need to do so." The Chief Constable Hopkins and Co. didn't agree with the HMI's assertion that they don't attempt to prevent or investigate crime well enough and performance has declined. GMP's standard, ill considered denial would ultimately catch up with it (GMP) the following year. At the end of 2020, it was placed into special measures after HMI visited again, largely as a result of the same failures which just continued and worsened, led from the top as usual.

It was not only due to the failure to record crime and monitor victims, but the way GMP treated the Manchester public in ignoring the initial report by the Inspector of Constabulary and responded to the criticism effectively with two fingers to 100 HMI recommendations, some five years old, but remaining outstanding. Inevitably and yet unsurprisingly with GMP it was deliberately failing to accept the Inspectorate's latest assessment. Such deliberate failures, fuelled by the speedily growing illusion of being 'untouchable' and above the law even to the point of critiquing their own investigative body.

Dr Graham Smith, a senior law lecturer at Manchester University, who had been called in by Deputy Mayor Baroness Beverley Hughes to investigate GMP's Professional Standards Branch which deals with internal bad conduct issues In the past the so called Professional Standards Branch had exhibited mind boggling bias to the equally mind boggling indiscretions of the senior ranks whilst sacrificing the junior ranks 'for the figures'. He regarded the acquittal of senior officers charged with several offences arising from the Hillsborough crowd control and resultant deaths as yet another example. He believed GMP to be a 'case study' in that kind of behaviour.

There has always been a tendency within the GMP at all ranks to lean towards the culture of obfuscation, denial, secrecy and an instinct to defend the indefensible as displayed during 2008 and 2020 under CCs Peter

Fahy and Ian Hopkins. To pompously tell the HMI that they had "got it wrong in their critical report was stupidly wrong. The risk of repetitional damage is extremely important to policing and chief officers at any expense especially in the knowledge that 'they can literally get away with murder'.

Greater Manchester's puppet Police and Crime Commissioner Tony Lloyd also put out a statement in sympathy with the Grainger family...

"I have enormous sympathy for the family of Anthony Grainger as we are now three years on from his death and they are really no closer to finding out what happened to him" he said "They will be rightly disappointed by the collapse of this case. The family and the wider public deserve to know what took place during the police operation that led to Anthony Grainger's death" he added "I can only now urge that the coronial process is expedited to bring these issues to a conclusion as quickly as possible so the family can finally have the answers they seek. It cannot be right for anyone involved – and that includes the police officers involved in the operation – that we are three years on and there is still a significant amount of time to go before it comes to an end. This does not serve the public interest.

"I do not believe that it was ever right to spend the best part of a year pursuing the truth by using health and safety legislation" he explained "Health and safety laws are in place, rightly, to protect workers and the public in the workplace. They are not intended to sit in judgement on policing operations such as these, as the collapse of this case has shown.

"Central Government must review this case to ensure the proper lessons are learnt" he added "We cannot have years go by in tragic cases like this before proper conclusions can be drawn. We cannot have major matters of public policy being determined by health and safety legislation that was not drawn up with this kind of case in mind. I will be raising this directly with the Home Secretary."

This comment on twitter seems to say it all ... "So what the so called Independent Police Commissioner can offer the Grainger family is that Central Government should review the case! Can I remind Lloyd that it is HIS job as elected by the Public, to hold the Police to account and not defer or ramble on about Health and Safety. Lloyd is just a clone of GMP and a puppet of the Chief Constable. He should be challenging GMP as to why they are not prosecuting all concerned'.

Surely this has to be worth repeating ... yet again.... Rotten to its' Core.

Throughout the Inquiry, Anthony Grainger's family has tried to discover the truth as to why he died, and, after listening to the evidence surrounding the shooting, have now accused GMP of *'a catalogue of failings'*, *'incompetence'*, *'staggering ineptitude'* and *'shocking attempts at a cover up'*. "Anthony was a committed family man. He adored his children and was a loving son and brother. Over the last four months we as a family have had to listen to evidence revealing a catalogue of failings in the Greater Manchester Police (GMP) operation that led to his death.

"Police incompetence was prevalent in each and every aspect of the operation, from the gathering of intelligence to the briefing of firearms officers and the actions of such officers in the bungled arrest of Anthony. "We suspected incompetence on the part of GMP, but the

Inquiry has revealed levels of staggering ineptitude way beyond what was expected. Officers were not competent to perform their roles. There was a firearms training department in disarray. A slapdash approach was taken to gathering and verifying intelligence and there was a failure to properly plan an operation, which not only exposed Anthony to risk but also innocent members of the public.

"At the start of this Inquiry GMP were encouraged to adopt an open and honest approach. Lessons had to be learned and this could only be achieved with openness. Anthony's mother, Marina, does not want any other mother to have to go through what she has been through. "Sadly, GMP have completely failed to act with the openness called for. The evidence has revealed concerted and shocking attempts at a 'cover up'. Officers have attempted to conceal evidence and mislead the investigation, with key documents destroyed and withheld, accounts and logs embellished and the production of statements carefully stage managed.

"GMP have done their upmost to conceal the truth is indicative of GMP's approach to this shooting. They shot and killed an innocent man yet the emphasis throughout has been on covering up the failings that caused such killing. "The family have absolutely no confidence in GMP or their willingness to learn from this incident. Until they stop trying to cover up their wrongdoing lessons will not be learned and other mothers run the risk of the same knock at the door and the same terrible news that Marina received in March 2012."

R.I.P. Anthony Grainger and God Bless his grieving family.

The unnecessary death of Jordan Begley

An inquest was held at Manchester civil courts of justice over a period of five weeks in 2015 to report on the death of Jordan Begley and police conduct and use of a Taser.

Lawyers for Donnelly the man who fired the Taser and four other officers unsuccessfully sought a permanent anonymity order which would have prevented their being identified at the inquest. In February 2015 Manchester Coroner Nigel Meadows refused the anonymity order, and named PC Donnelly, PC Mills, PC Peter Fox, PC Dave Graham and Sgt. Andrew Wright as the officers who were present at the scene. Meadows said he had not been persuaded by arguments that the officers would face reprisals if their identities were publicised.

Donnelly, Fox, Graham, Mills and Wright, all serving GMP officers, gave evidence. In June 2015 Wright denied colluding with other officers regarding his evidence. Medical experts who gave evidence said the Taser was "unlikely" to have contributed to Begley's cardiac arrest. The coroner said the inquest had "been a long case with a lot of evidence" which had been "different and inconsistent". Is that not a consistent description of police evidence in so many matters and certainly The Anthony Grainger enquiry.

Could Dorothy Begley have ever considered the devastating outcome having initially called police on the evening of 10 July 2013. Her son Jordan Begley had become upset following an argument with neighbours who had accused him of stealing a handbag and was threatening to take a knife outside. Whilst she was in fear that the situation would deteriorate, causing her to fear that there would be "a murder" as he had threatened to use a knife. She did not tell Begley she had called the police.

Armed GMP officers rushed into Begley's dining room in Gorton. In typical GMP over reaction, highlighted in TV show Force Manchester, eleven officers were deployed. Begley was initially outside the house but agreed to go inside with the officers. A standoff developed, which ended with PC Terrence Donnelly drawing his Taser X26 and opening fire. In a display of poor training if any at all, under the 'leadership' of Peter Fahy the Taser shot lasted nine seconds and was from a distance of only 70 centimetres. Donnelly was described as having entered "a high state of alert." Fahy speak for hysterical bullying. Begley was said to be immediately restrained when he offered minimal resistance.

Jordan Begley was a thin build, slim, with health issues. The officers left Begley lying face-down with his hands cuffed behind his back.

The inquest was told that P.C. Donnelly had been made aware that Begley was potentially in possession of a knife based only on his Mothers initial phone call which clearly said that it was only a threat. Donnelly told the inquest that Begley's hands were in his pockets, and that he asked him to show his hands to determine the whereabouts of a weapon, and to stop moving.

According to Donnelly, Begley continued to approach him, after which he told him to stand still. In my days of Yates Wine Lodges he would have been kicked in the balls which always had the desired effect. P.C. Donnelly, in what can only be described as wanton bullying and cowardice deployed the Taser. In evidence, Dorothy Begley said her son had been "doing exactly what they wanted him to do" when the Taser was used.

The inquest jury's verdict said that after Begley was forced to the floor the officers did not attempt to determine whether he was conscious, and ignored the fact that he did not cry out or speak. When he was turned over on to his back it became clear that he was in distress. Sergeant Andrew Wright said Begley had an "ashen" colour to his face and a "golf ball"-sized lump on his head when he was rolled over, and that his breathing was irregular. Officers removed his handcuffs and attempted to revive him using a trauma kit.

Begley died in hospital at 10 pm on 10 July, around two hours after the incident, from a cardiac arrest. Begley was 23 at the time of his death. His funeral, was paid for by the police, which certainly appeared to be a display of accepted guilt.

In August 2013 Dorothy Begley said she believed her son's death was due to a case of mistaken identity relating to a 25-year-old man from Sale in Greater Manchester also named Jordan Begley, who was on the run from prison. Begley said that on the night of her son's death an officer had questioned her about links to Sale. In absolute Peter Fahy fashion, Assistant Chief Constable Dawn Copley said police were "not aware of any evidence to support that suggestion at this time."

The jury took four days to conclude in a verdict on 6 July that the use of the Taser did not directly cause Begley's heart to stop, but the restraint and the Taser "more than materially contributed" to a combination of stressful factors which triggered cardiac arrest. Other factors included Begley's alcoholism, his drug abuse, a dispute with neighbours, and the confrontation with police which followed. The jury also found that Donnelly had acted "inappropriately and unreasonably" in using the Taser for longer than was necessary, and found that the two punches delivered as "distraction blows" by one officer were unnecessary. The verdict said "there was no need to punch twice without even checking his first response to the first punch." The jury also found that the officers were "more concerned about their own welfare" than that of Begley. The ruling marked the first time an inquest jury had found the use of a Taser to have contributed to a death.

Begley's family were dissatisfied with the outcome of the inquest and that they intended to sue the GMP. In what was an excellent comment Dorothy Begley called for the immediate introduction of police body cameras and questioned why the officers involved had not been disciplined. She described the decision as "fantastic" and said "After two years of fighting everybody, fighting the system, Jordon's day has come. That is all I ever wanted. The last two years have been hell." Dorothy Begley's lawyer, Mark McGhee, said the inquest's outcome would extend "far beyond the death of this one individual".

Peter Fahy protege, A.C.C Dawn Copley, added for GMP, said the verdict "raised a number of serious concerns, including the way the Taser was used, the use of force by the officers after the Taser was deployed and

... the communication between the officers who attended Jordon's home." Copley said the GMP would "examine the jury's findings in detail" Clearly as good as an admission of guilt in relation to any lack of real level of expert training. Corroboration of such thinking flowed from the National Police Chiefs' Council which called for an independent body to examine the medical evidence and determine whether safety advice on Tasers should be changed in the light of Begley's death.

Copley would have served the public interest had he considered the existing statistics on Taser use by GMP officers and the none existent training which must be at the root of such deplorable figures.

GMP Chief Constable Peter Fahy, true to form defended the use of Tasers by GMP and said the record of British police in terms of force was "remarkable." Has Peter Fahy ever consulted any actual research before uttering such nonsense in relation to GMP alone.

A report on the use of the Taser by UK police and particularly GMP they reported ...

In 2019 alone, Greater Manchester Police's use of Tasers increased 73% from 832 incidents in 2017/18 to 1,442 incidents in 2018/19. This rate of increase exceeded the national average of 39% as well as that of comparable forces such as the Metropolitan Police which reported a 49% increase in the use of Tasers. In 2018/19, Greater Manchester Police reported more incidents involving Tasers (1,442), whether discharged or not, than any other force with the exception of the Metropolitan Police. In 2018/19, Black people were subject to the use of Taser by Greater Manchester Police at nearly 4 times the rate of white people. In 2018/19, Greater Manchester Police reported more incidents involving the use of Tasers against children under the age of 18 than any other force with the exception of the Metropolitan Police. In total, Greater Manchester Police reported 118 such incidents including eight against children under the age of 11.

So! there we are with the truth and should Peter Fahy have been investigated by the Home Office as an inveterate liar in relation to the conduct and so called leadership as Chief Constable of a once great Force.

Rest in Peace Jordan Begley.

Operation augusta ... "a beacon of good practice"?

Started by GMP in 2004, because of the general outcry in the wake of the heart breaking case of Victoria Agoglia a fifteen year old girl who, whilst in care was sexually abused 'in plain sight' of officials.

She died of a drug overdose in 2003. She had, two months earlier reported the fact to her carers that she had been raped and injected with heroin by an older man. No action was immediately taken but later as a result of pressure from various media outlets, 50-year-old Mohammed Yaqoob was arrested and charged. He had been forcibly injecting her before his sexual assaults but was later cleared of manslaughter and jailed for three-and-a-half years for administering the noxious substance. Was that British Justice at it's best?

At her inquest in 2007, yet another Coroner with his own dubious agenda, Simon Nelson concluded that the authorities could not have foreseen her death, recording a narrative verdict and referencing her propensity to 'grant sexual favours'. What an absolute failure of the supposed independence of the Coroners office. The verdict was blatantly untrue and must have been based on lies provided by GMP. This conclusion is to be challenged by the family who fifteen years later have been granted permission.

After Victoria's death, Greater Manchester Police (GMP) launched an investigation in 2004 into child sexual exploitation in south Manchester called Operation Augusta. But this was closed a year later.

An independent review into Operation Augusta was commissioned by Greater Manchester Mayor Andy Burnham only as a result of the undeniable, horrendous publicity caused by a 2017 BBC documentary The Betrayed Girls. The programme focussed on Victoria's death and the subsequent rubbish police operation. The review established that Operation Augusta had identified at least 57 victims and 97 potential suspects. Whatever version of this saga you choose to read, these figures differ but the fact remains that the victims have been recently (2021) estimated at around four hundred and the perpetrators in the hundreds.

The report outlined how senior GMP officers had chosen to under-resource the investigation and then make the dubious decision to close it down in 2005. The Greater Manchester Mayor's Office published a review of this so called investigation in January 2020, which raised concerns about the conduct and decision-making of some of the officers involved. On close examination it could be seen that the Burnham's report did not name names as is the norm for Burnham and local media as though naming names in the Senior Ranks of GMP was a poisoned chalice.

Throughout his years as Police and Crime Commissioner, Burnham showed no real interest in controlling the hopelessly out of control GMP, relying only on misleading information fed to him by the Force itself.

Burnham deserves no credit for commencing this enquiry. He was backed into a corner and it had been fifteen years before the review was eventually published. That is fifteen years of continuing sexual abuse of very young white girls by many members of the Asian Pakistani community. The publication revealed only that un-named officers are being investigated for their conduct in the supervision and direction of the conduct of Operation Augusta which of course commenced in 2004. During its so called investigation involving police and social services it claimed the fanciful figures of almost 100 potential suspects and over 50 potential victims of child sexual exploitation raised its 'fictitious' head yet again.

Whatever the figures they certainly did not reveal any corresponding number of actual arrests.

The review found that Operation Augusta was closed down by unnamed senior officers in 2005 only a year after it opened. The detectives at the pointed end were actively establishing the potential enormity of such an investigation. A complete investigation, the likely cost and the numbers of detectives necessary to cope with such estimated volumes was seen to be impossible. In a total abandonment of the child victims one of the esteemed ranking leaders stated that 'all lines of enquiry had been successfully completed or exhausted' and the investigation was to close "in order to free up resources". This was blatantly untrue

The review, which forensically reopened and examined Manchester council records dating back the best part of two decades, concluded social services 'failed to protect her'. "she had been abused 'in plain sight' of officials". Abusers were able to pick up girls from care homes in and around the city's Curry Mile and abuse them, the damning report reveals.

The 150 page report refers to senior officers in key roles at the time by rank and title but were referred to under the anonymity of alphabet letters for public consumption. At a meeting in April 2005, an officer named only as 'Chief Superintendent A' said he was 'unable to put permanent staff into Operation Augusta and that the operation would finish on 1st July 2005'. However the concerns regarding accusations of racial prejudice were always present . At one of its early meetings in July 2004, concern was expressed about 'the risk of proactive tactics or the incitement of racial hatred'. The report added 'there were concerns amongst some at GMP that Op Augusta was focusing on a gang of largely Asian Pakistani men'.

From my point of view, it is very difficult to conclude how such racial hatred could not be an end result when it was always Asian Pakistani older men grooming and raping fourteen years old white girls.

The fundamental flaws in how Operation Augusta was planned and financed did, in fact damage the investigation. Apparently there was 'no central responsibility' for the investigations regarding child sexual exploitation. The junior ranks 'at the pointed end" revealed offences which were uncovered throughout three police divisions, resulting in the inevitable 'conflict' about which division should provide the necessary officers and funding, giving absolutely no consideration to the continuing abuse and suffering.

GMP appeared to attempt to hide behind two offences and the focus was on a racially-motivated murder and the murder of a child in the city centre. These long-running investigations were said to be running at the same time as Augusta. An obvious solution would have been to absorb these investigations into Operation Augusta which would benefit from the additional detectives.

The anonymous senior officers are actually the current chief constable of West Midlands Police, Dave Thompson, the retired chief constable of North Yorkshire Police, Steve Heywood, who was the head of GMP's public protection unit at this time, Dave Jones who was the head of GMP's CID at the time and Tony Cook who is now at the National Crime Agency. Assistant Chief Constable Dave Thompson has now confirmed he was 'Chief Superintendent A' but has insisted: "I would not have closed an investigation like this." Look at the rank, is that not yet another example of GMPs promotion procedures ... "Get in the shit and get on'?

The enquiry concluded "We believe, from the evidence that we have seen, that the decision to close down Operation Augusta was driven by the decision of senior officers to remove the resources from the investigation rather than a sound understanding that all lines of enquiry had been successfully completed or exhausted", the authors said. "How could three senior detectives fail to have a 'sound understanding' of the entire workings and failings of an operation which they headed".

These are senior officers who had probably climbed the ranks and served under Chief Constables Todd, Fahy and Hopkins until they reached the dizzy heights, giving them the authority to simply stop an investigation into the grooming and raping of young white girls by gangs of Asian Pakistanis after only twelve months. Then to follow with a totally false claim that the investigation was complete before claiming it was under resourced. Just how many Peter Fahy type statements would follow with the expectation that the moronic public and Andy Burnham would believe anything. During their service we had seen the unbelievable failings of uniformed Inspectors at the Manchester Arena bombing and the destruction of 80,000 crime reports to improve the dismal detection rate by the CID. Highlighted during the reign of CC Hopkins but going much deeper into the terms of previous Chief Constable.

Not to be confused with Andy Cook ex Merseyside CC and HMI, Detective Superintendent Tony Cook was Augusta's senior investigating officer Tony Cook, now incredibly, head of operations for child sexual exploitation at the National Crime Agency and who appeared to cooperate with the enquiry. He stated that Operation Augusta wanted to focus on 25 victims to prevent the operation getting out of control.

He told the inquiry: "In agreement with the gold strategic multi-agency group, the terms of reference were kept deliberately tight and focused on a precise number of victims due to the scale of the task and resources available. "I had concerns not only from our small team getting quickly swamped by a rising number of potential number of victims and offenders, but also that subsequent new reports could feasibly get allocated to the Augusta team". "In which case we would have had not only to investigate these but also manage associated safeguarding risks with a very small number of staff."

In Burnham's selective style of minute taking, no minutes of the 'gold' meeting on April 22nd at the town hall could be found although an experienced detective of the old school kept a log of the meeting noting that an update had been given, 'press strategies discussed' and the operation's end date confirmed, the report reveals.

The report continues "Finally, the investigation strategy placed too heavy a reliance on victims' willingness to make complaints. As resources and time ran out, activity became reduced to closing down the majority of the cases because the child declined to make a formal complaint. This was to be proved totally false later. Critically, the problem that Operation Augusta had been set up to tackle, namely the sexual exploitation throughout a wide area of a significant number of young white children in the care system by predominantly Asian Pakistani men, had not been addressed." It had clearly been addressed as comments above prove.

Superintendent Dave Jones,(get done and get on) who retired as Chief Constable of North Yorkshire Police in April 2018, is understood to be the officer identified in the report as head of CID command. He did not provide any material to the inquiry. The official report says it had received no response from him. He had even been shown documents to prompt his memory in addition to a list of questions. He stated that he 'could not recall the detail and would not be able to assist'. Absolutely unbelievable and to accept such a refusal by a serving senior police officer is clearly very concerning.

Chief Super.Dave Thompson, referred to as Chief Superintendent A is now Chief Constable of West Midlands Police.(get done and get on) He says he has 'no recollection' of discussion about resources, despite Mr Cook's log. He said "At this time, I was the local police commander for one district of the City of Manchester. I was not in charge of criminal investigations. "I have never been involved in the Operation Augusta investigation. I have no recollection of the investigation which was led by the Greater Manchester Police's Serious Crime Division.

He continued "the report references from another officer's notes that I was at a meeting where resources were discussed". "Whilst I have no recollection of this discussion and no other documents are held by GMP in this case I do not believe an investigation of this type initiated at a force level would have been terminated by a local commander. "It is clear Greater Manchester Police and Manchester City Council should have done a better job. 'As a member of the force at that time, I am very sorry we did not do a better job. However I am very clear I would not have closed an investigation like this." What can you say to that, now a Chief Constable of the failing West Midlands force, passing on his experience of so many dubious acts.

Can you believe the following final statement of the enquiry "Even though it went nowhere, Op Augusta was considered by force top brass to be **a beacon of good practice** because, for the first time, a social worker was embedded with the detectives, the report reveals. A commendation was handed to the team.

An inquest returned an open verdict and an investigation by West Midland Police, the force which later employed Dave Thompson as Chief Constable, concluded C.C Todd had not put GMP at risk despite his reputation as a lothario. The inquiry interviewed 39 women he knew. It is unclear what role, if any, he played in shelving Op Augusta. They need look no further than repeated statements of Chief Constable Todd who believed **that such actions would damage community relations.**

However his successor Peter Fahy, never to be regarded as believable, in an ITV interview in 2014, said he was 'quite happy' to look at Victoria Agoglia's death again.

Only after being pressed as a result of her grandmother Joan Agloglia, in the wake of the Rochdale sex grooming scandal. She had shouted from the 'rooftops': "These men are still walking about, she needs to be put to rest and I hope if anyone is watching and they do know something, even if it's the smallest thing, to come forward so that social services will know there's a lot of people that still know they never helped these young girls." In his perfected slippery style Peter Fahy later said that "he could not recall the ITV interview". He said "he believed the Agoglia case would fall under one of the reviews which were instated following the jailing of the Rochdale sex grooming gang in 2012. "It clearly wasn't," he said.

Peter Fahy repeated what he had told the authors of the inquiry report ...

In typical style, he appeared to be perfectly relaxed whilst he misled the interviewer and diverted the question. He added: "I gave my recollection to the enquiry and fully co-operated and along with everyone connected with GMP hugely regret that more was not done in this case. Major improvements in the way GMP protracted vulnerable children were made during my time but we cannot be complacent."

"As well as examining the past we need to look at what is happening now - nationally there are huge difficulties in the care system, there has been a huge drop in convictions for sexual offences and there have been limited improvements in the way courts deal with victims. We are now seeing even more serious exploitation of children in county lines gang activity.

The Operation Augusta investigation remained dormant during Peter Fahy's tenure and for the few years that followed when Ian Hopkins replaced him in 2016.

It was only in the summer of 2018, after the 'early findings' of the Mayor commissioned report, highlighted failure by police and social services that action was taken. Chief Constable Hopkins authorised another look at Op Augusta because of the reports damning findings. Incredibly Hopkins denied any suggestion he had tried to stop the damning report being made public and stresses that he defied legal advice suggesting the force wasn't obliged to co-operate with the inquiry. He said: "There have been claims that Greater Manchester Police has tried to stop the review of Operation Augusta being published. Nothing could be further from the truth. Contrary to these reports, we have cooperated fully with the review team and acted with transparency and integrity throughout."

A social media comment of January 2017 says it all ... We have MP's and politicians bending laws around themselves, along with local councils and the GM (Gestapo-Manchester) Police force. Paedophile rings within institutions for MPs to get their jollies off in. All neatly covered up by 'friends in high places' to save their own miserable necks (under the misnomer of things being in the interests of 'National Security'). Not little cover ups. We're talking full blown cover ups that stink to high heaven. And we sit back and take it like sheep.

The death of Victoria Agoglia led to Operation Augusta and the more shocking aspect of this whole affair being, to this day no investigation has taken place. At the inquest into her death yet another clearly police biased Coroner ruled "there was no evidence of a gross failure to meet Victoria's needs that would have had a significant bearing on her death". And that there could be no inference that the events leading to her death were "reasonably foreseeable". As a real illustration of existing police bias, the existing coroner has refused to release relevant documents to the official enquiry.. On the evidence it makes it impossible to agree with the coroner's judgement. In a joint attempt to deliver justice for Victoria and her family five Manchester MPs have written to the Attorney General calling for a new inquest.

Her family's lawyers said "the original 2007 inquest concluded authorities could not have foreseen her death. The family have been given permission to seek a fresh inquest." Twenty years on, her family said 'they were now one step closer to justice".

Public law associate Claire Macmaster, is representing them, and they demanded a new inquest which recognised Victoria as a victim of child sexual exploitation. "This is a milestone in my client's pursuit of justice for Victoria. My client is understandably anxious to ensure that circumstances leading up to Victoria's death are understood within an accurate factual context," she said.

Solicitor General Michael Tomlinson KC has granted permission for the family to seek a new inquest at the High Court. A government spokesman said it was now a matter for the court to decide if an inquest will be granted. A separate investigation into three ex-senior officers who led the investigation was discontinued in 2022 by the police watchdog.

Yet another unbelievable comment by The Independent Office for Police Conduct (IOPC) when they said 'the decision was made as there was no indication the officers had breached standards'. Fat dripping off a chip?

IOPC Director of Major Investigations Steve Noonan: "This has been a lengthy but necessary process, and it has taken some time to gather the information required to make a decision whether it was necessary to investigate, and who should conduct the investigation. "The Mayoral review raised many questions about the actions of those involved in Operation Augusta. We have now decided it is necessary to investigate the individual conduct of these three former GMP officers who were all involved in either supervising or setting the direction of Operation Augusta."Though the content of the Mayoral review has been analysed as part of our decision to begin an investigation, it was not a specific investigation into the actions of the officers involved. We now need to establish and examine all the available evidence. The investigation is in its early stages." ... Don't hold your breath.

Always to 'jump on the band wagon' with yet more self protecting bull, Mayor of Greater Manchester, Andy Burnham, said: "When I commissioned the independent review into child sexual exploitation, I wanted to send the clearest of messages to victims that supporting them is my top priority and that I won't let the passage of time nor any other consideration be used as an excuse for not giving them the truth, justice and accountability that they deserve. "Given the seriousness of the issues revealed by the review into Operation Augusta.

It is important that they are properly investigated and that is why I welcome this decision by the Independent Office for Police Conduct. It is only through robust, impartial investigation that we can truly establish what happened at the time and ensure any mistakes are not repeated. "Since 2005, there have been undoubted improvements in the investigation of child sexual abuse, not least in Greater Manchester. But we must never be complacent. There is more that we need to do to right the wrongs of the past and improve how we support people going forward.

In Greater Manchester, we must have a zero tolerance approach to child sexual exploitation of any kind and an absolute determination to root it out wherever it is found. Did he really say 'impartial' in the same breath as 'The independent Office for Police Conduct? Ex police investigating serving police being 'impartial'?

As I write in February of 2023, GB News, Journalist Charlie Peters in conjunction with Maggie Oliver and her Maggie Oliver Foundation have totally exposed the honesty of all the 'feel good' 'aren't we clever' B.S. statements by Andy Burnham who clearly has no idea and is basically the puppet of GMP and the forces 'tail wagging the PCC dog example.. The IOPC through Steve Noonan features no better and of course the GMP leadership of what was thought and acclaimed to be the past.

I can do no better than copy the devastating article in its entirety and trust Charlie Peters of GB News will welcome the accolade.

The grooming gangs scandal is still claiming scores of victims an exclusive GB News investigation has found, as thousands of historical and modern survivors have come forward to a charity supporting victims since 2020. This broadcaster has seen an exclusive copy of The Maggie Oliver Foundation's (TMOF) annual report, which reveals that it is currently working on over 50 live group-localised child sexual exploitation cases.

The charity has also supported over 1,000 survivors of child sexual abuse and exploitation through its legal advocacy and emotional support services since 2020. At least 400 survivors say they were failed by the police in some way last year GB News has reported. In 2022 alone at least 400 survivors contacted TMOF having been failed by the police in some way. Approximately 55 per cent of all of its cases from the last three years involved some form of sexual exploitation, with the average age for abuse to start being just 12-years-old.

The foundation, which was launched by Maggie Oliver, a former Greater Manchester Police officer who exposed the Rochdale grooming gangs scandal, has found that child sexual abuse and exploitation carried out by organised networks and gangs are increasingly continuing from the victims' childhood into adulthood. ts cases have also become more violent, with methods of coercion deployed by abusers becoming increasingly threatening and adopting modern methods of surveillance.

The Maggie Oliver Foundation said that perpetrators were regularly contacting, threatening and exploiting their victims through Snapchat and other apps that allow for online communication to disappear. The MOF told GB News that even after a decade since Oliver blew the whistle on the Rochdale case, it is still seeing some police officers across the country judging girls reporting these crimes as making "lifestyle choices".

GB News has seen case studies for survivors that the MOF is currently supporting.

One survivor, kept anonymous as they continue their case, contacted the foundation seeking legal advocacy and emotional support due to historic and ongoing sexual exploitation. She says she was the victim of child sexual exploitation by a group of perpetrators from the age of 13. She is 28 now but her abuse and exploitation has continued well into adulthood, including a recent gang rape and attempted strangulation.

On one occasion, she told her perpetrators she had been made pregnant so they kicked her in the stomach.

The MOFoundation said it is still seeing some police officers across the country judging girls reporting these crimes.

In order to make her meet with them to be trafficked for sex, the perpetrators have sent photographs of her family members and their homes, threatening to harm them if she does not comply. Police are aware of her historic and ongoing abuse and exploitation. But despite repeated attacks and clear evidence of abuse, the foundation said that "she has not been safeguarded and these attacks have been allowed to carry on. She has been called a 'prostitute' by police officers when reporting her abuse yet has never received any money in exchange for sex".

In another case, also seen by GB News, another survivor's mother approached the foundation with concerns about police handling of an investigation of sexual exploitation and blackmail of her 16-year old daughter by an adult male. The survivor was in what she thought was a sexual girlfriend-boyfriend relationship with the offender, but he had coerced her into sharing intimate photographs, which he subsequently sold. She was also blackmailed, with the offender threatening to share the images and harm her family unless she extorted money from friends and family.

The foundation said that her abuser is suspected of abusing another 15 girls using similar strategies of coercion.

The survivor family said: "The police have not done anything to protect [our daughter] and during the whole process have failed to keep us up to date with their handling of the case, failed to return our calls and as a family we feel they have left us in the dark.

"I actually feel like giving up on it all. It's so unfair as victims we're the ones left suffering, filled with worry and what ifs. Absolutely deflated. Such a sad mad bad world."

When the family asked the investigating officer if they had an update on the case, they reportedly received the following response: "To be honest, as of yet, no. We have been running with a lot of live jobs which is making looking at any of my crimes a nightmare... I'll be putting in some overtime to get it sorted."

During the GB News Investigates production, titled "Grooming Gangs: Britain's Shame", this broadcaster spoke to survivors, activists and whistleblowers across the country. In the film, Maggie Oliver told this broadcaster: "It is not a historical problem. It is going on today. Very little has changed. We have seen trials, but all too often these children are still being judged and fobbed off and that is not good enough."

Jayne Senior MBE, the Rotherham whistleblower who exposed the scandal in the South Yorkshire town, told GB News that authorities are still underestimating the extent of grooming gangs across the country. n Rotherham, the 2014 Jay report found a 'conservative estimate' of 1,400 victims, since revised by the National Crime Agency to 1,510. Senior thinks it could be higher. She told GB News: "I would put my conservative estimate between 1750 and 1800, because I remember the name of every child that came to Risky Business".

Maggie Oliver told GB News it is 'not a historical problem. It is going on today' She added: "But what we have to remember is that's the children we knew [about]. How many children just in Rotherham alone didn't come forward, didn't tell anybody what was happening to them, didn't report their abuse, and they've still not spoke about it. So we'll never know that real number."

Maggie Oliver said: "Child sexual abuse and exploitation by 'grooming gangs' is a current problem. We see through our work at The Maggie Oliver Foundation that, if anything, these gangs are getting more sophisticated in their tactics and the problem more widespread. "Access to mobile phones and apps like Snapchat makes young girls so much more accessible to these criminals. It's so important that the public are aware of this so they can spot the signs and we can keep the pressure on police and statutory services to take these crimes seriously and protect those at risk from these dangerous men."

A source close to Home Secretary Suella Braverman told GB News: "The Home Secretary is appalled by these findings of GB News. Grooming gangs are a stain on our country. "The Home Secretary is committed to ensuring support and justice for the victims of these heinous crimes.

"She will not shy away from further measures to crack down on abusers and end the despicable exploitation of vulnerable young girls and women."

Let us all hope that Stephen Watson the current C.C.of GMP is to 'get a grip' without any Home Office directives. It appears to be the case and was started with the removal of Asian Pakistani Mohammed Hussain, once his Assistant Chief Constable but now at North Yorkshire Police following in the dubious steps of named Dave Jones when Chief Superintendent and now the retired Chief Constable of North Yorkshire. What a strange coincidence and is this tiny force a dumping ground for GMP rejects, to claim a full pension.

Operation greenjacket

Operation Greenjacket is claimed to have started in May 2019

Assistant Chief Constable Mohammed Hussain joined GMP in October 2018 with what appeared to be a perfect CV. Unfortunately his fictitious claims of successes with regard to preventing horrendous incidents of child abuse were put into heart stopping context.

Chief Constable Stephen Watson joined GMP with a hard nosed reputation in June 2021 following 'fall guy' Ian Hopkins with a declaration to clean up the mess of his predecessors. Note the plural. Six months later January 2022 Assistant Chief Constable Hussain resigned and moved to the outbacks of North Yorkshire Police as Deputy Chief Constable. A force with only 1042 male officers and 619 females, one being the temporary Chief Constable Lisa Winward and appointed as the infamous Dave Jones (resigned) (of Anthony Grainger and Operation Augusta) of damaging fallout fame. Did C.C Jones fall before he was pushed as damaging criticism from Justice Teague and the various investigations featured earlier continued to swirl around him. The same maybe said about Hussain and GMP.

In May 2019, Operation Green Jacket, a multi-agency operation was setup with the much heralded Hussain as the first ethnic in such a position. He was at the helm with the acclaimed aim of identifying, supporting and safeguarding victims of child sexual exploitation. The duel aim was also to identify offenders and bring them to justice, regardless of whether the offences are historic or current. Great words but that was where it ended as It appears that no arrests were made until twelve months later when on Thursday 30 April 2020, a man in his 40s was arrested on suspicion of sexual activity with a child when in a position of trust and misconduct in a public office. The man in question was employed by Manchester City Council's Children's Social Care and had been bailed pending further enquiries. Whilst enquiries were ongoing, the man was suspended from his duties. In fact the arrest was nothing to do with any investigations by Operation Greenjacket as he had been identified by colleagues in the department but falsely claimed as the first arrest, unbelievably in its' first twelve months.

Following the findings of the Child Sexual Exploitation (CSE) Assurance Report that was commissioned by the Mayor of Greater Manchester Andy Burnham. It was said, Chief Constable Ian Hopkins requested a peer review to analyse its approach and practices to the Operation Green Jacket investigation. This review was undertaken by national policing leaders which in truth, should have given no comfort at all. "Taking learning from national best practice a number of recommendations were made which have been implemented by the investigation team to ensure the operation is as robust as possible to support victims and bring offenders to justice."

Operation Hydrant: It's strange that, despite my fanatical interest and research I have never heard of this Operation despite its countrywide claims. It was said to be a British police investigation into allegations of "non-recent" child sexual abuse.

It is claimed to co-ordinate a number of other investigations by police forces throughout the United Kingdom. It is headed by Simon Bailey the Chief Constable of Norfolk Constabulary. WHO? Since 2013, he has been with Norfolk a backwoods force known only for sheep and sister shagging by City based officers. A search of WikiPedia found Bailey to have the shortest entry I have ever seen. Bailey is also the National Police Chiefs Council lead on child protection. He is acclaimed to have previously worked as a detective, and was involved in the investigation of a murder which began after the Jimmy Saville scandal prompted more complainants to come forward.

In May 2015, eight months later Operation Hydrant was claiming it had information on "1433 suspects of which 216 are deceased, 666 suspects related to institutions, 261 classified as people of public prominence, of which 506 are classified as unidentified, and 357 institutions have been identified within the scope of the operation".

By December 2015, there were claimed to be 2,228 suspects under investigation by Operation Hydrant, of whom 302 are classified as of "public prominence", including 99 politicians and 147 celebrities from the media, and 1,217 operated within institutions including 86 religious institutions, 39 medical establishments, 25 prisons/young offenders institutes, 22 sports venues, 10 community institutions, 81 other institutions such as guest houses, and 6 unknown). 286 were dead, and 554 classified as unknown or unidentified. Of the prominent suspects, 39 were from the music industry and 17 from the world of sport. Where was the media and how did I never get a whiff.

In July 2019, the BBC reported: "Some 7,396 possible crimes on its database have now had a final outcome. Of those 2,043 - or 29% - ended in a conviction." Well they kept that quiet. This is clearly a poorly veiled public relation exercise with storage of collated information from forces throughout the UK, repeating whatever they are told without corroboration ... and GMP observers all know how that ends.

Talking of fantasists, yet another Peter Fahy style statement direct from the Cheshire Constabulary text book. "Despite the challenging situation caused by the Coronavirus pandemic, the operation was declared to be a top priority for GMP with officers continuing to provide support to a number of victims in addition to investigating a number of suspects". National Police Chiefs' Council lead for child protection, Chief Constable Simon Bailey, said: "Following the peer review commissioned by GMP, it's been recognised that Operation Green Jacket is progressing significantly and I am encouraged by the strength and approach adopted by the force" Being a detective of minimal experience he must have taken the fictional author's (Fahy's?) word which by now was being regarded as highly unreliable in all areas of the legal profession but continuing to remain under the local medias' radar.

For that matter where did Operation Hydrant appear from in this context and where is it now? "It's important that police forces continue to work together to tackle child sexual exploitation and a lot can be learned from this Operation Hydrant peer review. In order to continue to protect and support children across the country, Op Hydrant allows national best practice to be shared nationally with all police forces".

"Policing will always explore different avenues and opportunities to ensure that children are protected as much as possible. It is challenging and equally important that forces commit sufficient resources to support victims and pursue suspects, the set-up of Operation Green Jacket is effectively addressing both these issues." The words of an inexperienced 'detective' condescending and oblivious to the truth.

Mohammed Hussain's arrival from West Yorkshire Police came four months after CC Ian Hopkins, told the long suffering citizens of Manchester that he intended to step up recruitment of ethnic minority officers in the wake of the Arena bomb attack. "GMP has been trying to increase the number of officers from Manchester's diverse communities for four years. Greater Manchester Police's new Assistant Chief Constable will be the force's highest ranking Asian police officer" CC Hopkins said there is 'strong support' from Muslim communities to the recruitment drive. It is well documented that the employment of Hussain was rushed without real employment procedures clearly to fill the Ethnic Asian hole. In 2007 during the nutcase 'reign' of C.C Michael Todd, one of the highest ranking Asian officers in Greater Manchester Police force is taking his employers to a tribunal alleging racial discrimination. Detective Inspector Bal Singh, who has has been decorated for his service to the police, is suspended and has been under investigation for eight months.

He was arrested by the GMP internal investigations department November 2006 and accused of money laundering.

The charge was eventually dropped but despite this he says he is still threatened with disciplinary action over two minor traffic offences. His case has become a source of anger and concern among the Asian community and, among Asian and black officers in GMP who feel his ordeal is being prolonged un-necessarily. GMP's commented as usual "these charges and say they will "robustly" defend the force against any allegations of racial discrimination at an employment tribunal." The usual internal report admitted that a "disproportionate" number of visible minority ethnic (VME) police officers had been involved in disciplinary proceedings. It found that while Asian and black officers make-up four per cent of GMP they make-up more that 10 per cent of the officers subject to disciplinary investigations. The report advances reasons why this might be the case speculating that investigators may have a conscious or unconscious racist approach but adds there is no evidence to support such a conclusion. It maybe that the so called racist officers had also raided the goat farmer, boarding house Pakistani in Didsbury.

So there it is GMP's obsession with protecting it's own doesn't stretch to its much acclaimed ethnic minority. Clearly they don't help themselves by continually getting caught and must 'serve' with the same untouchable ethic as the Asian Pakistani paedophiles.

The conduct of Hussain, particularly his desperate claims of suspect numbers and victims should be examined closely. They should be treated as additional proof of 'blind' and 'rotten' employment procedures, readily adopted and later proved to be yet another failure.

Clearly, a leader, totally out of his depth and clinging to glowing media reports based on fictional blurb.

In January 2022 Hussain took up a position in North Yorkshire Police. Having already printed incredible bullshit for Yorkshire media consumption, mostly copied from the pen of Hussain himself, there was only a one line mention from The Manchester Evening News of his departure which was strange to say the least.

The various North Yorkshire journals had heralded Hussains appointment, clearly gleaned from the many MEN glowing reports and without any original information.

The following, a typical example of such rubbish, is not now the cringe worthy bilge one would normally struggle through without the benefit of the above knowledge which now gives it all a hint of tongue in cheek humour.

Assistant Chief Constable Mabs Hussain, proudly and with firm resolve stated: "This operation remains a top priority for GMP with officers doing everything they can to provide victims of child sexual exploitation with appropriate support from specialist agencies and continuing to work to bring offenders to justice.

"The landscape of policing is undoubtedly challenging at the moment in light of the global pandemic, Operation Green Jacket has continued during this unprecedented period and remains very active with a team of dedicated detectives within our Major Incident Team working alongside partners every day to identify and support victims". "We are completely committed to ensuring victims receive the right support and as a result of detectives meticulously reviewing historic files and pursuing new lines of enquiry, the scope of the investigation has grown with officers engaging with a significant number of victims and assessing a number of suspects "Whilst we have made an arrest, our investigation is continuing and I would encourage anyone affected by the case, requiring support or with information that could assist our investigation to get in touch via the dedicated email address."

My thanks to Neil Keeling, noted to be the Chief Reporter of The Manchester Evening News for the following input of the 18.3.21 which appears to consist of unverified fantasised and glowing claims of GMP in his unofficial capacity as 'public relations for GMP'. Remember he speaks with Assistant Chief Constable Mohammed Hussain, himself an Asian Pakistani with family roots in Bradford, West Yorkshire.One of many such articles reads ...

... A new police unit to investigate child sex grooming gangs in Greater Manchester has already identified more than 800 offenders.It is running three major investigations into historic abuse of young girls in Manchester and Rochdale. GMP's Force Child Sexual Exploitation Unit, has 54 officers and staff and has been launched at a cost of £2.3m. A year in the planning It comes in the wake of stinging criticism of the force for previous failings when investigating such crimes. Across the force there are now 70 investigations which involve multiple victims of child sexual exploitation. A total of 468 victims have been discovered of whom 332 have been identified. Police say there are 809 offenders of whom 540 are known. In addition there are "hundreds of cases" where a single victim is involved. The new unit will focus on large and complicated investigations and is currently handling three major operations. Never a mention of offenders being charged, court appearances or prison sentences except for one small group to be identified later.

In failing to recognise such unprecedented bullshit and corruption of actual figures he continues... One,

Operation Exmoor,(true report) has identified ten new victims in Rochdale aged 9 to16 who were sexually abused between 2008 and and 2013. A wide range of alleged offences committed against them includes rape and sexual assault. It was begun after a review of Operation Span, an investigation into an infamous child sex grooming gang led by Shabir Ahmed, known as "Daddy". Ahmed and eight others were convicted and jailed for a series of sex crimes committed against five girls who were abused and then 'shared' at sex parties across the north west between 2005 and 2008, although details of their crimes only emerged in 2012. After the victims were initially not believed, a shelved investigation was resurrected as Operation Span and the victims vindicated.

A second investigation which the new CSE Unit is handling is Operation Green Jacket. It was launched in May 2019 as a response to the flawed Operation Augusta. After the death of Victoria Agoglia, aged 15, in 2003, Augusta, was set up to see if there was a wider issue of child sexual exploitation in south Manchester. Victoria was sexually abused and injected with heroin. Officers managed to identify a network of nearly 100 men potentially involved in the abuse of scores of girls via takeaways in and around Rusholme, but Augusta was shut down shortly afterwards due to the fear of causing racist unrest amongst the Asian Pakistanis and claimed to be 'lack of resources' and even then diluted to 'rather than a sound understanding' of whether lines of inquiry had been exhausted. Hardly any charges were made against the men identified by the operation. Eight of them later went on to commit serious sexual crimes, including the rape of a child, the rape of a young woman, sexual assault and sexual activity with a child.

Operation Green Jacket has assessed 122 perpetrators, and 82 have declared themselves as victims. Of course Operation Augusta claimed that the victims would not cooperate. It now claims to have identified 122, or 100 or 57 or 400 take your choice. Perpetrators of whom eight have been arrested as suspects via so termed 'unhelpful' victim information. Of the eight arrested four relate the case of Victoria Agoglia leaving a balance of four. Well that's dedicated detectives at their best with 'skilled' leaders.

Assistant Chief Constable, Mohammed Hussain, said: "Operation Exmoor is an investigation instigated at the end of 2019/2020. What I asked for was, that all victims that had been seen as a result of Operation Span and had received the level of service that we would expect today from Greater Manchester Police. "From that we identified ten victims who provided further investigative opportunities. We have identified 142 offenders linked to the victims and 46 of them have been recognised as suspects. But there is a lot of work to do with the victims. "Is this the same victims previously claimed as unhelpful.

The unit is also running a third major operation, also in Rochdale, but due to operational sensitivities no further details are being released. But police are confident it will result in a large number of charges. The Deputy Chief Constable added: "We will take any opportunities to bring offenders to justice and, importantly, provide support for victims. Our door is continuously open." "There are some horrendous things which happened to these girls which disgust me. That's why we are so focused on making sure it gets the level of support it does.

Hussain states that the CSE Unit "is not a gimmick." This has been in the planning since last year. I am grateful to the Mayor, Andy Burnham, he has supported and helped to finance this team." In what appeared to be a likely 'kiss of death' he stated "senior, very experienced officers are in charge." Then in total conflict, "If you want to make a difference you have got to have people who are passionate and care. If it means knocking someone's door for something they did 20 years ago we are going to do it." It would be difficult to envisage more 'senior and very experienced senior officers than the very senior officers named in the Anthony Grainger shooting. Remember the totally discredited Chief Superintendent David Thompson and the obstructive and disinterested Chief Constable David Jones. Now they are certainly a 'kiss of death' to any reference to "very experienced senior officers" Hussain/Keeling continues, "What I don't want is a repeat of the past. I am not saying we will never make mistakes, we will because we are human. But when we make a mistake, we will apologise and do all we can to put it right. "What I want to make sure of is that we are not intentionally because of our lack of focus making mistakes."

In addition to investigating large scale and complex cases, the unit will also have strategic oversight of all multi-victim/multi-suspect CSE investigations taking place across Greater Manchester. Yet again further concerns as representatives of other failing agencies are 'roped in' for window dressing and will undoubtedly have little input. He says "Officers will work closely with dedicated representatives from the Crown Prosecution Service (CPS), Child & Adult Social Services, mental health services and Independent Sexual Violence

Advisors (ISVA). The ACC added: "I'm incredibly proud to be able to update the public on the latest significant step we are taking to tackle the sexual exploitation of children in Greater Manchester.

So who do we believe ? ... GB News and Maggie Oliver or this rehash of past failures. Remember the earlier complaint? When the family asked the investigating officer if they had an update on the case, they reportedly received the following response: "To be honest, as of yet, no. We have been running with a lot of live jobs which is making looking at any of my crimes a nightmare… I'll be putting in some overtime to get it sorted."

This honest reply by a hard worker at the pointed end appears to be in conflict with the following ..." At full capacity, the unit will be made up of 54 officers and staff whose overriding priority will be to dedicate their specialist skills to investigating large scale and complex CSE investigations. "This will provide consistency in our approach, as well as a specialist focus on victims and investigations. With this significant dedicated resource we will be able to progress complex investigations in a more focused and timely manner; allowing us to disrupt, investigate and convict those responsible for this abhorrent crime swifter than we ever have before.

"It is important to note that this team is not the only resource we have to call on in our campaign to tackle the exploitation of children. "The work of the unit investigating the most serious and complex cases will be in addition to the work of the 10 Complex Safeguarding Teams currently located in each of our policing districts. "Actions speak louder than words, and I believe that the establishment of this new dedicated unit clearly demonstrates our ongoing commitment to protecting children and bringing those responsible for abusing them to justice." Seventeen Years Too Late "GMP is not the GMP of 15 years go. We have done a lot of work in the last two and a half years in this field. The amount of investment into this shows the force's dedication". "We are going to do everything we can to bring the perpetrators before court. I think the victims in Operation Green Jacket have been extremely brave to support the investigation when we have potentially failed them in the past and give us the opportunity to right the mistakes we made. It is a great leap of faith by them."

On the 3rd November 2020 only five months before the Neil Keeling, Manchester Evening News epic of the 18th March 2021, Assistant Chief Constable Mohammed Hussain is alleged to have given an interview to Isobel Frodsham, then of the Independent who, as the rest of the media must have believed such a high ranking officer of such a 'respected force' would only give facts that did not require verification. She innocently wrote ... Operation Green Jacket is multi-agency investigation into child exploitation during 2004 and 2005. It was launched in May 2018 and included a new probe into the death of 15-year-old Victoria Agoglia. The teenager, who had reported to the police that she had been raped, died after being injected with heroin in 2003. Miss Agoglia was one of the victims involved in the latest arrests.

"Three men have been arrested on suspicion of rape of a girl under 16 as detectives continue to investigate child sexual exploitation under the Operation Green Jacket inquiry. G.M.P. said one man, 41, had also been arrested on suspicion of indecently assaulting a girl under the age of 16, on suspicion of causing the prostitution of a girl under 16 and the supply of Class A and B drugs. The second, a 49-year-old man, was also arrested on suspicion of indecently assaulting a girl under the age of 16. The pair remain in custody. The third man, 38, was arrested last month on suspicion of the rape of a female under 16 and supplying a Class A drug. He was bailed pending further enquiries.

The arrests all relate to separate victims as part of the operation. "In total, six men have been arrested as part of Operation Green Jacket and enquiries are ongoing", the force said. Assistant Chief Constable Hussain said "in addition to the inquiry there are 73 live investigations which are ongoing and in relation to child sexual exploitation. They involve multiple victims or perpetrators across Greater Manchester. A total of 480 victims have been identified so far in the investigation and police are assessing more than 650 perpetrators".

He added: "Since January this year, a total of 54 individuals have been prosecuted for child sexual exploitation offences resulting in 120 years' of custodial sentences. The media would have shouted these figures from the roof tops if there was any element of truth." A further 13 individuals have been convicted and are awaiting sentencing and ten others have been charged and are awaiting trial. These prosecutions have been achieved amidst the backdrop of a global pandemic which has brought challenges to the criminal justice system. "Whilst we have made further arrests, Operation Green Jacket is continuing and I would encourage anyone affected by the case, requiring support or with information that could assist our investigation to get in touch via the dedicated email address."

"Mohammed Hussain's arrival from West Yorkshire Police comes just four months after GMP's C.C Ian Hopkins, stated he intended to step up recruitment of ethnic minority officers in the wake of the Arena bomb attack. 'GMP has been trying to increase the number of officers from Manchester's diverse communities for four years - and Mr Hopkins said in May there is 'strong support' from Muslim communities to the recruitment drive. The potential value of recruits from minority backgrounds as a source of intelligence, has been recognised after the atrocity in which Salman Abedi murdered 22 people and injured hundreds."

It is worth having a peep at his career history. ... Mohammed Hussain joined North Yorkshire Police as Deputy Chief Constable in January 2022. He always preferred to be known as 'Mabs' clearly dropping his real name because of the obvious leanings to potential racist comments.

He was born in Bradford and after working for a short period with the Inland Revenue he started his policing career with West Yorkshire Police in 1996. When working for West Yorkshire Police Mohammed served at every rank as a detective including Detective Chief Inspector. His colleagues knew him 'fondly' as Mabel which appears to say it all. He was promoted to Superintendent in 2012 only sixteen years after joining and is 'said' to have worked in a variety of uniformed operational and strategic roles. As Chief Superintendent he was the Commander for Wakefield and also spent time as the Commander for Leeds District. In short he was a 'desk jockey' and whatever experience he is supposed to have had 'at the pointed end' came to an end and never to be resurrected.

Such a rate of accelerated and protected promotion surely ensured that he never kept in touch with the turbulent streets of West Yorkshire and the masses of young Asian Pakistanis who were becoming increasingly restless. The TV programme which features West Yorkshire traffic cops, illustrates the command such Asians have over what are being considered as 'No Go Areas' where a stolen car cannot be followed for fear of attacks. Traffic Police are now taunted by decoy stolen cars which they will chase into an estate only to be obstructed and surrounded by what can be fifty young Asians. The cops are in such a position that they cannot enter such areas unless 'team handed' and supported by the higher ranks but you never see an officer over the rank of sergeant.

At Greater Manchester Police ACC Mohammed Hussain was said to be responsible for specialist crime: major investigation teams, serious and organised crime teams, forensics, safeguarding, and public protection. Well! we all know how that story ends. He was a Specialist Firearms Commander and a Gold Public Order Commander.

In following the GMP mandate for repetitive confusion and In taking the lead of Operation Greenjacket which effectively was tantamount to 'turkeys voting for Christmas'. Hussain chose to introduce more so called 'Operations' all of which are referred to 'under the umbrella' of Operation Greenjacket.

Having managed to confuse the entire issue with a minimum number of arrests it appears CC Watson recognised Hussain's many failures through the fog of accumulating bullshit and encouraged the termination of his services. 'Luckily' North Yorkshire Police had a vacancy. Hussain joined as Deputy Chief Constable in January 2022 which effectively despite the title is a demotion, after having been Assistant Chief Constable at Greater Manchester Police since October 2018. The actual number of senior officers in relation to the number of working constables was akin to the Mexican Army of Alamo days, when everyone was a General.

The UKs second largest force, now with a 'hard nosed' Chief Constable in Stephen Watson who no doubt recognised the years of inactivity in the arrests of Asian Pakistani child abusers whilst the Asian Pakistani ACC led on so many Operations. As I have said, but worth repeating he appeared to be in 'some difficulty' and 'out of his depth'. So apparent since the GB News exclusive with Maggie Oliver. Despite the valiant efforts of her Trust and the saving of so many young girls, the problems of the gangs of Asian Pakistanis remains

So many separate Operations with so many proclaimed staff members which must surely in reality have an overlap of staffing but claimed as separate Operations just for the believing media consumption.

OPERATION SPAN ... DECEMBER 2010, Greater Manchester Police (GMP) launched Operation Span to investigate a large group of men who were suspected of sexually exploiting children and young people in Rochdale.

OPERATION HYDRANT ... JUNE 2014 Operation Hydrant was to deliver the national policing response, oversight, and coordination of non-recent child sexual abuse investigations concerning persons of public prominence, or in relation to those offences which took place within in Greater Manchester.

OPERATION GREENJACKET MAY 2019..Operation Green Jacket is multi-agency investigation into child exploitation during 2002 and 2005. It was launched in May 2018 and included a new probe into the death of 15-year-old Victoria Agoglia. The teenager, who had reported to the police that she had been raped, died after being injected with heroin in 2003. ACC Hussain in one of his early dubious exercises in number counting claims that Operation Green Jacket has assessed **122** victims - 82 of whom have declared themselves as victims. It has identified **124** perpetrators of whom **eight** have been arrested as suspects. Of the eight arrested **four** relate the case of Victoria Agoglia.

OPERATION LYTTON ... JULY 2020 It was widely reported that a total of 84 charges were made under Operation Lytton, by Greater Manchester Police, into non-recent child sexual exploitation. It should be noted that only fifteen at the most appeared in the local media, which to say the least is very surprising and maybe deliberately misleading. For example eight men have appeared in court accused of being part of a grooming gang who sexually abused girls as young as 12 in Rochdale. This incident is continually repeated in other contexts.

The men were accused of "widespread sexual exploitation and abuse" of two girls aged between 12 and 16 between 2002 and 2006, Manchester Magistrates' Court heard. The success of the BBC drama Three Girls has shone a national spotlight on the grooming scandal in Rochdale.Despite running the child sex exploitation grooming gang and forcing one young victim to call him "daddy" - Shabir Ahmed, 59, claimed that the girls knew what they were doing.

His evil, at the heart of the gang surfaced when he claimed during the trial that the victims of abuse were actually prostitutes. The girls were the real ringleaders of the scandal, he claimed. He argued that they had enough 'business acumen' to have won The Apprentice. Despite his outbursts during the trial at Liverpool Crown Court, he was among nine men that were convicted in May 2012. Jailing them, Judge Gerald Clifton said: "You have all been convicted by the jury after a long trial of grave sexual offences which were committed between the spring of **2008 and 2010**"These involved the grooming and sexual exploitation of several girls, aged in their early teens. "In some cases those girls were raped, callously, viciously and violently. "Some of you acted as you did to satiate your lust, some of you to make money, all of you treated them as though they were worthless and beyond respect."

In a separate trial District Judge John McGarva told prosecuting lawyers: "I think it would be useful to give a nutshell account of what we are dealing with." Charlotte Rimmer, prosecuting, told the court: "We are dealing with a case, known as Operation Lytton, an investigation into allegations brought by two individuals, between 2002 and 2006, when these two females were aged between 12 and 16. "These are allegations of widespread sexual exploitation and abuse, following grooming, by a number of defendants in the Rochdale area.

OPERATION SHERWOOD ... JUNE 2022. Operation Sherwood is a dedicated team of police officers and support staff whose remit it is to investigate **non-recent** cases of child sexual exploitation featuring within the IRT's report in Oldham. It is also shown in media reports that this team are part of GMP's CSE Unit of specialist officers dedicated to investigating historical cases of CSE across Greater Manchester. This team are part of GMP's CSE Unit of specialist officers dedicated to investigating historical cases of CSE across Greater Manchester.

OPERATION EXMOOR ... APRIL 2022. A new police unit to investigate child sex grooming gangs in Greater Manchester has already identified more than 800 offenders. It is running three major investigations into historic abuse of young girls in Manchester and Rochdale. GMP's Force Child Sexual Exploitation Unit, has 54 officers and staff and has been launched at a cost of £2.3m.

A year in the planning It comes in the wake of stinging criticism of the force for previous failings when investigating such crimes. Across the force there are now 70 investigations which involve multiple victims of child sexual exploitation.

C.S.E. UNIT ... March 2021 It appears that the C.S.E. (child sexual exploitation) GMP's CSE Unit of specialist officers dedicated to investigating historical cases of CSE across Greater Manchester was the front runner.

Then various Operations emerged for reasons which are not readily apparent if there is a crux of 'dedicated officers' as repeatedly claimed but in reality appear to overlap and therefore giving a false representation of the real facts.

Having followed such a dubious history can you believe... The new unit will focus on large and complicated investigations and is currently handling three major operations. A total of 468 victims have been discovered of whom 332 have been identified. Police say there are 809 offenders of whom 540 are known. In addition there are "hundreds of cases" where a single victim is involved.

OLDHAMS COMPLEX SAFEGUARDING UNIT ... OCTOBER 2022.

prevents and reduces child sexual exploitation (CSE) and child criminal exploitation (CCE).

"**Operation Exmoor,** has identified ten new victims in Rochdale aged nine to 16 who were sexually abused between 2008 and 2013. A wide range of alleged offences committed against them includes rape and sexual assault". "It was begun after a review of **Operation Span,** an investigation into the infamous child sex grooming gang led by Shabir Ahmed, known as 'Daddy'. Ahmed and eight others were convicted and jailed for a series of sex crimes committed against five girls who were abused and then 'shared' at sex parties across the north west between 2005 and 2008, although details of their crimes only emerged in 2012. After the victims were initially not believed, a shelved investigation was resurrected as Operation Span and the victims vindicated.

Repeating what I have already penned above but I feel necessary to repeat additional points. A second investigation which the new CSE Unit is handling is Operation Green Jacket. It was launched in May 2019 as a response to the flawed Operation Augusta. Operation Augusta was not 'flawed'. It was a disgrace of leadership, poor training and most of all belief in an investigation which required sympathy and patience with the complainants. After the death of Victoria Agoglia, aged 15, in 2003, Augusta, was set up to see if there was a wider issue of child sexual exploitation in south Manchester. Victoria was never believed when she reported the fact that she was being sexually abused and injected with heroin. She was never believed and regarded as a fantasist but kept a secret detailed diary which was held in her belongings and stored away for several years. The diary was only discovered when real detectives started an enquiry as they should have, from the beginning. Her belongings were examined and the diary discovered.

Assistant Chief Constable Hussain said: "Operation Exmoor is an investigation instigated at the end of 2019/2020. What I asked for was that all victims that had been seen as a result of Operation Span and had received the level of service that we would expect today from Greater Manchester Police.... F.F.S." From that we identified ten victims who provided further investigative opportunities. We have identified 142 offenders linked to the victims and 46 of them have been recognised as suspects. But there is a lot of work to do with the victims."

The unit is said to be also running a third major operation, also in Rochdale, but due to operational sensitivities (usually means it isn't) no further details are being released. But police are confident it will result in a large number of charges. It hasn't to date.

The ACC added: "We will take any opportunities to bring offenders to justice and, importantly, provide support for victims. Our door is continuously open." "There are some horrendous things which happened to these girls which disgust me. That's why we are so focused on making sure it gets the level of support it does. "It is never nice when the Senior Investigating Officer briefs you on the circumstances surrounding the horrendous abuse victims suffered. You can't help but feel for that victim.

Again commenting on the CSE Unit and apparently recognising later criticism, he added: "It is not a gimmick. This has been in the planning since last year. I am grateful to the Mayor, Andy Burnham, he has supported and helped to finance this team." Officers were invited to join the unit and senior, very experienced officers are in charge. "It you want to make a difference you have got to have people who are passionate and care. If it means knocking someone's door for something they did 20 years ago we are going to do it."

When the entire structure is studied in context it really does promote absolute disbelief and considerable doubt that so many 'Operations' can be staffed fully and operated as described in the trusting media, when the overall manpower at the 'pointed end' is lacking in the first place.

ANDY BURNHAM ... What more critical, repetitive drivel attributed to him, can be said?

I have no intention of repeating all the Burnham negative nonsense which has been adequately covered previously.

What can you say and remain somewhat polite, well not a lot.... Andrew Murray Burnham was born 7 January 1970 in Aintree, Liverpool. is a British politician who has served as Mayor of Greater Manchester since 2017. He was a professional politician and served as the Labour M.P. for Leigh from 2001 to 2017. Having little real competition he served in various cabinet positions.

He served in Gordon Brown's Cabinet in the treasury from 2007 to 2008, he was Culture Secretary from 2008 to 2009 and Health Secretary from 2009 to 2010. He served as Shadow Home Secretary from 2015 to 2016.

Clearly in the knowledge that even a chimpanzee would be voted in by the resident Labour supporters he was selected as Labour's candidate for the new Greater Manchester Mayoralty. So confident he stood down as Shadow Home Secretary in 2016 and an MP at the 2017 General Election. Incredibly with a 'brain dead' majority of 67% he won the 2017 mayoral election and was re-elected in election of May 2021.For his role of securing more money for local Northern communities during the Covid Pandemic he was dubbed the "King of the North by the media. Burnham was elected to the new role on 5 May 2017 with a majority of 67%. Upon taking office, he became entitled to the style of Mayor. In his mayoral victory speech he said "Greater Manchester is going to take control without the strings of London"

"We are going to change politics and make it work better for people." In truth the turnout of the 'chimpanzee' voters was only 34%.

George Osborne, Conservative must have had a brain fart when in November 2014, the position of Police and Crime Commissioner was removed and its responsibilities subsumed into the mayoral office. Did he ever consider the effect such a change would have on the conduct of an already corrupt, poorly trained and badly led police force.

The issue of homelessness in Greater Manchester became Burnham's popular 'bandwagon' and was a major focus of his mayoral campaign. This was a neutral subject which would have no opposition. He even pledged to donate 15% of his mayoral salary to charities tackling homelessness if elected. After his election he outlined his plan to launch a "homelessness fund", with money going to homeless charities and mental health and rehabilitation services. He pledged to end rough sleeping in Greater Manchester by 2020.

Of course having secured the vote the target was ignored and whatever money was raised appeared to go towards exes rather than the homeless. It appears that Labour voters do not go as far as a Mayoral ego trip. A theme of failure and stance changing claims, throughout his tenure.

I mention the homeless of Manchester because I can write with some authority. During this period I was a practicing Christian, possibly rueing my chequered past. I took a great deal from the Pentecostal Sunday service at Audacious Church in Salford with all the singing, scruffy young pastors and great sermons. I volunteered for the Tuesday evening, feeding and clothing of an average of 80 homeless of both sexes. I was the chef for eighty three course meals with helpers until I could not stand due to a painful leg. I then sorted the masses of donated clothing, this time with assistance from a couple of homeless lads.

It is a great regret that I eventually suffered a below knee amputation and ceased walking my Christian pathway. However, early into my Christianity, I wrote to Burnham, offering my services and giving him the benefit of my knowledge of the homeless, in any case. He was employing individuals with absolutely no knowledge of the homeless in positions which only, as I saw, the ability to fabricate the figures, appear busy and never offer any practical financial assistance to the homeless via several similar charities throughout the City.

Dealing with the homeless is difficult, they are human beings on 'life's scrap heap' often with drugs and drink problems and a tendency to violence to condescending town hall types. Many are ex army, returning from overseas service to a divorce and no job and no where to live. They needed properly guided help and not media headlines.

There is little point in repeating all that has gone before with the many proclamations of Burnham in previous chapters as he 'ducked and dived' various serious issues with his bland platitudes. Let us just tip toe through the tulips of Burnham Bollocks without any real subject or context.

"I don't consider it a failing... I don't run Greater Manchester Police", says Andy Burnham as his term ends with GMP in the humiliating position of being in Special Measures.

On the campaign trail for re-election as mayor, insisted "he held a troubled force to account throughout a turbulent term", one that ended with the Chief Constable exiting and GMP in special measures If there is one subject generating political heat during the 2021 mayoral campaign, it is policing. Since 2017 GMP, for which the mayor has political oversight, has been on a rollercoaster. the Manchester Arena atrocity occurred days after the mayor took office, with all the trauma that entailed.

"But GMP has also faced, and continues to face, serious questions over its leadership's competence and culture over an extended period". "They include, in the last four years, major concerns around the roll-out of the computer system iOPS and the impact on officers and victims; whistleblowers warning of cultural failures spanning years; the blistering verdict of the public inquiry into Anthony Grainger's shooting, which found evidence from senior officers was 'seriously misleading' and 'lacked candour; 'failures to submit evidence to the early stages of the Manchester Arena inquiry in 2019 and a string of critical inspectorate reports in 2018, 2019 and twice in 2020, most of them highlighting failures to protect vulnerable people. "All are examples to have rocked GMP during the first mayoral term, a period that culminated in Her Majesty's Inspectorate of Constabularies, Fire and Rescue Services confirming woeful levels of crime under-recording last year and that victims were being 'denied justice'. "

His term ended with GMP in special measures. Burnham insists policing has not been the biggest failure of his first term. "No, I don't consider it a policy failing, for this reason: I don't run Greater Manchester Police," He actually said he did, when it suited. Can you believe, he was voted in for a second term? "The job is to hold them to account and you've got to be judged on the extent to which they've been held to account. "As you know, within days of coming into office I challenged them around Child Sexual Exploitation and I think there has been a substantial change within the force on that particular issue.

So! Mr Andy Burnham, bull shitter extraordinaire what change was that, Ask Maggie Oliver and her hardworking Trust, about the truth of that ridiculous statement. And then the HMIC report comes to light.

"So my job is not to run GMP. I've got two things I can do - two big levers, if you like. "One is to fund them and the other is to change the leadership if things are not going right. And I've done both of those things to put them back on the right path." He is also quick to highlight the review of the fire service that was undertaken immediately after the Arena attack. 'A similar process' is now taking place in GMP, he notes. F.F.S Burnham!

"I inherited a severely weakened police force. They'd had seven years of cuts, they were 3,000 staff down; 2,000 frontline officers, 1,000 staff. "That is what I inherited." "So in my view, I'm repairing the damage of Conservative and Lib Dem cuts," he says. "If you move on to the second point about accountability, as I say, you've got the nuclear option, if you like, which is removing the leadership. You do not have the ability to intervene day-to-day. Yes you do, if you accepted the responsibility that came with the job.

"And we were often faced with a pushback of 'we are independent'. That is a common thing that all police and crime commissioners get - you can't just go roaming around the organisation, it's just not how it works. It is, if you have the 'balls'"But they were implementing a massive upgrade in the IT system that had been planned from way before my time, way before," he responds. "So there were big things that were happening within the force that needed stability, if you like; the crises we faced, but also that change. "And then, obviously what happened late last year - I would say I did act quickly and I did act decisively to bring in new leadership."

One frustration for journalists - and others - throughout the last four years has been getting to the bottom of how exactly the force's senior command is scrutinised. Is that the same journalists who accepted all he said at face value. Is it the same journalists who accepted Mohammed Hussain and his continual claims, printed word for word without a probing question. Was it the same journalists who gave Hussain one embarrassed line on his departure to the barren lands of North Yorkshire.

"Police and crime panels, held in public, albeit not always very regularly, have discussed few of the greatest calamities facing the force over the past four years, with the exception of iOPS - but only once it had been introduced and caused frontline outcry, as opposed to during its development, when delays were racking up and vast amounts of public money" .... What the hell does that mean?

So there they are, all the recent comments by Andrew Murray Burnham, an itinerary of bland excuses for total failure of a man who actually believed that Police hierarchy could not be as blatantly dishonest as his continual words of support, laughing all the way to 80,000 lost crime reports and the Manchester Arena Terrorist Attack only two examples of so many incidents which could have been prevented with diligent training and supervision. Can you believe for this repetitive crap he is paid £110,000 plus expenses.

Will C.C Stephen Watson take a firm hold and mark the end to Burnham's failures?

The end

P.S.

I was to offer a final conclusion as an end to this history of failure and corruption but what can I say, GMP appears to be working harder, the Town Hall appears to be taking an interest and a few more coppers are being prosecuted, even to the rank of Inspector, but that's where it ends. I hope you have been as amazed as I and I actually thought I had seen it all. Seeing all the corruption fabrication and perjury without a trace of a prosecution, actually in context, over fifty years is breath taking ... you could hear the fat dripping off a chip. Cabal of Corruption will never be happy and why should he? He should have been the Chief Constable by now. At the moment the book cover says it all and all that remains is once again in real Mancunian ... FFS - 50 years of GMP.

Research references

- The Salford Star. Excellent original reporting. C.C Fahy, IPCC, Lloyd, Graham Grainger reporting, but now no more.
- The Guardian Newspaper, excellent factual reporting.
- The Independent.
- Isobel Frodsham.
- The Telegraph.
- The Manchester Evening News, Neil Keeling for police bias.
- The Manchester Evening News, Jennifer Williams ex Political Reporter. Ground breaking.
- The Bolton News. Lewis Finney.
- Neil Wilby. Campaigning Journalist. Incredible well researched reporting
- Mike Greensmith The Artworks, Hayfield. Derbyshire. Book covers, general support.
- @UKCorruptPolice...Paul Ponting .. saying it as it happens. Follow!
- @OldhamEye.
- @Whistleblowerat ... Cabal of Corruption. Real GMP practices, comment. Follow!
- @CorruptionCause ... Noble Cause.

John Barlow. Support & Research throughout.

Milton Keynes UK
Ingram Content Group UK Ltd.
UKHW041020090823
426580UK00001B/9

9 781803 814810